the HOMESELLER'S KIT

Fifth Edition

Edith Lank with Dena Amoruso

DEARBORN™
TRADE
A **Kaplan Professional** Company

This publication is designed to provide accurate and authoritative information in regard to the subject matter covered. It is sold with the understanding that the publisher is not engaged in rendering legal, accounting, or other professional service. If legal advice or other expert assistance is required, the services of a competent professional person should be sought.

Vice President and Publisher: Cynthia A. Zigmund
Acquisitions Editor: Mary B. Good
Project Editor: Trey Thoelcke
Interior Design: Lucy Jenkins
Cover Design: KTK Design Associates
Typesetting: Elizabeth Pitts

Published by Dearborn Trade, a Kaplan Professional Company

Printed in the United States of America

01 02 03 10 9 8 7 6 5 4 3 2 1

Library of Congress Cataloging-in-Publication Data

Lank, Edith.
The homeseller's kit / Edith Lank with Dena Amoruso.—5th ed.
p. cm.
Includes index.
ISBN 0-7931-4439-6 (pbk.)
1. House selling. I. Amoruso, Dena. II. Title.
HD1379 .L325 2001
333.33′8—dc21 00-012908
CIP

Praise for the Previous Editions:

"Edith Lank is real estate's Dear Abby."

–*USA Today*

"Edith Lank is real estate's Q & A guru."

–*The Boston Globe*

"Edith Lank is considered the Dr. Ruth of real estate. . . . It's Lank's soothing words which calm the remorseful buyer reeling from panic attacks after signing a real estate contract. It's her sage advice which catapults the prudent penny-saver into a real estate mogul. And it's her wit, charm, and clarity which distinguishes her columns."

–*The Miami Herald*

"For most of us, the single largest purchase we will make in our lifetime is our home. Doing it right the first time is made considerably easier with this trilogy of homebuying/selling books [*The Mortgage Kit, The Homebuyer's Kit, The Homeseller's Kit*]. Lank, a syndicated columnist and real estate consultant, has painstakingly gathered the essentials and made them readable/practical. . . . Each of Lank's books is replete with payment/mortgage tables, glossary, charts, check-off lists, sample forms, and innumerable helpful hints and strategies for doing it right the first time."

–*Library Journal*

"Now prospective homesellers can get experienced, practical advice on how to fix up, market and sell their home, from a leading real estate expert. *The Homeseller's Kit,* written by national real estate columnist and author Edith Lank, tells how to sell a home for the most money and with the fewest headaches."

–*Bloomingdale (IN) Herald*

"If you are selling your home, Lank's *The Homeseller's Kit* is must reading. Lank's years of experience and knowledge are there for the taking."

—*Tri-City Herald*

"Whether you are selling your home or buying one, this book will answer most of your questions. The author is Edith Lank, an experienced real estate writer and teacher who knows her subject very well. . . . Her valuable insight into how agents operate make the book well worth studying. . . . This is an excellent book for sellers and buyers who want to know what to expect. It is simple, nontechnical, and easy-to-read, with insights that give the reader the confidence to sell a home."

—Robert Bruss, Syndicated Real Estate Columnist

"Lank, national real estate columnist and author, tells how to sell a home for the most money. . . . She offers advice on how much to ask, how to prepare the house for sale, when to use an agent and how to judge a buyer's capability to afford your house. She also covers recent law regarding home selling (Fair Housing and human rights laws), FHA/VA mortgage regulations, tax-saving strategies, charts, tables, and checklists."

—*St. Petersburg (FL) Times*

"*The Homeseller's Kit* and *The Homebuyer's Kit* provide as thorough a coverage of the homebuying/selling process as you are likely to find. Lank is a veteran real estate practitioner whose writing reflects her knowledge of life in the real estate trenches."

—*The Real Estate Professional* (rated *The Homeseller's Kit* one of the 10 bestselling real estate books in the United States)

Contents

Preface

Thousands of letters have come in to my syndicated real estate column, radio, and television shows from would-be homesellers, those currently involved in the process, and others smarting from wounds received. (Those with happy, successful sales don't usually write to a columnist.)

So when my son and daughter-in-law put their first home on the market and sought to buy a larger one (grandchildren!), I had ample advice to give them, and that was the genesis of this book.

Everything I've learned is set forth to help you with the adventure. The book includes advice for selling on your own and unique information—found in no other book I know of—on making the best use of a broker if you do retain one.

One of the most frequent queries I receive concerns the income tax consequences of a sale, so the book concludes with a chapter on just that topic. The text guides you from the decision to sell to selecting a good agent (and dismissing a poor one); preparing, pricing, and showing your home; negotiating a sales contract and making sure the buyer obtains financing; ensuring a smooth and timely closing; and on through to an analysis of those tax ramifications.

For this fifth edition, Dena Amoruso has come on board to add her special expertise.

If you are selling your home, you face changes in your life—sometimes exhilarating, sometimes worrisome. I hope this book smooths the way, and I'd enjoy hearing how it goes.

You're welcome to write me at 240 Hemingway Drive, Rochester, NY 14620, with comments, suggestions, or questions. My e-mail address is edithlank@aol.com.

CHAPTER

1

To Sell or Not to Sell

Americans move around a lot. Statistics from the National Association of REALTORS® indicate that the average household in the United States moves once every seven years. Whether you are selling a home for the first time or are a seasoned home selling veteran, putting your home on the market is frequently a time of mixed emotions, among them anticipation, anxiety, uncertainty, and sometimes relief.

When You Have No Choice

You may have no choice in the matter. A corporation may couple a promotion with a transfer across the country. Or you yourself may decide that it is worth uprooting the family for a career opportunity in another area. If yours is a military family, you must accept the fact that you may often spend only two or three years in one place.

It can be a pleasant milestone that suggests your move: an increase in income permitting you to buy a larger home, the marriage of your last child, retirement. Or you may be forced to sell your home because of a dramatic life change: divorce, death in the family, debilitating illness. And for some who buy, move into, fix up, and sell real estate as a part-time or full-time hobby, it can be business as usual.

Perhaps you are unable to carry your mortgage and are facing foreclosure. In that case, immediate action is essential, as discussed at the end of this chapter.

But when your motivation is the need for more living space, you are faced with a choice: Should you add on to your present home or buy another?

The Case for Adding On

If you presently enjoy a pleasant neighborhood with familiar faces, a helpful mail carrier, a school you have confidence in, or a place of worship within walking distance, you may prefer to stay put. It's much easier to improve or expand the property you have now than to start all over again in a new neighborhood. You can retain the rose bushes you've been nurturing, the kitchen you worked so hard to wallpaper, and your low-interest mortgage.

It is satisfying, also, to plan precisely the home improvements you've had in mind. In adding on, you could relocate the washer and dryer where they're most convenient for you, build a media center into the new family room, or knock out the wall next to your master bedroom and create that private hideaway you've always dreamed of.

To make the decision practical, ask yourself: Is my present house a modest one compared to its neighbors? If so, additional investment in it may be prudent.

Consider a neighborhood where houses sell for approximately \$180,000. Your home, though, is a bungalow worth only \$150,000. It is probably safe to spend \$25,000 expanding your property. Then, if you have to sell, it should not be difficult to find a buyer willing to pay \$180,000 (or at least \$175,000) to live on that particular street.

The Case for Moving

Suppose instead that you own a particularly impressive house on a $150,000 street, property that would be worth more than $180,000 in another part of town. As it stands, the house might bring $155,000. Beyond that, buyers with more to spend will look in more prestigious areas.

It is obviously ill advised to invest money in improving such property. An extra $25,000 spent on additions would increase the potential price by only a few thousand dollars, if that.

A given street, in other words, will support only a given price range. It is economically unwise to overimprove a house for the neighborhood.

Few improvements repay you dollar for dollar for what you invested. Even in the most favorable circumstances, the expansion or improvement of a house seldom raises its value by the amount of money spent. Some exceptions may be energy-saving modifications or the updating of older kitchens and baths when all the homes around you have already taken those steps. If you live in an area where it's swimming weather only about three months of the year, the installation of a swimming pool, for example, may even reduce the number of potential buyers. The idea of pool maintenance the other nine months of the year may not appeal to them. Elsewhere, if it's pool weather from April until October, you may be able to recoup around half the money you spend in the long run. Even in the Sun Belt, some potential homebuyers will have nothing to do with a pool and its maintenance; others may find it pleasant, but will shy away from paying more for a property with one in the backyard.

One danger in adding on to a house is the factor called *functional obsolescence.* Appraisers lower their estimate of value for a house if its parts do not match. A new wing, for example, may turn a three-bedroom house into a five-bedroom house. If the original small kitchen is retained, however, the house may not serve the needs of a five-bedroom family. And if the home still has only one bathroom, the same holds true.

Besides the possibility of not recouping investment costs on the eventual sale, there is the consideration of your present outlay.

Even with the expenses of selling and buying, you may find that it costs less to move to a larger home. You might even pick up, at a bargain, a house that has been generously expanded by homeowners who cannot recoup *their* costs.

If you are trying to decide whether to add on, look at nearby houses on the market. Open houses, usually held on weekend afternoons, allow you to visit freely without making appointments. This preparation for your sale is valuable for several reasons. For now, concentrate on how your home compares with those presently on the market.

Figure 1.1 will help you make your add-on-or-sell decision.

Although asking price is not relevant to this particular decision, it is helpful to make a note of that figure. Ask also how long the house has been on the market.

While you are viewing these houses, make notes on the salespeople and brokers you meet, observing their techniques if you intend to sell on your own, and estimating their capabilities if you intend to list with a real estate broker.

For Older Homeowners

"My home is paid up and costs me practically nothing." Such a statement is infinitely comforting to someone who lived through the Great Depression. Many older people feel safe in a house that is free and clear. This emotional satisfaction is probably worth more than the house itself for some homeowners.

The drawback is that it may prevent you from selling a house that no longer serves your needs, for a paid-up house is actually as expensive as any other form of housing.

Because you paid $8,500 for your home after World War II, it can be difficult to understand what is implied when you are told that your property may be worth $200,000. You have never seen that money, but it is yours. If you sell your house, you can add to your cost basis whatever you've spent on permanent improvements over the years, and you can take your profit tax-free under the special provisions the IRS offers home sellers of any age (see Chapter 13). After selling expenses are subtracted, you might clear $185,000.

FIGURE 1.1

Add On or Sell and Buy Elsewhere: Worksheet

	Which is better in:					
	No. of Bedrooms	**No. of Baths**	**Lot and Location**	**Garage**	**Sq. Ft.**	**Condition**
Your House						
House No. 1						
Your House						
House No. 2						
Your House						
House No. 3						
Your House						
House No. 4						

That $185,000, invested in safe, fixed long-term investments, can yield thousands of dollars per year. Add to that the money you presently pay for property taxes, homeowners insurance, and maintenance costs. You could probably sell your home and realize sufficient income for the purchase or rental of an apartment or other housing in an active adult community, retirement, or resort area.

It is important to realize that as the owner of a paid-up home, you do have an option. Each day that you remain in your home, you are making a decision to keep your money in the house instead of in an income-producing investment.

This is not to say that every older homeowner should move. Those who are comfortable should, of course, remain where they are. The gardening and small repairs that bedevil some homeowners are satisfying activities for others. The emotional stress of uprooting can be a serious consideration. The point is, if you'd prefer to move, you probably can. You are not tied to your house.

Reverse Mortgages

For seniors who do want to remain at home, obtaining a *reverse mortgage* can sometimes solve financial difficulties. This type of loan allows you to tap the equity in your home without having to prove any credit or income qualifications. Instead of sending in a payment every month, you receive a check from the lender. Closing costs and interest are added to the debt, which builds up gradually against the property. No repayment is due until you sell the house or leave it permanently. AARP (American Association of Retired Persons) has a home equity information center and a free book; for a copy, call 202-434-3525 or visit them on the World Wide Web at <www.aarp.org>.

One important consideration in favor of moving, however, is the advantage of doing so before you are forced to. If you plan to move to a warmer climate, a single-level house, or an apartment eventually, you will have the benefit of better decisions when you are not under pressure. You are more likely to receive full market value for your home if you have time to spruce it up for the market, show it during favorable months of the year, and consider offers at leisure.

Your choice of retirement housing, also, will be more satisfactory if you are free to visit resort or retirement areas before making your decision, house-hunt or apartment-hunt without haste, and choose your own pace for moving.

When to Put Your Home on the Market

In a good market, supply and demand are in balance–there are about as many home seekers as houses on the market–and, in an ideal situation, unemployment is low, the economy is in good shape, and plentiful mortgage money is available at reasonable interest rates.

Sustaining a perfect market is rare, however, and at any given time, your community is likely to have a *sellers' market* (not enough houses to satisfy demand) or a *buyers' market* (surplus housing stock so that buyers can call the shots).

Where does your town stand at any given moment? Most real estate brokers know what sort of market prevails. To judge for yourself, look for statistics on the following:

- Unemployment
- The average number of days homes stay on the market
- Relative housing prices

When unemployment runs high (large local factory closing, corporations downsizing), workers leaving the area may flood the market with houses, and the few buyers remaining are able to pick and choose.

Real estate brokers should have figures for *days on market* (DOM) showing the number of days elapsed between the time houses go on the market and the dates of contracts for sale. In a buyers' market, DOM runs several months or more.

Because many sellers have no option but to accept whatever price the buying public may offer, price levels falling near or even below those of the previous year are indications of a buyers' market.

Catching a Sellers' Market

If you are in no hurry to sell, you will certainly try to catch a sellers' market. Except in resort locations, spring and early summer usually yield the highest prices. More buyers are active then, as many families hope to move before the school year begins. Spring starts early in real estate; activity usually heats up as early as February.

No Point in Waiting

If you are selling one home and buying another, it doesn't make much difference where in the cycle you find yourself because you will have an advantage at one end or the other.

Although fewer buyers are looking in the depths of winter, those who do plow through bad weather are usually well-motivated and ready to deal. If your circumstances dictate a winter sale, there is no need to worry. The shortage of listings at this time of year can work to your advantage. While others decide to wait until after the holidays, you may just be the only game in town, and that's good.

When you have decided to sell your house, the off-season can be the most favorable time to list it. Six months before you expect to move is almost a minimum for best results. Even if satisfactory buyers for your home appear promptly, the complicated paperwork involved in mortgage application, and the dovetailing of your needs and the buyer's, can result in problems if you are pressed for time.

If your house is not sold before you must move, you could be in the unenviable position of paying for two places at once. Because a vacant house seldom shows as well as one with furniture in place, your empty house may sell less readily or bring less money. (If you are selling a modestly sized home, however, where the clean emptiness may create spaciousness in the eye of a potential buyer, the reverse may be true.) Check with your insurance agent as to how long you may keep insurance coverage on an empty house.

Although houses have certainly been turned over in less than a week, in unusual circumstances or with no new mortgage involved, it is best to allow three to six months whenever possible. You are most likely to receive the highest price for your house if you draw from the largest possible pool of buyers. An unhurried approach to your sale is the best guarantee of sufficient market exposure.

If You Are Facing Foreclosure

With many mortgages, a homeowner can technically be subject to loan foreclosure after even one late payment. Lending institutions, however, are not eager to foreclose; many will work with a borrower who faces temporary problems.

SELLER'S TIP

When listing your home on the market:

- Remember that spring is the most active time of year
- Check the current number of houses on your market
- Allow at least three months before expected sale

Your first step, if trouble looms, should be to confer with your lender in person, if possible, or by phone (for starters) if your lender is an out-of-town institution. Your mortgage servicer is required by law to have a toll-free phone number, or to take collect calls.

Sometimes temporary payment schedules (interest only, FHA intervention for as long as a year) can be arranged to help deal with the problem. Sometimes a mortgage can be refinanced for a longer period, to lower your payments.

When you receive written notice that foreclosure is being instituted, the worst response is to ignore it and hope the threat disappears. Once the procedure gets too far along, considerable legal fees will have been incurred. Even if you could raise the money to pay off the loan and stop the process, you would be liable for extra costs.

Why not simply give up and wait to see what happens? Here are two very good reasons:

1. If the house is sold at a foreclosure auction, the proceeds may not cover the outstanding loan, accumulated back payments, and the load of legal costs. In some states, the lender is likely to seek a *deficiency judgment* against you personally. The judgment—money you still must pay—could cripple your attempts to get back on your feet.

2. Once you have gone through foreclosure, you will have to wait *at least three* years from the final date of foreclosure even to apply for another mortgage loan. From a lender's point of view, a foreclosure contained in a bankruptcy is a heavy stain in an individual's credit history. Even if you are facing the most disastrous of financial pictures, try to sell the house before a foreclosure takes place. Bankruptcies dictate that consumers wait a minimum of two to four years from the discharge to apply for another mortgage, but guidelines for a credit recovery from either foreclosure or bankruptcy vary by the type of loan and lending institution used.

In any event, bankruptcy will not wipe out your present mortgage, even if it postpones foreclosure for a few months. If real estate values have plunged in your area, the best move is to ask the lender to take your house back and forgive the debt (deed in lieu of foreclosure). Your attorney can explore this matter for you. Occasionally, and if you can prove you are nearly destitute, a lender agrees to accept a *short sale,* canceling the debt in return for whatever the property brings on the open market.

But if your house can be sold for a sufficient sum to clear the mortgage, prompt action is essential. Get in touch with a real estate broker and list the house immediately, at rock-bottom price for quick sale. If called in early enough, your broker or lawyer might persuade the lender to hold off foreclosure for a few weeks. Many investors are out there looking for bargains in just such situations. You might be able to salvage your credit reputation, avoid extra legal fees, and even realize leftover equity, if any.

Anyone facing foreclosure has special need for an attorney even though, in such a situation, additional fees are a burden.

CHAPTER

2

Agent or FSBO

What percentage of homeowners sell on their own, without using brokers? It all depends on whom you ask, but the figure was about one out of every ten a decade ago, and has probably risen to around two out of ten today.

This book, then, will offer advice for every stage of how to do it on your own, but will concentrate on how to get the most out of a broker.

Selling by Owner

As soon as you advertise your own home for sale, you become what is known in real estate circles as a *FSBO* ("fizz-bo," For Sale by Owner). What motivates a FSBO? The stated objective is usually to sell a house at full market value and pocket the commission that may have otherwise been paid to a broker. Some owners may not be able to gather an adequate down payment on their next home without every dime of equity from their current one, so their reasoning is understandable. Often, though, the sellers are intrigued by the challenge of a new task and believe that they have the time, patience, and knowledge that it takes to sell it themselves. Many look forward to mastering a new skill and hope to do it as well as professionals.

Most FSBOs do quit and list with brokers, usually within a month, as they begin to realize the study, effort, and expense involved in selling a house. Some tackle the job with zest, however, and carry through the whole transaction. Those who succeed are usually sophisticated in business and financial matters or have done a considerable amount of research.

As a seller, you can eliminate the broker, but you cannot eliminate the expenses incurred and the work performed by the broker. *Fee-for-services* brokers are gaining popularity, offering homesellers unbundled services, like contract-writing, listing in Multiple Listing Services, performing a comparative market analysis, or assisting with pricing. And there are also *discount brokers,* offering both scaled-down selling assistance and multiple listing exposure.

FSBOs and the Web

FSBO Web sites for the pure owner-seller (those who refuse to pay any fees or commissions to any outside person) come and go. Where real estate experts predicted the Internet would be a natural haven for FSBO sellers, they have discovered inherent problems with them. In her research, Blanche Evans, author of *Homesurfing.net,* discovered that one problem home shoppers cite is the lack of volume in a given area. People like to browse through many listings, comparing pictures, prices, and neighborhood amenities without having to go to several different sites. Another problem seems to be the lack of professionalism and sophistication with which the listings are displayed (one may have a page of descriptive text on a home and the next listing may have three lines), and yet another is an absence of photos.

Professional broker Web sites, like Realtor.com, on the other hand, have thousands and thousands of listings to browse through, giving home shoppers a wealth of information with which to narrow down their decisions on areas, neighborhoods, homes, and seller terms.

FSBO Proposition Not a Piece of Cake

Many people think the job consists of finding someone who wants to buy your home, but that is only the tip of the iceberg. Ensuring that buyers are financially qualified, agreeing on a proper sales contract, and seeing the transaction through all the paperwork down to final closing are important tasks. That is why serious FSBOs who plan to stay in it for the long haul may use a fee-for-services or discount broker as opposed to totally going it alone.

Answer the questions on the "Doing It on Your Own" quiz in Figure 2.1 before you decide whether to become a FSBO.

The Agent's Pitch

A FSBO's first classified ad may bring more calls from real estate agents than from prospective buyers. Instead of cutting off hopeful brokers, you can learn a great deal by chatting with them at length. If you feel you have sufficient sales resistance, remember that inviting a broker into your home involves no commitment on your part. You may even tell them ahead of time the purpose for your invitation and they will not be insulted, because they hope to make a favorable enough impression to earn your listing if you change your mind. You can obtain free information about the local market and educational pointers on what is involved in home selling. After each interview with an agent, note your impressions on a form like the one in Figure 2.2.

Expect the broker to give you a classic *listing presentation,* which will make some or all of the following points:

- *The ability to handle tension, complications, and disappointment* is one of the prime requisites for a good real estate agent. Every transaction is different, posing new challenges. Your agent should protect you from as much headache as possible, using expertise to anticipate, head off, and absorb many of the problems in your sale.
- *Selling a home involves emotional upheaval.* It can be difficult to free yourself of sentimental ties, view your house dispassionately, and regard it simply as a piece of merchan-

FIGURE 2.1
Doing It on Your Own

YES	NO	Do you have . . .
❑	❑	1. leisure time for studying, preparing, answering phone calls, showing the house?
❑	❑	2. the ability to handle disappointment or rejection?
❑	❑	3. extra time to explore the market before you must sell?
❑	❑	4. a good lawyer who specializes in real estate?
❑	❑	5. some sophistication in financial matters?
❑	❑	6. a realistic, nonemotional approach to your home?
❑	❑	7. access to credit bureau information?
❑	❑	8. the ability to ask prospects face-to-face about their assets, income, and credit rating?
❑	❑	9. good negotiation skills?
❑	❑	10. patience?

Passing on the quiz is 70. Unless you answered "yes" to at least seven of the ten questions, seriously consider using a broker.

dise. Thus (your would-be agent will argue), many homeowners employ brokers for much the same reason that surgeons prefer not to operate on their own relatives.

- *A concrete marketing plan is essential.* Advertising, fliers, agent tours, open houses, and strategy may be explained in hopes of leaving you with an impression of competency and professionalism.

An agent knows the market, and a good one has ways of procuring the highest possible price for your home. Every agent has heard stories of how "my brother-in-law sold his place himself for full price the first day," and the broker refrains from mentioning

FIGURE 2.2
Agent Interviews

Keep a record of those agents you talk to; there's no telling where you'll be a month from now. It will help if you can recall some details about them.

Agent's Name ____________ **Firm Name** ____________
Address ____________ **Phone Number** ____________

	YES	NO
Called at a convenient time?	____	____
Identified self promptly as agent?	____	____
Sounded cordial?	____	____
Offered useful information?	____	____
Asked permission to call later?	____	____

Agent's Name ____________ **Firm Name** ____________
Address ____________ **Phone Number** ____________

	YES	NO
Called at a convenient time?	____	____
Identified self promptly as agent?	____	____
Sounded cordial?	____	____
Offered useful information?	____	____
Asked permission to call later?	____	____

Agent's Name ____________ **Firm Name** ____________
Address ____________ **Phone Number** ____________

	YES	NO
Called at a convenient time?	____	____
Identified self promptly as agent?	____	____
Sounded cordial?	____	____
Offered useful information?	____	____
Asked permission to call later?	____	____

Agent's Name ____________ **Firm Name** ____________
Address ____________ **Phone Number** ____________

that a house that sells within a few hours is usually severely underpriced. There isn't much satisfaction in saving a 6 percent commission if you lose 10 percent of true market value–unless, like the brother-in-law, you are blissfully unaware of what has happened.

Buyers who deal with a FSBO are taking on their own challenge, forgoing many of the services of an agent, in hopes of picking up a bargain. They expect the saved commission to be passed on to them. Some buyers prefer to deal directly with principals, as in buying a used car from a private party, and have prepared themselves for all of the realities and extra legwork they can expect.

This is not to say that there are indeed instances where everything can line up–correct asking price, selling price, a nonemotional, amicable closing, etc.–but those instances seem to be a successful few. Not much research exists on FSBO sales, because private parties need not report their experiences to any official sources.

Why Use an Agent?

Some of the classic reasons for using an agent, which you will hear as soon as you start interviewing them, include the following (see Chapter 3):

- *Out-of-towners and relocated executives,* especially when short on time, usually search a new community with brokers. They are valuable, well-motivated prospects who need to buy promptly.
- *The agent deals with a pool of buyers and acts as a matchmaker.* Fewer than 5 percent of buyers purchase the house they first call about. Your one classified ad is fishing with a single hook; the agent is fishing with a net. Prospects are sorted out and the appropriate ones directed to your home.
- *The agent tries for 24-hour coverage* by telephone, Internet, pager, and voicemail, and expects to work weekends and evenings when buyers need service. When the agent is unavailable, backup service is usually arranged. This means that you won't be tied down.

- *The agent screens prospects.* Everyone who comes to your house should be looking for property like yours, capable of buying it, and (unless you are using a discount broker) accompanied by the agent.
- *Buyers are even more nervous than sellers.* They find agents' expertise soothing, speak to them more frankly than to homeowners, and believe them more readily because they have more than one house to sell.

What the Agent Does

Some of the tasks you must be prepared to accomplish yourself as a FSBO include the following:

Market analysis. Pricing your house properly is half the job of selling. An agent will conduct research, often before your initial interview, so that you will have the data needed to arrive at the proper listing price.

Information. At the time your house is listed, the agent will collect detailed information about the property. The material will be used not only for assisting possible buyers in choosing which homes to view, but for writing advertisements, drawing up a purchase agreement, and arranging the eventual transfer of title.

Fixup advice. It can be difficult for you to view your home with an impartial eye. Being skilled in looking at houses as buyers see them, the agent can offer valuable suggestions for showing your home off at its best.

Interim services. If you must leave town for a vacation or move before the house is sold, you can expect a real estate agent to supervise the property, pick up papers, arrange for lawn care or snow removal, and check for signs of vandalism or fire. Neighbors seeing anything suspicious usually call the number on the For Sale sign, and the agent is available in an emergency.

Advertising. These costs are usually borne by the real estate firm, which decides on the size and frequency of advertisements. You may be asked for suggestions, but you'll find that the agent is experienced in writing ads, making up and distributing marketing fliers, and getting Internet exposure.

Qualifying prospects. Unless each house-hunter who visits your property is financially capable of buying it, then you, the agent, and the prospects themselves are just spinning your wheels. The agent has an established technique for judging buyers and will obtain information about income, assets, and credit rating within the first few minutes of conversation. The process is called qualifying the prospect. Many agents now have laptop computers handy with loan-qualifying software to make almost instantaneous judgements as to whether a buyer is a real player or not.

Matchmaking. "Buyers are liars" is a catchphrase in many real estate offices. The implication is not that buyers deliberately tell falsehoods but rather that they are motivated by many subtle influences of which they themselves are unaware.

A family explains to an agent, quite sincerely, that they are interested only in a four-bedroom colonial in Sunny Meadows. For three months, the agent shows them every four-bedroom house that comes on the market. Finally, when yet another one is listed, the agent calls to give them first chance at it, only to be told, somewhat apologetically, that they bought a house the preceding week. They had been out on a Sunday, visited an open house and fallen in love–with a three-bedroom ranch in Hidden Valley. They liked the big trees! Buyers are liars, concludes the agent.

The agent, therefore, develops skill in reading between the lines, listening carefully, and helping people find out more about their motivations than they know themselves. A large part of the work involves skillful dovetailing of buyers' needs with available homes. The agent's filing system or computer will contain a database of appropriate prospects for your particular house.

Appointments to show. You can expect your agent to clear appointments with you in advance, accompany all prospects, and (with some exceptions) conduct the actual showing of your home. It is universal real-estate etiquette to call first on every showing, even when a *lockbox* arrangement has been set up. It is also customary for the visiting agent to leave a business card behind as proof that they were there and for your agent to collect and follow up on. Chapter 8 examines in detail all the reasons, if at all possible, why you should not be present. An overzealous owner can jinx a sale. Every good broker has developed a skilled, professional technique for showing property to best advantage.

Open houses. For the same reasons, your agent may recommend that you leave the property during an open house. This period, usually a weekend afternoon, is advertised as a time when the public is welcome to visit. Special signs invite all comers, and the agent will devote several hours to your property that day. Most agents know open houses do not really sell homes. It is rare that those coming through on their own will buy that particular house. You must decide together whether regular open houses make good marketing sense or if just one or two at the beginning of the listing period will suffice.

Reports on progress. While your home is on the market, you should receive periodic calls from your agent, even if only to explain why nothing is happening. Astute listing agents follow up on any showings of your home by outside brokers (these visitors usually leave their business cards on a kitchen or entry countertop), looking for expert feedback on the pricing and marketability of your home. They'll ask why the buyer-broker's clients wanted to see your house, why they may have decided to pass on it, or whether they just may be back for a second look, and will report this information back to you.

Contract negotiation. The agent's tact and diplomacy are most directly displayed in achieving a written agreement with the qualified buyer who wants your property. Knowledgeable in finance and real estate law, with the experience of past transactions to draw from, the agent serves as a buffer between buyer and seller, skillfully smoothing the path to a satisfactory agreement.

After the contract. Although many buyers are prequalified with a lender before beginning their search for a home, the agent can often arrange financing for your purchasers if they are not represented by their own agent. Expertise in finance is often the major factor in your successful sale. In many areas, it is not unusual for the seller's agent to guide the purchaser to a lender that suits the buyer's needs and offer help with the mortgage application. During what constitutes a nervous time for all, particularly the buyer, the agent continues to serve as liaison, also staying in touch with lawyers and the escrow or title company.

Transfer of title. In the matter of final settlement, local customs differ widely. In some areas, real estate brokers run a closing session; in others, the agent is not even present. Check to see how ownership transfers in your area.

After the sale. The broker will keep all papers dealing with your sale readily available for a designated period of years.

SELLER'S TIP

Selling your home without an agent requires:

- Ensuring that an interested buyer is financially qualified
- Doing your own advertising and marketing
- Detaching yourself emotionally from your house
- Executing a proper sales contract
- Staying in touch with your buyer's lender, escrow officer, and/or attorney

If You Are Selling on Your Own

Don't pay too much attention to the broker who has "just the right buyer" for your property; that may simply be an attempt to get a foot in the door in hopes of talking you into listing. If, on the other hand, there really is such a prospect, you might allow the broker in and offer to pay a small commission if that specific prospect does end up buying your home. A simple written memorandum of the agreement, signed before the buyers enter, will prevent misunderstandings later. You may even want to offer a fee to any buyer's agent and notify buyer-only agencies about it.

You may find yourself contacted by agents who represent buyers. They will be legally bound to represent their clients' best interests, not yours. If the buyers are compensating them, you have nothing to lose by letting them view the property. If, as is common, they expect to be paid by the seller, they are probably requesting a modest commission. Whether you'd go along with that is your choice, but you should have an understanding before the broker brings clients over. The written memorandum would apply only to the one particular house-hunter the broker represents.

CHAPTER

3

Finding a Good Agent

If you are selling on your own, you can safely skip this chapter, although it might be helpful to read over the material on the differences among agents, brokers, salespersons, and REALTORS®. Take a look also at the final section of this chapter: the matter of lawyers.

The Agent

Every business or profession makes subtle distinctions in rank. The difference between an *associate professor* and an *assistant professor,* for example, has considerable meaning in the academic world. So it is with real estate. Before starting your search for the best of all possible agents, you should know the significance of the different terms you will encounter.

An *agent* is a person who is empowered to act for another. A *real estate agent* is a limited agent, retained by you for a single purpose–to find a buyer for your property. It is worth noting that the person you hire is your agent and not the buyer's. Real estate agents are licensed in two general categories, *broker* and *salesperson;* their licenses are issued by the state.

The Salesperson

An entry-level license is issued to a salesperson (sometimes called "the agent"). A specific broker takes legal responsibility for the salesperson's acts, closely supervising him or her. Obtaining a salesperson's license usually involves study, examinations, and continuing education; further standards are set by each state. It is a mistake to assume that a salesperson is necessarily an uninformed beginner. Often an expert agent chooses to remain associated with a broker rather than to establish a separate office.

The Broker

Only a broker may collect commissions from the public. These fees are then shared with the salesperson according to a prearranged schedule; a 50/50 division is common. The salesperson provides the legwork on a transaction, and the broker furnishes supervision, backup resources, and office expenses. The salesperson must work for one specific broker and may not receive fees from any other person. Because of the irregularity of their income, most salespersons are not strictly employees, but rather independent contractors who receive no salary or benefits, and who arrange their own Social Security, income tax, and retirement programs.

The REALTOR® or Realtist

A REALTOR® is a broker who chooses to join a private organization, the National Association of REALTORS®, and usually a local Association or Board of REALTORS® as well. Although the state licenses brokers and salespersons, the decision to become a REALTOR® (the word is capitalized and trademarked) is a personal choice. The REALTOR®'s salespersons may join as REALTOR-ASSOCIATES®.

The REALTOR® subscribes to a code of ethics that goes beyond state regulations. A local Multiple Listing Service (MLS) is usually associated with a Board of REALTORS®. A smaller, similar organization, the National Association of Real Estate Brokers, designates its members as Realtists, who also subscribe to a strict code. Some agents belong to both organizations.

The coined and trademarked word, REALTOR®, has become only too successful with the public. The National Association of REALTORS®, eager to keep its exclusive use of the word (like the owners of Xerox, Kleenex, and Coke), was distressed to find in a recent survey that more than half of the people questioned thought any real estate agent was properly referred to as a REALTOR®.

Finding an Agent

You should base your selection on these four criteria:

1. Is the agent currently active in your area?
2. How skilled and successful has the agent been?
3. How comfortable and confident do you feel with the agent?
4. How much marketing and exposure does the agent routinely promise for a home listing and what methods are planned?

A logical first choice is the person who sold you your home. If you were impressed with the service you received, by all means get in touch with that agent. Former clients are the most gratifying source of business, and you should receive a cordial welcome, with the promise of a particularly conscientious job. If you bought your place 20 years ago, however, ask how active the agent is now, and in which neighborhoods, and whether, perhaps, he or she now represents buyers exclusively.

Referrals from friends, relatives, your lawyer or banker, coworkers, or neighbors are good sources of possible agents. All are in a position to tell you what sort of service they received.

Remember, though, that the agent who did such a great job for your aunt will be of little value to you if he or she operates on the other side of the county. Agents specialize, and no one can be expert in too large a geographic area. You want someone who deals every day with buyers looking in your area, who has on hand a complete inventory of neighboring houses on the market, and who remembers prices, problems, and trends from several years back.

SELLER'S TIP

Look for an agent who:

- Deals every day with buyers in your area
- Has on hand a complete inventory of neighboring houses on the market
- Leaves you feeling confident in his or her abilities
- Has a concrete marketing plan that is used with each listing

If you are involved in a company transfer or are starting a new job in a strange town, your employer may refer you to an agent in its relocation network. Company transfer arrangements, in fact, often include extensive assistance with real estate. Appraisals of your present house, guaranteed minimum price, payment of commissions and legal fees, carrying your old mortgage for several months, and house-hunting and moving expenses may be offered. Your employer may even subsidize some of the interest payment on your new house if the rate is much higher than it was on your old mortgage.

Although you may not be obligated to list your house with any particular agent, those recommended by your company are probably expert and eager to do a good job to maintain their relationship with your firm.

Friends and Relatives

What about your friend Harry and cousin Daphne who are in the real estate business? The question is touchy. Consider several points:

- If Harry operates on the other side of town, or is in business only part-time, or is now an exclusive buyer's agent, he may not be the right person for your house.
- Doing business with a close friend or relative can be a good way to jeopardize the relationship.
- Daphne may feel hesitant about taking money from you and end up donating valuable time instead.

If you have confidence in your friend, you may want to go ahead with the listing. If you decide not to, an explanation is in order. Feelings will be hurt if your decision is discovered when someone in the office scans the computer printout of new listings and says, "Hey, isn't this guy over on Marshall Parkway your cousin? Did you know he was listing his house?"

Instead, call your friend a few days before listing and explain that you want to deal with a firm nearer home. You might also ask for an opinion of the company you plan to use. The courtesy of an advance explanation will ease the situation.

Ads and Open Houses

To find agents active in your neighborhood, start with the weekend classified advertising section or search the Internet on sites like Realtor.com, inputting your zip code or geographic location. You should be reading the ads regularly in any event, before listing your home, to familiarize yourself with the current market. Brokerage offices or individual salespersons who have several nearby listings are good candidates for your consideration.

Conduct a survey of For Sale signs in your area and pay attention to Sold signs. REALTORS® consider the latter to be their very best advertising, and with good reason.

On a weekend afternoon, drive through the neighborhood and visit open houses. You'll build a valuable background of information on properties competing with yours, and you can meet agents and judge their methods. The one who lounges in the living room chatting on a cell phone, and who waves you through the house by yourself is one to cross off your list. Use Figure 3.1 to take notes on the agents you meet.

Although the last entry on the "Open House Impressions" table may not strike you as a desirable quality, it is. If you were a bona fide buyer, such questions would enable the agent to offer good service.

Agents hosting open houses usually do more than simply try to sell that particular house. Open houses provide an excellent opportunity to meet prospects, and the agent may come prepared with information on similar properties and listings for the entire area, should the specific house being shown not interest the visitors.

When it becomes apparent that you are not interested in buying the house, a skilled salesperson, if not busy with other visitors, will invite you to sit down and discuss real estate further. This is the time for you to explain frankly that you are trying to gather background information before putting a nearby house on the market. It's not likely that you'll have to guide the conversation after that!

Sometimes another agent or an agent's assistant is assigned to hold an open house. Verify first that the person with whom you are chatting is indeed the one named on the sign outside. Agents who don't hold their own listings open may be too busy or have too many listings to give yours the attention you would like.

Even if you are pleased with the first agent you meet, it is prudent to talk with at least three, allowing them to inspect your house and make their listing presentations. Call firms active in your area and ask them to send an agent to talk with you. You may ask for a specific salesperson whose name you have seen on signs. If you don't, either the broker in charge will assign the call or the agent answering the phone will handle the request.

An excellent way to meet prospective agents is to allow them to present themselves. Put a For Sale by Owner sign on your lawn for a day or two and place one or two small classified ads. You may hear from more agents than you do buyers. Each agent who calls

FIGURE 3.1
Open House Impressions

Visit open houses and keep score on how agents behave.

Agent's Name, Phone Number, and Firm:

1. ______________________________
2. ______________________________
3. ______________________________
4. ______________________________
5. ______________________________
6. ______________________________

Agent:

	1	2	3	4	5	6
Greeted you at the door						
Introduced self						
Offered a business card						
Asked your name						
Asked you to sign in						
Furnished a fact sheet on the property						
Showed you through in a professional manner						
Asked personal questions						

is obviously interested in your neighborhood, enterprising, and presently free to take on listings. You won't hear from those who are inactive or currently swamped with work. And you may hear from many rookie real estate agents with enough enthusiasm to make your head spin.

You might find yourself flooded with house-hunters on that day, and even receive several written offers that evening. This may mean that you have mistakenly priced your house too low in the ad. Your best bet is to set the price higher than you think appropriate; the ad is intended simply to see which agents will contact you.

How to Judge an Agent

There is no simple answer to whether you will be better served by a man or a woman, salesperson or broker, young or old, small office or large, independent firm or one bearing a nationally franchised name. In the end, the decision comes back to your own feelings about the abilities of the salesperson you are considering. Nothing matters as much as the particular individual you choose.

Women earn as much as men in real estate for the number of hours worked, which makes it clear that they are equally effective. Either is capable of selling your home successfully.

A recent survey of homesellers ranked the agent's ethics, the fair treatment of all parties, knowledge of the community, and mastery of financing techniques in order of importance. Few considered the size of the firm as an important factor.

Your own feelings must guide you in choosing between an experienced older salesperson and an energetic young one. The enthusiastic beginner, if properly trained and supervised, can often turn in a superior job. The broker may accompany the beginning salesperson on a listing interview. Then you can judge whether the newcomer is receiving proper supervision and how the two work together. On the other hand, you may prefer an experienced broker with a proven track record.

Part-timer or full-timer? Many feel that only the full-time salesperson is worth trusting with a listing. The premise is that there is a greater commitment to selling real estate. On the other hand, the salesperson whose spouse is a department head at the university or a line worker with many acquaintances at the local factory often has contacts with newcomers who might want your property. Although the full-time salesperson is probably a better bet, there might be good reason for you to prefer a specific part-timer. In that case, ask the broker in charge of the office if help will be available to back up your listing agent when he or she is unavailable.

The question of an independent office versus one associated with a well-known franchise also arises. Independent and small offices continue to exist, and their success makes it clear that they are selling or they would not remain in business. Avoid those large firms that specialize in commercial properties, with perhaps only one or two salespersons in their residential department. Their services could be too limited.

What about the broker who is also a REALTOR®? Although many good independents choose not to join the National Association of REALTORS®, the fact remains that REALTORS® do subscribe to a code of ethics that goes beyond state regulations. Local boards have established complaint procedures and offer an opportunity for the client to submit issues to the REALTOR®'s peers. Most important, more than 80 percent of REALTORS® belong to local Multiple Listing Services, which are of great benefit to both buyers and sellers.

Tests to Apply

Identification. The well-trained, ethical agent always starts a telephone conversation or a visit to your house with "Hello, I'm Sal Salesperson of Bravo Brokers." If you suspect that some of the respondents to your one-day ad are salespersons who have not identified themselves, resolve never to do business with them.

Disclosure. Required in writing by most states these days, and recommended everywhere, is a broker's early disclosure of agency. You can expect a good broker to discuss, early on, the various fiduciary duties that will be due to you as the seller (see Chapter 5), and the fact that you could have some responsibility for your agent's actions. *Your liability for the actions of subagents should also be explained (see Chapter 4).*

Phone calls. One early test of effectiveness is the agent's handling of telephone calls. This will demonstrate how easily you can reach your listing agent (the agent who would list your property for sale) and more importantly, how prospective buyers would be treated. Most busy agents arrange for office coverage beyond normal business hours: a pager, a cell phone, voicemail, and e-mail. Children answering the agent's home telephone should be trained to record each call politely and accurately.

How quickly should your calls be returned? Remember that even the most efficient agents can be involved in situations where they cannot return calls immediately. They may be working with out-of-towners, meeting them early, orienting them to the community all morning, taking them to lunch, visiting houses all afternoon and, because the visitors have no other business in town, even extending the house-hunting far into the evening. If your calls are returned at 10 PM, you may hear the explanation, "I was working with out-of-towners."

If a day or two goes by without your calls being returned, cross that agency off your list. You don't want potential buyers of your home to receive such treatment.

Preparatory homework. When agents arrive for a listing presentation, that initial interview in which they try to sell you on their services, they should demonstrate some preparation. They may have verified your property tax figures and lot size, or obtained a preliminary title report. This is not an invasion of privacy but the use of public information freely available. Agents might also have a record of what you paid for the house and a comparative market analysis detailing recent sales for comparable properties. Such groundwork indicates a professional approach to the job at hand. Agents are likely also to be armed with statistics on how many listings and sales they have had in your neighborhood.

Personal questions. The agent who is interested in serving you must determine your needs. Questions such as "When do you need to move?" and "Where are you planning to go?" are not impertinent. Rather, they demonstrate the kind of information gathering that marks a skilled agent. You want someone who can ask similar questions of prospective buyers.

Recent transactions. If the salesperson does not volunteer information on recent dealings, ask. Ask also about training and courses of study in real estate. You may eventually decide to go with a personable newcomer, but you should know how long your agent has been in the business and what kind of success he or she has achieved.

Price recommendations. A knowledgeable homeowner has been known to mention a ridiculously high asking price just to test the reactions of potential listing agents. The agent is in a delicate position and is torn at this point: sounding pessimistic about securing that price, the agent runs the risk of losing your listing. But a professional salesperson knows that an overpriced listing receives little attention, and merely wastes time and advertising dollars.

A good agent will try, as tactfully as possible, to talk you out of an unreasonably high price. While hesitating to criticize your house, an agent may make suggestions for enhancing its appeal. Beware of the agent who agrees readily to your ambitious price and promises a sale within a week. Houses are not supposed to sell that quickly. Some agents, when met with resistance to list a home at what they would consider a relatively reasonable price after offering all their expertise, will turn down a listing. They may explain that they are not prepared to spend marketing dollars and time trying to sell a home priced too high to appeal to buyers.

You do not, on the other hand, want to list with a person who demonstrates no enthusiasm for your property. An agent should not play on your fears or denigrate your house in an attempt to pick it up at a bargain. Of course, you may encounter someone who is by nature reserved and unenthusiastic. Even if that doesn't turn you off personally, it probably will repel others. You are better off with an agent who gets reasonably excited about your house and conducts business in an open and friendly manner.

Educational background. The beginning salesperson may have studied only the material required by the state for licensing. As time goes on, however, top agents are most likely to attend seminars, real estate conventions, training sessions, and college courses in appraisal, finance, e-commerce, or construction. In some states, continuing education is required every few years. There's no harm in asking during your listing interview about the agent's background. Don't be surprised if it is in teaching; many trained and experienced teachers enter real estate.

Many agents now make it their business to become cyber professionals, knowing the ins and outs of the World Wide Web in finding buyers for their listings. The National Association of REALTORS® even has a special designation, called e-PRO, for agents who have completed training of this kind. If this appeals to you, call the brokers or REALTOR® association in your area and ask if any of their agents hold that designation.

Cooperation with other brokers. It is rare that Multiple Listing Services are not available in a particular area, but if that is the case, ask whether the agent cooperates with other offices that might want to show or sell your house. Such arrangements must be made with the offices' broker, not by the individual salesperson who may be speaking with you; office policy is well established in this matter. You should work with an office that will cooperate fully with others.

On occasion, you may encounter a member of a Multiple Listing Service who intends to evade its rules by keeping your listing under wraps for a while. Here are some tipoffs: the broker discourages a sign on your lawn, "forgets" to date the listing you sign, or suggests a price far above the figure you would accept, effectively keeping exclusive control. Other brokers will be unable to talk buyers into viewing your property, and your agent alone will know that you would take less for it. A broker who suggests that you require your agent to accompany other brokers who want to show the house could effectively block their efforts and sabotage the usefulness to you of the Multiple Listing Service.

If your home is eventually sold by a cooperating broker from another company, you are not normally responsible for any extra commission. Discuss this point, just to make sure. Ask what share of the commission will be offered to the agent from another firm who might produce your buyer. In some communities, a 50/50 split is common, but the listing brokerage can set its own figure. If not enough is promised to a cooperating firm, other agents in a multiple listing system may not be motivated to work on your property, thus cutting down on the pool of potential buyers.

Ask also about your listing office's policy on buyer brokerage. If another agent is being paid by the buyers to represent them, will your company cooperate in showing the property and negotiating a sales contract? If you are asked to pay for the buyer's broker, will your company consider appropriate adjustments to commission?

Commissions. Immediately cross off the list any agent who tells you that commissions are set by law or by the local Association of REALTORS®. This just isn't so. Commission rates are *completely negotiable* between you and the agent, although a salesperson requires the broker's permission to change the office's customary rates. Chapter 4 discusses guidelines on commission rates.

Competition. During the listing presentation, agents are eager to convince you that their service is the best you can find. Pay attention to the way they speak of other offices. REALTOR® ethics and general business standards suggest that they refrain from knocking the competition. If you have a sad story of someone else's ineptitude to tell, an agent might properly reply, "I'm sure I can handle this to your satisfaction; give me a chance to see what I can do." An agent who criticizes another's practices may later cut corners on something else.

Types of Listings

An explanation of the types of listing contracts open to you will be found in the next chapter. One arrangement, however, should trigger a red flag. If an agent proposes to guarantee you a certain sum from your sale in return for the chance to keep anything over that amount, you have been offered a *net listing.* This arrangement is open to so much abuse that it is illegal in about half of the states. You can view with suspicion any practitioner who suggests it.

At first, the net listing may sound seductive; you receive the agreed-upon sum from the sale of the property, and the agent assumes all the risk that the sales price is not higher. But any number of complications may arise. The agent might be tempted to block an otherwise attractive offer; although the law requires that you, as the client, must come first, the agent's own interests have in this case become paramount.

Of course, you will want to calculate what you might net from your sale, as explained in Chapter 6, but this is a different matter from entering into a net listing.

The Guaranteed Sale

In some circumstances, you may need to know that you can count on a certain minimum sum by a given date. Some offices can offer you a *guaranteed sale.* In essence, it is a promise to buy your property at a discounted price if it has not been sold by your deadline. Any guarantee should be in writing, and you need assurance that meanwhile the office intends to market the property aggressively and to try for a higher price.

In a broker-guaranteed sale, the broker is justified in offering a price below market value. The broker buys your house at wholesale. It is worth much more to the homebuyer who intends to live in it. Some of the broker's costs, if he or she does buy your house and then sells it again, include an average of three months' taxes, insurance, utilities, and lost interest on the investment while the house is vacant. Legal fees for buying and again for selling, maintenance, emergencies, and points (explained in Chapter 10 and in the glossary) must all be considered. The broker will also include the lost commission on the eventual buyer, who might otherwise have been sold another house.

If a guaranteed sale is contemplated, the broker should explain these factors to you and furnish an estimate of true market value. The broker should counsel you to price the house attractively yourself in hopes of selling it at retail within your time limit.

Some large corporations will offer you a guaranteed sale in your relocation package, assuring you of a certain agreed-upon price for your home, but allowing you, say, 30, 60, or 90 days in which to get your home sold through their referred agent for a higher price. If, at the end of that period, your home remains on the market, you would have agreed to accept the buy-out, and that, as they say, would be that.

Neighborhood Expertise

While you are interviewing agents, stay alert for the one who is familiar with special programs at the local elementary school, serves on the Scout committee, and knows why the fast-food operation was turned down for the spot on Main Street. Local expertise is vital to good service and usually indicates an agent who is genuinely interested in real estate. He or she may make routine visits to the city planner's office, checking on what may be slated for residential, commercial, or retail areas around existing neighborhoods.

Do You Need a Lawyer?

The law does not require you to have legal representation to sell a house. In many areas, local custom does not expect it either. Nevertheless, you are well advised to have access to an attorney, no matter where your home is located.

In many areas of the eastern United States, sellers routinely expect to employ attorneys to help prove that they can furnish marketable title to the property, to draw up the deed that transfers the real estate, to field problems, and to represent them at closing. In other parts of the country, transfer may be effected by title companies or special escrow companies, which perform many of the same tasks, and attorneys are only brought into the picture if there is need of expert legal advice.

It is always appropriate to discuss fees in advance. The law firm may charge a percentage of the sales price of your home, or bill you by the hour for services actually performed. Extra charges are acceptable if an unforeseen snag arises, but a lawyer should be able to estimate the likely cost of your transaction.

Remember that lawyers specialize, and that you want one who is active in real estate. Start your search with a lawyer who has performed other services for you; consider the one who represented you when you bought the house.

Beyond that, you can request a list of lawyers from your real estate broker. Your agent knows which attorneys are active in real estate work. You need not fear conflict of interest; the lawyer is well aware of fiduciary duty to you as a client.

Lending institutions can be a source of information in this matter. Call a local savings and loan office to ask about law firms that handle their own real estate transactions. This is a particularly good way to find a good attorney in a strange town.

For quick legal advice, your employer may offer legal-matter benefits to its employees by phone, or as a starting point for further engagement.

In states where attorneys are routinely retained for real estate transactions, the law does not forbid them from representing both you and the buyer, although ethics discourage the practice. It is common in small towns where there may not be much legal talent to choose from. The lawyer must withdraw, however, if a conflict arises.

When you select your lawyer (preferably before starting to market the house), be frank about any problems, with either the property or your own situation. Unpaid judgments, an impending divorce, an electric system that you know violates code—all represent exactly the sort of complications for which you'll want legal assistance. Attorneys spend much of their time heading off trouble. If you employ an attorney and conceal your problems, it's like seeing a physician and concealing your symptoms.

CHAPTER

4

The Listing Process

This chapter deals with the process of listing your home for sale through a broker. Read it even if you are selling on your own, because without an agent, you will be listing the house with yourself, and your first task will be carefully gathering the information detailed here.

If You Invite Agents

The agents you have invited to your home for listing presentations have the task of convincing you that they are the right persons to handle your property. These initial interviews will cost you nothing, and you will not be obligated in any way. Even if you like the first agent who calls, it can be educational to talk with several others before making your decision. If you are planning to interview several agents, inform them at the outset that you will do so before making any decisions.

The *listing* is an employment contract under which you agree to pay a commission to the broker for securing a purchaser who is ready, willing, and able to pay the price and comply with the terms that you have specified. Strictly speaking, this contract might be enforceable by the broker even if you were not the owner of the property, and even if the transaction were never completed. In theory, the broker's function is completed when he or she finds a buyer who satisfies the requirements you have specified. In practice, the listing contract often contains provisions further regulating the payment of commission that protect both you and the broker. You may want your lawyer to review the contract before you sign it.

Types of Listings

Oral. In approximately half of the states, a listing need not be in writing to be enforceable. Although the statute of frauds in all states requires that real estate contracts be in writing, a promise to pay a licensed broker a commission for aid in selling real property can be an exception. Even accepting the services of a broker, without any promise to pay commission, has sometimes been held by the courts as an implied contract of employment.

Net. In a net listing, the sellers agree to a certain figure as their share of the selling price. Monies beyond that sum remain with the broker as commission. As previously pointed out, this type of listing is seldom in the seller's best interest, and it is illegal in most states.

Open. On a country road, one may come across an isolated house with three or four For Sale signs in its yard, each bearing the telephone number of a different agency. This house is being marketed through open listings. The owners have promised a number of agents that they will pay a commission to the firm that produces a satisfactory sale. If the owners should sell on their own, no commission would be payable to anyone.

The open listing is often used in rural areas that lack multiple listing arrangements so that the seller may use the services of several agents in nearby towns. Its simplicity is attractive, and it appears to be in your interest. Any particular agent, however, may lack the incentive to invest heavily in advertising or to spend time marketing your property. If a competing office effects the sale, the hours and money spent are not reimbursed in any way. It can be difficult to obtain maximum effort from those with whom you have open listings.

Exclusive. These listings fall into two categories, *exclusive agency* and *exclusive right to sell.* With the first, you retain the right to sell the property on your own without owing a commission, and that constitutes the major difference between them.

Exclusive agency promises that the listing office will be your only agent. If anyone is to receive a commission, that firm will be the one. You retain the right, however, to sell the property yourself without paying a commission. In effect, you are in competition with your own agent.

Exclusive right to sell is promise of commission if the property is sold by anyone during the listing period. Even if you sell it yourself, you still owe a commission. With the protection this affords, a listing office is theoretically motivated to go all-out on the assignment. Figure 4.1 (courtesy of the Greater Rochester Association of REALTORS®) is an example of an exclusive-right-to-sell-contract.

Multiple Listing

In a Multiple Listing Service (MLS), your agent shares the listing with a number of other brokers. If one of these finds the buyer, your original firm will receive a share of the commission, usually around 50 percent, depending on local custom. You will not be liable for any extra payment.

A listing that is thus shared might, in theory, be any of the types mentioned, but exclusive right to sell is the type most often required by a Multiple Listing Service. It is difficult to understand that you can sign an exclusive right to sell with hundreds of different offices; somehow that doesn't seem very exclusive. In a few Multiple Listing Services, each firm becomes your subagent, unless you have specifically stated otherwise. Some sellers fear that they could be held liable for misrepresentations or human rights violations that might be made by cooperating brokers who have been accepted as their subagents.

FIGURE 4.1 Exclusive-Right-to-Sell Contract

LISTING BROKER'S COPY

GREATER ROCHESTER ASSOCIATION OF REALTORS® , INC.
EXCLUSIVE RIGHT TO SELL CONTRACT

THIS FORM IS FOR USE BY MEMBERS OF THE GREATER ROCHESTER ASSOCIATION OF REALTORS®, INC. ONLY FOR THE PLACING OF PROPERTY LISTINGS IN ITS MULTIPLE LISTING SERVICE.

REALTOR® EXCLUSIVE RIGHT TO SELL, EXCHANGE OR LEASE CONTRACT. COMMISSIONS OR FEES FOR REAL ESTATE SERVICES TO BE PROVIDED HEREUNDER ARE NEGOTIABLE BETWEEN REALTOR® AND OWNER. IT IS UNDERSTOOD THAT THE GREATER ROCHESTER ASSOCIATION OF REALTORS®, INC. (Including its MLS) IS NOT A PARTY TO THIS LISTING AGREEMENT.

1. **OWNERSHIP OF PROPERTY AND POWER TO SIGN CONTRACT.** I am the Owner(s) of the property located at ______________ ______________ (the Property). I have complete legal authority to sell, exchange or lease the Property. I have not entered into any other agreement which would affect the sale, exchange, lease, or transfer of the Property; except as follows: (name or specify agreement.)

2. **EXCLUSIVE RIGHT TO SELL, EXCHANGE OR LEASE.** (Check and complete either (a) or (b)).
(a) ______________ I hereby hire ______________ (REALTOR®) to sell or exchange the Property and I hereby grant to REALTOR® the Exclusive Right to Sell the Property for the price of $ ______________ or any other price that I later agree to, and upon such terms and conditions as I may agree to or to exchange the Property upon such terms and conditions as I may agree to.
(b) ______________ I hereby hire ______________ (REALTOR®) to lease the Property and I hereby grant to REALTOR® the Exclusive Right To Lease the Property for a rent of ________ per ________ or any other rent that I may later agree to, and upon such terms and conditions as I may agree to.

3. **MULTIPLE LISTING SERVICE.** I authorize REALTOR® to submit the information contained in this listing agreement and the applicable Greater Rochester Association of REALTORS®, Inc. Profile Sheet relating to the Property to the Multiple Listing Service of the Greater Rochester Association of REALTORS®, Inc. (MLS). REALTOR® will submit such information to the MLS through REALTOR®'s MLS terminal (or by first class mail or telecopy if REALTOR® does not have a MLS terminal) **within 48 hours** of my signing this Contract, excluding Saturdays, Sundays and holidays. REALTOR® shall retain this listing agreement and the Profile Sheet for at least six years.

4. **PAYMENT TO REALTOR®.** (Check and complete either (a) or (b), or both).
(a) ________ I will pay REALTOR® a commission of ________% of the sale price of the Property as set forth in the purchase and sale contract that I sign, or $ ______________, or a commission of ______________ if the Property is exchanged.
(b) ________ I will pay REALTOR® a commission of ________% of the gross rent for the Property as set forth in the lease contract that I sign, or such other compensation arrangement as is agreed upon in writing, a copy of which is attached.

5. **AUTHORIZATION REGARDING OTHER BROKERS.** I authorize REALTOR® to cooperate with other brokers, including brokers who represent buyers (with the understanding that such "buyers' brokers" will be representing only the interests of the prospective buyers), to appoint subagents, and to divide with other licensed brokers such compensation in any manner acceptable to REALTOR®, such other brokers and me. I understand and agree that if the commission provided for in Paragraph 4 is divided, it will be divided as follows: ______________

6. **PAYMENT OF COMMISSION.** I agree to pay to REALTOR® the commission set forth in Paragraph 4 on the "closing date" specified in the purchase and sale contract or when I sign a written agreement to exchange the Property or when I sign a lease for the Property. I will pay this commission to REALTOR® whether I, REALTOR®, or anyone else sells, exchanges or leases the Property during the life of this Contract. REALTOR® has earned the commission when I am provided with a written purchase offer which meets the price and other conditions I have set or when the purchase and sale contract becomes a binding legal commitment on the buyer, or when I sign a written agreement to exchange the Property, or when I sign a lease for the Property. At the closing of the sale of the Property, my representative (such as my attorney) is authorized to pay to REALTOR® the commission agreed to in Paragraph 4 from the proceeds of the sale of the Property.

7. **DUTIES OF REALTOR® AND OWNER.** REALTOR® will bring all offers to purchase, exchange or lease the Property to me. I agree to refer all inquiries about the Property to REALTOR®. I agree to cooperate with REALTOR® in showing the Property to possible buyers or renters at any reasonable hour. I agree that REALTOR® may photograph the Property listed for sale, exchange or lease.

8. **SUBMISSION OF OFFERS TO PURCHASE.** **Check One**
I agree that any offers to purchase, exchange or lease the Property shall be submitted through: ________ the listing broker ________ the selling broker

9. **FOR SALE, FOR RENT SIGN.** Authorization to install a "for sale" or "for rent" sign placed on the Property: ______ Yes ______ No

10. **LOCKBOX.** Authorization of the use of a lockbox. I understand that neither REALTOR®, any cooperating broker, the Greater Rochester Association of REALTORS®, Inc. nor its MLS shall be responsible for any theft, loss or damage attributed to the use of a lockbox. ______ Yes ______ No

11. **PROPERTY CONDITION DISCLOSURE.** I have completed and delivered to REALTOR® a Real Estate Transfer Property Condition Disclosure Statement concerning the condition of the Property: ______ Yes ______ No

FIGURE 4.1 Exclusive-Right-to-Sell Contract (Continued)

12. LIFE OF CONTRACT; SALE, EXCHANGE OR LEASE OF PROPERTY AFTER CONTRACT ENDS TO A PERSON WHO WAS SHOWN THE PROPERTY DURING THE LIFE OF CONTRACT. This Contract will last until midnight on ______________, 19______. However, if I sell, exchange or lease the Property within ________ days after this Contract ends (the "Effective Period") to a person who was shown the Property by Owner(s), REALTOR® , or anyone else during the life of this Contract, I will pay REALTOR® the same commission agreed to in Paragraph 4 of this Contract. I will not owe any commission to REALTOR® if such sale, exchange or lease occurs during the life of a Greater Rochester Association of REALTORS® , Inc. MLS Contract I enter into after this Contract ends but before the expiration of the Effective Period.

13. PUBLICATION OF PROPERTY DATA. I agree that REALTOR® may provide MLS with information, including the selling price, about the Property upon final sale of the Property. I further agree that REALTOR® may provide MLS with information, other than price, prior to final sale of the Property.

14. INFORMATION ABOUT PROPERTY. All information about the Property I have given REALTOR® is accurate and complete, and REALTOR® assumes no responsibility to me or anyone else for the accuracy of such information. I authorize REALTOR® to obtain other information about the Property if REALTOR® wants to do so. REALTOR® will use sources of information REALTOR® believes to be reliable, but is not responsible to me for the accuracy of the information REALTOR® obtains. I authorize REALTOR® to disclose to prospective purchasers and any other persons including other brokers any information about the Property REALTOR® obtains from me or any other source. I understand that New York law requires me to give certain information about heating and insulation to prospective purchasers if they ask for it in writing before a purchase contract is signed.

15. NON-DISCRIMINATION. I understand that the listing and sale, exchange or lease of the Property must be in full compliance with local, state and federal fair housing laws against discrimination on the basis of race, creed, color, religion, national origin, sex, familial status, age or disabilities.

16. RESPONSIBILITY OF OWNER(S) UNDER THIS CONTRACT. All Owners must sign this Contract. If more than one person signs this Contract as Owner, each person is fully responsible for keeping the promises made by the Owner.

17. RENEWAL AND MODIFICATION OF CONTRACT. I may extend the life of this Contract by signing a renewal agreement. If I renew this Contract, REALTOR® will notify MLS of the renewal. All changes or modifications of the provisions of this Contract must be made in writing, signed by Owner(s) and REALTOR® .

18. LIST OF BROKERS. I hereby certify that REALTOR® has provided me with a list of names and addresses of all MLS member companies.

19. OWNER'S LIABILITY FOR CONTRACT TERMINATION. In the event this Contract is terminated prior to the time specified in Paragraph 12 for any reason other than REALTOR® 's fault, I will be liable for and agree to pay all damages and expenses incurred by REALTOR® , including without limitation costs for advertising the Property.

20. ATTORNEY'S FEES. In any action, proceeding or arbitration arising out of this Contract, the prevailing party shall be entitled to reasonable attorney's fees and costs.

21. NOTICE TO HOMEOWNERS. The Secretary of State, State of New York, requires that the following explanation be given to homeowners and acknowledged by them in the listing of property:

EXPLANATION:

An "exclusive right to sell" listing means that if you, the owner of the property, find a buyer for your house, or if another broker finds a buyer, you must pay the agreed commission to the present broker.

An "exclusive agency" listing means that if you, the owner of the property find a buyer, you will not have to pay a commission to the broker. However, if another broker finds a buyer, you will owe a commission to both the selling broker and your present broker.

Owner(s) understands that this Contract grants REALTOR® the exclusive right to sell the Property.

Acknowledgement of Explanation:

_______________________ OWNER(S) SIGNATURE   _______________________ OWNER(S) SIGNATURE

In consideration of the above, I accept this Contract and agree to its terms and conditions. Date: __________

_______________________ OWNER(S) SIGNATURE   _______________________ OWNER(S) SIGNATURE

_______________________ Print Owner(s) Name   _______________________ Print Owner(s) Name

In consideration of the above, REALTOR® agrees to use best efforts to find a purchaser. Date: __________

_______________________ Print Name of REALTOR®   _______________________ Print Name of Broker or Salesperson

_______________________ Signature

9/91

REALTOR

Members of Multiple Listing Services can also, if desired, accept listings that will be truly exclusive to one firm. Although MLS is usually the most efficient way to market your property, you might prefer to deal with a single office. If you desire a *silent sale* (one that is not publicized), multiple listing is not for you because the system widely disseminates information about your house.

What to Negotiate at Listing Time

Commission rates are always negotiable between you and the listing broker. Rates in a given community may cluster around 6 or 7 percent, but can be considerably lower; thus discount brokers continue to do business. Some types of real estate commonly listed at higher rates are vacant land, farms, resort property, inexpensive parcels, and property that is difficult to market.

In an area of expensive homes, on the other hand, you may be able to negotiate lower fees than a firm's usual rate. Before making any such arrangement, however, you must consider a number of factors. Will the contract be placed in a Multiple Listing Service where the lower commission rate won't motivate cooperating brokers? Does the broker who operates below usual rates have a sufficient budget for advertising?

You may be approached by a discount broker who offers limited, unbundled services, called a *fee-for-services* broker. If you are prepared to handle some tasks in marketing your home and wish to hire an agent for just one or two of the many services he or she offers, this may be the arrangement for you. *Discount brokers,* on the other hand, operate much like the full-service broker, but without as much personal assistance for tasks like open houses, advertising, and accompanying buyers to your home. If you use one, make sure that your home will be entered in the multiple listing system with enough commission offered to traditional firms that may produce a buyer.

Sellers have been known to make separate agreements with a member of a multiple listing system. They may offer a higher total commission if the fee must be shared between the seller's and buyer's agents, but lower if the listing agent *double-ends* the sale, by bringing you a buyer on his or her own.

The duration of a listing is also a matter for discussion. One month is too short a period for the agent's protection; some of the marketing techniques will just be getting under way. One year, on the other hand, is unfair to the seller, unless rural property is being marketed. In general, property that is correctly priced should sell within three months, except in depressed markets. The agent may ask for a six-month period instead, or even write in a six-month expiration date without asking your permission. Remember that the length of time is at your discretion and that you want the contract to contain an expiration date with no automatic renewal. Check all these points before you sign the listing contract. Some agents will not entertain listing a house for less than three or six months, if they believe that their up-front investment of marketing dollars and time does not warrant doing so.

Details to Discuss

You and the agent will discuss many items relating to your house besides the terms of the listing contract, such as the following:

Can a For Sale sign be placed on your property? You must decide whether to give permission. Do so by all means. The sign is one of the best advertisements your home can have. It gives the firm's name and telephone number, and may also state "by appointment only" so that you will not be bothered by unexpected callers. Some even display "talking ad" phone numbers, giving buyers the opportunity to drive by and listen to a recording about the house. A sign should not be placed, however, if the neighborhood is overloaded with property for sale, if local regulations forbid signs, or if you have an overriding need for privacy regarding your sale.

Will the broker hold open houses? The proper time to discuss this possibility is at listing time. Sellers don't realize that few sales result from open houses, but if you want the broker to schedule them, talk about it now.

Hours for showing must be discussed. It is wise to place as few restrictions as possible. You may not want your house shown on certain days of the week, or during certain times of the day. You may prefer that no one visit during the children's naps or when you are eating dinner. Some sellers request 24 hours' notice before a showing.

Every one of these restrictions, however, limits your chances for finding the right buyer. Out-of-towners in particular are often under rigid time limitations. They may need to find a house in one day, and those homes that can be viewed promptly stand the best chance of being chosen.

What about a key? Do not hesitate to leave one with your listing agent's office for use when you are not at home. The listing agent will notify other brokers that the key is available and keep careful track of who borrows it. If you dislike giving out the key permanently, do so at least when you go on vacation or leave town for the weekend; otherwise, your home is effectively off the market for those periods.

In some areas, it is common to use *lockboxes.* The lockbox is a gadget attached to your door, with your door key inside it. Each cooperating broker or agent has a lockbox code to enter in order to retrieve the key. The lockboxes retain that code as a record of who has used the key. Many brokers claim that lockboxes provide the best opportunity for showings, because a simple call to your home or a message left on your answering machine is all that is needed before buyers can be brought in. The MLS listing notes "Call First/Lockbox" to buyer agents. If potential buyers spot the sign and want to see your house, the agent can show it without an appointment, and agents armed with cell phones can place a quick call easily enough.

A lockbox on the door has helped sell many a home because of the ease and spontaneity it adds to house hunting, if you feel comfortable with it.

Pets on the premises. This is sometimes mentioned in the comments accompanying a multiple listing so that other offices are aware of the large dog in the basement or the cats in the garage.

For the best possible showings, it's best to house a large, noisy, or overly friendly dog with a friend, relative, or neighbor during the showings. As smitten as you are with your pet, others may be turned off and not wish to return for that all-important second look.

Special showing instructions. These can also be included: please turn down heat, back door must be slammed, shut off all the lights before you go.

Brochures or fliers. These are generally made up by the agent, and contain facts and interesting information about your house. They may include a photo, list of amenities, and special financing terms, if any. A supply of these can be placed in an entry or on a kitchen countertop. Sometimes a special brochure box can be attached to the For Sale sign. Ask the agent how often these brochures will be stocked, and offer to replenish the outside box if it becomes empty.

Financing Information

Financing possibilities may be detailed in the listing information. You will be asked to set the price you want, a topic that deserves a chapter all its own (see Chapter 6), and the terms with which you will sell. It is simplest to start with "all cash," for you can always accept different terms later. If you are willing to carry financing (hold the mortgage yourself), or if you have an assumable mortgage, these selling points should be mentioned at the outset.

Learn what types of mortgages can be offered on your specific house. Some lenders will not lend on homes with dirt road access, others will not lend on houses more than 100 years old. Your agent may need your loan number, and perhaps your specific authorization, to obtain information on your present loan.

If you are selling on your own, investigate for yourself. Talk with your mortgage holder to determine not only the present balance on the loan but also whether it will be of any value to the next owner of your house. Some old Federal Housing Administration (FHA) and Department of Veterans Affairs (VA) loans may be taken over (assumed) exactly as they stand by any buyer.

Newer VA and FHA mortgages and some conventional loans, particularly adjustable-rate mortgages, are "assumable with lender's approval." This means that the buyer must meet bank standards and possibly pay a higher interest rate than you do. Find out whether your present mortgage is assumable in any fashion and what closing costs (usually a small amount) would be involved.

Ascertain at this point whether you will be subject to a prepayment penalty if you pay off your old loan in full before the end of the term.

Find out from your agent whether new FHA and VA loans are available in your area and whether loan limits would cover your house. If so, they may be useful to many potential buyers. If these government-backed loans are available, you do yourself an injustice by stating that you do not want to see offers involving such mortgages. Although the house might have to pass a more stringent inspection or you might have to pay more points, your house is more easily sold when FHA or VA financing is possible.

Your agent should discuss at the time of listing whether you are likely to be asked to make specific repairs by a buyer's prospective lender. Consider these potential costs from the start. You will find a further explanation of repairs in Chapter 6.

If you are selling on your own, it is essential to estimate beforehand how much income a buyer might need to qualify for a mortgage loan on your property. To do this, call a lender and ask them to provide you with a fact sheet based on your asking price, which can be handed to a potential buyer when they tour your home. The lender can assume a typical down payment amount and use the going interest rate and terms for several different types of loans. Mortgage consultants are usually happy to do this, because your buyer may opt to use that particular lender, and the lender gets marketing exposure as well.

Of course, you can't guess how much a prospective buyer might have for down payment or how many other debts might cut the available loan amount. You should, however, study the material on qualifying ratios in Chapter 10, so that you have a rough rule of thumb to use when sizing up prospects.

Other Topics to Discuss

Certificate of occupancy. In some areas, you may be asked to furnish a certificate of occupancy for certain properties, particularly multiple dwellings. Your broker can explain what is involved. If this certificate is required, the listing should state clearly whether you agree to supply it.

Carryover stipulation. Your agent will probably use a standard listing form, which may include a carryover stipulation. This states that if the property is sold after the listing has expired to someone who first saw it while the listing was in force, a commission will be due. The provision protects the agent from exerting effort and investing money in your property while you wait out the listing and make a private deal with one of the firm's customers to avoid paying commission. The number of days this provision remains in effect can vary; 60 days after the listing expires is probably long enough.

Appointments through the listing agent. If you are using a Multiple Listing Service, you may have specific reasons for preferring not to talk with numerous brokers: a sick person in the house, perhaps, or a general dislike of telephone conversations. You may stipulate that all appointments be made through your listing office or that your own agent accompany everyone, even other brokers with their clients. Such restrictions, however, limit your chances of selling. If your agent is not available when another broker is ready to show property, your home may be ignored.

Accurate Information

Because other people will be making important financial decisions based on the information contained in your listing, it is essential that the details be as accurate as possible. Your listing agent should check lot size against your deed, survey, or preliminary title report, which will also yield a legal description of the property. Lot size can also be verified with the taxing authorities, who will furnish the *true tax* figures. Your tax bill may be misleadingly small (in some areas) if you are a veteran or a senior citizen, or are affiliated with a religious organization. It may be inflated, on the other hand, because of special assessments or unpaid municipal water bills.

Unless you are sure about the *square footage* of your home, it's best to measure before putting the house on the market. Use outside measurements, not counting basement or attic space. While you're outside, show the agent your *property lines.*

The old rule of *caveat emptor,* let the buyer beware, no longer has the force it once did in the sale of real estate. Disclosure laws throughout the country have changed considerably within the past decade, leaving you and your agent responsible for any misrepresentations. Not only must you answer questions truthfully, but you must also volunteer information on any hidden (latent) defect or major problem, particularly if it involves health or safety.

A hidden defect is one that is not readily apparent in a normal, prudent inspection. You are not required to say, "Come back here, you didn't notice the big crack in the living room ceiling," because the prospects could have noticed it for themselves. You should point out, however, that the septic tank is inadequate for the size of the house and requires frequent attention. If you do not do this, you may be setting yourself up for trouble in the future.

State laws vary in this matter, ranging from old-fashioned *caveat emptor* to California's elaborate disclosure form required of all sellers, which is reprinted in Appendix C.

Must you tell prospective buyers that a murder occurred on your property 20 years back? That someone committed suicide on the premises three years ago? That the neighborhood thinks your house is haunted? Matters like these are known as *stigmas,* and different states have different regulations about stigmatized properties. In some areas, you have no obligation to reveal occurrences (including health problems) that do not affect the physical condition of the property. Other states set a time limit, depending on how far back the problem occurred. In yet other states, only past court cases offer guidelines. If you have such a condition, it's prudent to consult your attorney or broker to find out just what applies in your area.

In some areas, you are required to have past utility bills available to buyers. If you haven't kept them, your utility company will furnish copies upon request. Buyers also welcome information about the type, thickness, and location of insulation.

Ground water contamination, previous flooding and its aftermath, soil containing an inordinate amount of rock or a questionable geological report; whatever may be construed as affecting future property value must be disclosed.

For houses built before 1978, buyers must sign acknowledgement that they have received specific written lead paint warnings. The notice must be given before a sales contract is signed.

At the time of listing you should reveal all *liens* (financial claims) against your property. Your mortgage or trust deed is probably the largest lien. Others may include back taxes, mechanics' liens (filed perhaps for that driveway work you refused to pay for), or personal judgments. Your agent and your lawyer will investigate problem areas. If you live in a master-planned or a multifamily area that has a fee-charging homeowners association, you must disclose this to a potential buyer as well. In this case, keep a copy of the local *covenants, conditions, and restrictions* (CC&Rs) handy for buyers' review.

You must also disclose, at the time you list the property, all you know about *easements,* such as the neighbor's right to use your driveway. Reveal any code violations (you know the plumbing isn't up to standards), and zoning variances (the house isn't really zoned for an attic apartment, but the city hasn't bothered you). If you are involved in a boundary dispute with a neighbor, mention it now.

Personal Property and Fixtures

What stays and what can you take when you move? All property is divided into two classes: personal and real. *Real estate* consists of the land and whatever is attached to it. *Personal property* (sometimes referred to as *chattels*) is movable. The tree growing on your land is part of the real estate. When it is cut into lumber, it becomes personal property that can be carried away.

SELLER'S TIP

When preparing information to sell your home, gather information to disclose:

- Lot size and property lines, and any easements
- Property tax and utility figures
- Financial or other claims against your property
- Any items that can be construed as affecting future property value
- Homeowner's fees and current association budgets
- Any existing covenants, conditions, and restrictions (CC&Rs) that apply to your neighborhood

In the opposite manner, personal property can become part of the real estate. A bathtub in a store is personal property that can be loaded into your station wagon. Take it home and hook it up to your plumbing system and it becomes part of the real estate. It becomes, in fact, a *fixture* (affixed to the property), which is a special term for chattels that have become real property.

You need to know this because many disputes in real estate transactions center around what does and does not remain with the property. In general, personal property may be taken away; fixtures must remain. To avoid argument, remove certain items before anyone views the property. If you plan to keep the large mirror in the hall that fits that spot perfectly, or—most commonly—the special dining room chandelier, the simplest solution is to replace these items before the house is shown. What they don't see, they can't want. If you are not going to do this, state clearly in writing, at the time you list, that you reserve the right to remove the specially cut area rug, the window air conditioner, the garage storage cabinets, or anything else the buyers might assume stays with the property.

Items that most often give trouble are lighting fixtures, drapes, satellite dishes, basketball backboards, play equipment, wood stoves, and pool equipment. The law holds that the items should remain if they are (1) permanently attached, (2) adapted to the use for which they were installed, and (3) intended to remain. It's best to forestall arguments.

Carpeting usually remains if it is attached to the floor. Appliances are removable unless they are built-in. Even if you are willing to leave freestanding appliances, do not mention them in your listing; they may come in handy as bargaining tools later.

In these days of Martha Stewart matching draperies, upholstery, pillows, and comforters, you may want to make clear whether you will take or leave any matching items (except for, perhaps, the matching wallpaper).

If you try to sell the house with its furniture, you are eliminating many potential buyers. Offer the house alone, noting that you would sell it with furnishings if so requested. You can always hold a garage sale, call a charity for pick-up, or hand furniture over to a consignment shop for later liquidation.

Supplementary Fact Sheet

Besides the information on the listing form, other data can be of value to house hunters. Your agent may prepare a standard information sheet. If not, you can create one.

If you are selling on your own, an informational brochure or flyer is essential and will contain much of the information that an agent's listing contract would include. Putting this together is a useful desktop-publishing project. Flyers can be distributed to area brokers if you are offering a co-op fee to a buyer's broker. They can also be handed out to neighbors, who may have friends or family considering buying a home in your area. Most importantly, a supply of brochures can be made available on an entry countertop to potential buyers as they tour your home or from an outside brochure box for passersby.

Room sizes and floor plans can be noted on your fact sheet. Mention carpet and tile types and descriptions. Describe the insulation, which is of ever-increasing interest. Include information on your landscaped backyard, extras you have installed in the home, such as closet organizers, and any special buyer incentives or financing being offered.

It's an excellent idea to go to the local elementary, middle school, and high schools that serve your neighborhood and gather information on test scores, programs, etc., to give to potential buyers. Families have been known to move to a particular area primarily for better schools, so offering information on them (even if you do not or have never had children attend them) is a good marketing tool. It's important not to make any guarantees about the schools, but refer buyers and their brokers to the school district phone number for more information.

This is the place for you to describe particular features you are proudest of and to list nearby bus or transit lines, shopping centers, golf courses, health clubs, and community colleges, in addition to neighborhood schools. (Omit from the list neighborhood places of worship, which could be interpreted as an attempt to attract certain prospective buyers in violation of fair housing laws.)

Use the sample fact sheet in Figure 4.2 as a guide for preparing yours.

Possible Exceptions to Commission

When you list the property, you may have in mind a couple who have expressed an interest in your house. You may even delay listing with an agent, losing valuable time waiting for their decision. There are two ways to handle this situation: You can turn their names over to the listing agent, or you can request a statement that no commission will be due if the property is sold to this couple. Many brokers will honor a request to exempt specific purchasers from the listing contract.

FIGURE 4.2
Sample Fact Sheet

Address: ______________________________ Price: ______________
Style: ______________________________ Taxes: ______________
Entry: ______________________________ Lot size: ______________
Living room: ____
____
Dining room: ____
____
Kitchen: ____
____
Family room/den: ____
____
Master bedrooms: ____
Other bedrooms: ____
____
Baths: ____
Office/den: ____
Basement: ____
Garage: ____
Backyard amenities: ____
Special features: ____
____
Facilities nearby: ____
Schools: ____
____
Financing: ____
____
Offered by: ______________________________ Phone: ______________

This information is believed to be accurate, but is subject to errors, omissions, prior sale, or withdrawal.

FIGURE 4.3
Your Reasons for Buying . . .

I chose this house because . . .

1. ______________________________
____
2. ______________________________
____
3. ______________________________
____
4. ______________________________
____
5. ______________________________
____
6. ______________________________
____
7. ______________________________
____

Keep these features in mind when you write your advertisement, or give the list to your broker.

The listing contract should be signed by all owners of the property, and in some states, this may include a spouse who is not an owner. A salesperson also signs the listing contract on behalf of the broker with whom you are entering into the contract.

It can be instructive, at this point, to make a list of the reasons you originally chose this particular house. Perhaps you bought because of the nearby transit line; then you bought a second car and haven't thought about public transportation since. But your original reasons may influence other buyers. Think back and enter the list in Figure 4.3.

CHAPTER

5

Some Legal Matters

Even if no broker is employed, most home sales are covered by the federal fair housing law, and sellers must be aware of the regulations involved.

This chapter also discusses the special legal obligations between principal and agent. Too few sellers or buyers are aware of these obligations.

Fair Housing Regulations

Both you and your broker must comply with a number of civil rights acts that are intended to protect the public from unfair discrimination in the sale of real estate.

The most sweeping, the Civil Rights Act of 1968, forbids discrimination on the basis of race or color. The law contains no exceptions, and it is clear that refusal to deal evenhandedly with a member of a minority race lays the seller and the broker open to severe penalties. Complaints are handled in federal courts.

More complex is the Federal Fair Housing Act of 1968. With some exceptions, this law forbids discrimination on the basis of race, color, religion, country of origin, sex, handicap, and the presence of children in a family. Any complaint receives prompt investigation.

In addition, your state might forbid discrimination based on other grounds: age, marital status, record of convictions, government assistance as a source of income, or political affiliation.

These prohibitions against discrimination apply not only to selling real estate but also to granting credit and renting living space.

Old-fashioned restrictive covenants that are contrary to these laws, such as a deed restriction forbidding the sale of property in a certain area to certain ethnic groups, are now illegal. Any such covenants remaining cannot be enforced.

Law of Agency

Every state now has its own definition of the law of agency, and some have even done away with traditional common law in this matter altogether. It is possible that in your state, every broker is assumed to be the seller's agent, or the buyer's agent, or even nobody's agent. Find out early on just what applies in your state.

The information that follows describes the special relationship that will apply once you have specifically hired a broker to represent you in the sale of your home. It describes the relationship between you and the person who is indeed your agent.

The law sets up a special set of duties and responsibilities between you and the broker with whom you have listed your home. Legally, your broker owes you a *fiduciary duty,* and you are known as the *client,* or principal. (Where the word *broker* is used in this book, it also applies to salespersons under the broker's direction and in some locations to cooperating offices in a Multiple Listing Service. All of these are subagents of the broker and bear exactly the same responsibility to you as does your listing broker—unless, as discussed in Chapter 4, you have disavowed the subagent status for cooperating brokers.)

Primary to the fiduciary relationship is a requirement that your broker put your interests above everyone else's, including the broker's own. The broker owes you first loyalty; anything short of that is considered a breach of duty. One of your agent's primary duties is to obtain the highest possible price for your property.

Note that buyers are *not* your broker's clients. Law requires a seller's broker to be trustworthy in dealing with buyers, and a good one knows the buyers well and identifies with their needs. Nevertheless, legally speaking, buyers are merely customers, and when push comes to shove, your broker's first loyalty is due you, the client.

Broker's Responsibilities

This fiduciary duty includes the following specific responsibilities.

Obedience. The broker must obey instructions, except when asked to do something illegal (concealing a hidden defect, for example, or discriminating against buyers of a certain race).

Information. Your broker must inform you of any facts, figures, or trends that may be helpful. If you are innocently ignorant of the market and plan to list your house at a figure well below its true worth, the broker cannot take the listing as a quick and easy sale or, even worse, buy the house through a cousin. The broker's duty is to inform you of the present state of the market and to suggest a price closer to the proper value. If your agent has knowledge of the shaky financial situation of a prospective buyer, those facts must be volunteered even if you do not request them. If the buyer tells your agent, "We'll pay more if we have to," your broker is duty-bound to pass that information on to you.

Not to buy. Brokers are specifically prohibited from buying real estate listed with them unless they disclose their interest in the transaction. They may not purchase through a dummy corporation or a relative. If you do sell property to a broker, you may well find the notification spelled out in the purchase contract itself: "It is understood that the buyer is a licensed real estate broker." In such a case, the broker should not charge commission and should make clear that he or she is no longer acting as your agent. Otherwise, the question of whose interests are being put first would arise, and conflict of interest would seem inevitable.

Present offers promptly. The broker is not permitted to screen or block offers but must present any written offer to you immediately, no matter how inconsequential the offer may seem. When the seller says, "Don't bring me anything under $200,000," and an offer comes in for $195,000, the broker faces a conflict between obeying instructions and presenting all offers. Unpleasant as the confrontation might be, most brokers would convey the offer.

Confidentiality. The broker may not divulge confidential information that is not in your best interest. The broker may not suggest an offering price under your listed figure without your authorization, or reveal the figure at which you have confided that you might sell. Although many people don't realize it, *this duty of confidentiality does not extend to the buyer dealing with a seller's broker.*

Accounting. The broker is required to maintain a separate escrow account in which the buyer's deposits are kept until time of transfer. You have the right to know the amount and form of any deposits. In the event of dispute, the broker should not return deposits to the buyer without your authorization. Each state requires deposit of the buyer's earnest money within a specific, short period of time.

Diligence. The broker also owes you continuous bona fide efforts to obtain a satisfactory purchaser for your house. This duty implies advertising, which is usually paid for by the broker, and showing your property.

Other Requirements

Real estate licenses are issued by the various states, and each state has set up additional regulations for brokers. Some of the more common ones are these.

Reveal extra profits. If the broker is receiving any fee in connection with your sale from an insurance company, mortgage broker, escrow company, home warranty insurer, or the like, your broker should reveal the amount of money involved.

Furnish copies. You and other parties to a real estate transaction are entitled to receive immediately duplicate originals of anything you sign. The first such document will probably be your listing contract, which may be in duplicate or triplicate form for this purpose. You shouldn't have to go to bed that night wondering what you signed.

No directed appraisals. Appraisers' ethics forbid a directed appraisal, which is specifically mentioned in some state laws. A directed appraisal is one elicited by instructions such as "See if you can come in at a high price," or "Remember that there's a contract to buy this place for $152,000."

Legal advice forbidden. Brokers walk a tightrope in this respect, for they accumulate a certain degree of expertise in narrow fields of law as they apply to real estate. Constantly alert to avoid the practice of law without a license, brokers may refer you to your attorney even though they know the answer to your question. In negotiating the purchase contract, brokers should refuse to draft an unusual provision, even when they know exactly what the wording should be.

Paying unlicensed person. It is illegal for the broker to pay any unlicensed person for help in a real estate transaction, and it is also illegal for anyone who is not licensed to receive a share of the commission. In some states, this prohibition against kickbacks includes even you, as the person who is paying the commission. If there is any adjustment or concession to be made, the broker may suggest, instead of turning back funds to you, that the commission rate be renegotiated to reflect the discount.

Commingling. The term refers to mixing the broker's own funds with money held in escrow, and the practice is strictly forbidden.

Representing both parties. On rare occasions, a buyer will offer to pay your broker for securing property. The buyer thus becomes a client, and the broker has a conflict of interest. The broker may not accept commissions from both parties, with one exception: if you and the buyer each know about the situation and agree to it, preferably in writing, the broker may then represent both of you. State laws, in recent years, have varied considerably in this matter. Your state may have set up specific duties for such dual agents, or it may prohibit dual agency altogether.

Concealing facts. Even under your direction, the broker may not conceal relevant information about your property. As the principal, you assume a certain amount of legal responsibility for the broker's acts, and you could be held liable for any misrepresentation on the broker's part, or on the part of subagents. *Caveat emptor* (let the buyer beware) is no longer looked upon as a way of doing business. You can even be held responsible these days for not disclosing items you may have been in a position to know about, but failed to look into.

Do you understand the agent's fiduciary duties? See Figure 5.1 for a quiz.

Your Agent's Duties

You can expect full-service agents to accompany all showings of your property to their own potential buyers. In cases where buyers' agents have called and made an appointment or arranged to use the lockbox key, clients must, of course, be accompanied by an agent for both access and for security reasons. Only in an emergency is it acceptable to send an unescorted visitor. You might, in such a case, receive a hurried phone call: "Those doctors I showed through yesterday are considering putting in an offer, and they'd like to go through the house again. I'm tied up here holding an open house, and we probably shouldn't delay them. Would you mind if they came over now? Please try to avoid any discussion of price or terms. Just smile and refer all questions back to me; that's safer at this point."

Communication is one of the agent's chief responsibilities, and the one most often neglected. Let your agent know, if he or she has not offered, that you would like a report after each showing, or at least a call once a week. A report every other week is

FIGURE 5.1
Quiz on Fiduciary Duties

YES	NO	Does your agent have the right to . . .
❑	❑	1. tell buyers nothing about your defective septic tank?
❑	❑	2. screen buyers for those who would be ethnically comfortable in your neighborhood?
❑	❑	3. conceal relevant factors about your financial difficulties from buyers?
❑	❑	4. conceal relevant factors about the buyer's financial difficulties from you?
❑	❑	5. keep the buyer's earnest money deposit in the broker's business account?
❑	❑	6. buy your property using a fictitious name?
❑	❑	7. accept a bonus from a grateful buyer without your knowledge?
❑	❑	8. keep confidential the fact that the buyers have said they'd pay more if they had to?
❑	❑	9. refuse to take a ridiculously low offer to you?
❑	❑	10. withdraw from your service—cancel the listing?

Answers: all no except 3 and 10.

probably the agent's goal, and it is easy to overlook this duty when things get busy.

Nevertheless, you'll want to hear how often the house is being shown. (Cooperating brokers from other offices who enter while you are away should leave identifying cards on your kitchen counter.) You'll want to know what potential buyers say about your property and what other brokers say, no matter whether the information is positive or negative. You may make future price adjustments or decide to improve something based on that feedback.

You are entitled to these reports even if only to learn that nothing is happening. A top agent will make suggestions in that case—ways to enhance your home's appeal. You may hear a tactful plea that you not participate in showings. Where price is the problem, the agent may suggest meeting with you to discuss steps that may be taken. If price is not the issue, you may eventually want to offer a bonus of a few hundred dollars to the successful salesperson. This news, disseminated through the multiple listing system, calls attention to your property, and occasionally achieves better results than lowering your asking price by the same amount.

If you are not receiving regular reports of progress, never hesitate to call and ask. Agents routinely make themselves available seven days a week by phone, pager, voicemail, and e-mail and don't resent your touching base with them in the evenings.

SELLER'S TIP

- If your property proves hard to sell at list price, consider offering a bonus to the successful salesperson rather than reducing your price by a small amount.

Keep yourself available. If you leave town on a vacation, alert your agent to keep an eye on the house. Make sure the property can be shown, and leave your temporary phone number with the agency. An offer can be communicated by pager, voicemail, telephone, and fax when quick action is needed.

Your agent will probably not bring you any oral offers. In every state, contracts for the sale of real property must be in writing. An idle question about whether you'd take $10,000 less than you are asking is of no value and can be harmful to you if answered. The agent would probably respond, "Let's put it in writing, and I'll see what they say." All written offers, on the other hand, must be presented to you immediately. The agent must be scrupulous about expediting offers from cooperating offices.

If You Have Complaints

Can you dismiss an unsatisfactory agent? Probably. Can you recover for damages suffered because of incompetence or breach of fiduciary duties? Possibly. For advice on either situation, talk with your attorney and the agent's broker.

Long before affairs reach such a state, however, you can take a number of different steps with complaints. The first and simplest step is to speak with the agent directly, communicating your dissatisfaction as openly as possible.

If this brings no results, talk next with the managing broker in the office. Don't be afraid to make a pest of yourself. If telephone calls don't bring satisfaction, write a letter (keeping it as brief as possible) indicating the next steps you intend to take. Most brokers are highly sensitive to sellers' complaints and will intervene promptly to straighten things out.

Next, before going beyond the immediate office, it may be wise to speak with an attorney. If you want to cancel the listing, in many cases you have only to ask. Depending on the terms of your listing contract, type of agency granted, and state law, you may be able to cancel at will, or you may be able to cancel with repayment to the broker for time and money expended. If you are told that the office does not cancel listings, a call from an attorney may break the deadlock. Multiple listing systems may look with disfavor upon a broker who picks up a canceled listing and resubmits it, so check the procedure if you plan to transfer to another MLS office.

If you want to blow the whistle on a broker, a number of options are available. The local chamber of commerce and better business bureau have no jurisdiction over agents. Neither does the Action Line or Help Column of the newspaper or television station. But a threat to complain to them touches a sensitive spot, for public opinion and reputation are of vital importance to the real estate business.

More serious is a complaint to the local Association of REALTORS®, if your broker is a member. The real estate industry is eager to retain as much self-regulation as possible and has set up procedures for enforcing its code of ethics. Your broker's action will come under serious scrutiny by his or her peers, and your problem will receive prompt attention.

Finally, any serious violation can be reported to the state licensing commission. This is strong medicine, for this body, in addition to lesser punishments, can deprive brokers of their licenses, putting them out of business. The mere mention of a plan to contact this body usually brings prompt response from recalcitrant agents.

In the event of a serious offense that has damaged you materially, your attorney can advise whether a lawsuit is in order. If you should win a suit against a broker who cannot be reached for collection of damages, some states have a recovery fund, to which brokers contribute regularly. This money is available if you are awarded damages that cannot otherwise be collected.

Where a relatively small amount of money is involved, you can represent yourself in small claims court at little expense. If you plan to do so, however, it's wise to discuss the case with an attorney beforehand for advice on how to proceed.

Your Responsibilities

Your primary duty is to compensate the agent as you originally promised. Unless otherwise provided, you owe a commission when a buyer is produced who is ready, willing, and able to purchase on the terms and at the price you stipulated, and who was secured by the licensed broker involved. The obligation might exist even without your acceptance of the offer. You could owe a commission even without a completed transaction, but many listing contracts and sales contracts provide that no commission will be paid until the sale is finally consummated.

You may be liable for a commission if you withdraw the listing to evade payment and then sell to someone first introduced to the property through the broker's efforts. You may also be liable if you sell the property yourself after having given exclusive right to sell. Sellers have been ordered by the courts to pay a commission even though a spouse refused to cooperate and thus blocked the transfer, even though some time elapsed before the seller completed the deal directly with the buyer, or even though the seller accepted the services of a broker without any written contract or promise to pay a commission. You may be liable if you simply change your mind and back out after a contract has been signed by both parties.

In practice, most brokers will not claim commissions in such situations if you have acted in good faith. Circumstances beyond your control can force a change of plans; the agent recognizes that fact and wants to maintain your goodwill.

Many sellers do not realize that they can be held legally responsible for certain real-estate-related activities of their agents. Problems of this sort are rare, but you should steer clear of any broker who seems shaky on ethics, fair housing laws, disclosure of defects, or similar legal landmines.

The Buyer's Broker

Movements have been afoot in state after state to clarify who truly represents whom in real estate transactions, because in the vast majority of cases, agent commissions are paid from a seller's proceeds. Growing in popularity is the employment of *buyers' brokers,* who owe fiduciary duties to the buyer. A buyer's broker is committed to obtaining not the highest, but the lowest, purchase price, and owes duties of confidentiality to the buyer, not to the seller.

Just as your agent cannot keep hidden defects confidential, however, so a buyer's broker is required to tell you about hidden defects of the buyer. If there was a bankruptcy last year, for example, you are entitled to know. Defects of the buyer take the form of inability or unwillingness to complete the purchase.

Various arrangements are used to compensate the buyer's broker, who may be paid by the buyer on a flat fee, commission, or hourly basis. In those cases, the buyer's broker should refuse to accept any share of commission originally promised by the seller. Sometimes the seller is asked to reduce the purchase price to compensate the buyer for this arrangement. Agents and buyers who agree to this purer form of representation resemble the attorney/client relationship, where allegiances are owed to the person engaging the attorney and ultimately paying the fee.

It is more common for the seller to agree to pay the buyer's broker fee, even with the clear understanding that that agent is putting the buyer's interest first. It is done simply to help the deal go through, because many buyers don't have much extra cash at closing time. The seller who pays a buyer's broker furnishes that money in place of the share of commission originally offered a traditional selling broker from a different firm.

This new field–buyer representation–is still being worked out. One perplexing question is referred to as the problem of *dual agency.* Some persons question whether a firm has a right to sell its own listings to someone who has retained that same company as a buyer's broker. Whose interests would be put first in that situation?

Even without a buyer's broker agreement, problems arise when a broker sells a house for an owner, acting as fiduciary agent, and then finds another house for that seller to buy. Where does primary loyalty lie in the second transaction?

At any rate, more homeowners should be aware that a seller's broker who violates fiduciary duty to the principal (seller) may have forfeited payment of commission, and may be liable for other damages.

Fee-for-Services and Discount Brokers

Some sellers who are willing to perform most or part of the brokerage work themselves list their property with fee-for-service brokers or *discount brokers.* These agencies offer a seller a limited list of services for a reduced commission or hourly or per-job fees. Fee-for-service brokers are gaining in popularity, because sellers who feel up to the task of handling many aspects of their own sale can engage other needed services piecemeal. These brokers can be used for services sellers feel unqualified or too busy to handle themselves, such as determining a price, helping respond to written offers, or helping with advertising and marketing.

When sellers engage the services of a discount broker, the primary responsibility of selling the home is left in the owner's hands. Some owners, in addition to hiring a discount broker to list their property in the local MLS, may also offer a buyer's broker a commission or flat fee for bringing them a buyer. In this case, the buyers of your home can have the services of their own agent to help them through a purchase of this type. Owner-sellers generally do their own marketing, such as placing classified advertising, creating flyers, and holding open houses, using the agent for the more complicated matters of the eventual transaction.

There are some blurred lines between the two types of limited services brokers. They are, however, licensed agents acting on your behalf for the services in which they are engaged.

Transaction Brokers

Some states have attempted to set up definitions for what are variously known as *transaction brokers* or facilitators (and possibly by other names). These licensed specialists act as agents for neither seller nor buyer. They offer expertise in every step of the transaction, but are bound by only certain duties, usually those of honest and straightforward treatment. They will neither receive confidential information nor pass it on to the other party, for example. They are permitted to take listings, show property to buyers, write contracts, negotiate in a neutral stance (no recommendations), take documents to closing, assist with the lender; all the things agents generally are perceived as doing, but without the liability of acting as agents. You may then call them go-betweens or licensees, but not agents, because agency is a relationship created between seller and the broker under the specific terms they determine.

To Sum Up

Probably the most important point for the seller, in today's shifting law of agency, is that the duty of confidentiality is owed only by the seller's own agent. It is unwise to confide to anyone else–buyer's agent, transaction broker, whomever–the lowest amount "we would really take for the property if we had to."

CHAPTER

6

Pricing Your Property

If you offered your house for sale at $2 million, it would never sell (or it would remain on the market until inflation caught up with your price). If you asked $100 for it, you'd have a sale before your advertisement even hit the papers. (The supervisor of the newspaper's classified ad department would be at your door five minutes after you called.)

So you need only search for the figure, somewhere between $100 and $2 million, that will attract buyers and at the same time bring you the most money. One point is clear: If you can sell for $100 in five minutes, and for $2 million in 20 years, obviously time and money are related in real estate sales.

If you are under no pressure to sell, you have the luxury of exploring the market, experimenting with price, and accepting an offer without pressure. This process is likely to yield the highest price.

If, on the other hand, you are working under a deadline, a no-nonsense price, slightly under true market value, will bring immediate action. When such a listing comes through the daily computer printout, one agent, idly reading, says to another, "Listen to this. A three-bedroom house in Suburban Heights for $170,000." And the other says, "Aren't they going around one-eighty over there? Won't last." Both reach for the phone to give the news to penny-pinchers they've been working with. The scene is repeated in any number of MLS offices, and that's one way houses are sold in a day.

A one-day sale, though, does not meet the standards set for *fair market value* of property. The concept of fair market value comes from the field of appraising.

Fair market value has been defined as the most probable price a property will bring if it has been widely exposed on the market, if sufficient time is allowed to find an informed buyer, and if neither party is under undue duress.

Pricing your property involves an attempt to estimate fair market value, depending on circumstances.

Factors to Ignore

Some sellers have misconceptions about where to start estimating value. Here are factors to ignore.

Your cost. Suppose you received your house as a gift; must you then give it away?

Your investment in improvements. You put in that purple kitchen because you enjoyed it, but you are not likely to find a buyer who feels that the house is worth $15,000 more because of it. Certain potential buyers may even calculate the cost of tearing it out and replacing it with something in green.

Reproduction cost. The money it would take to duplicate your house, building it from scratch, is its reproduction cost. Reproduction cost is usually estimated for property insurance purposes, but it is of little value in setting a sales price except for a newly built house. If the home you are selling is only a few years old, however, it may be wise to take a tip from what other new homes may be selling for in the area if they were outfitted and improved the way yours has been.

Assessed value. This figure, the result of a specific type of appraisal, is set by the taxing authorities as a basis for levying property taxes. No matter how often assessments are reviewed, and how sincere an effort is made to keep them in line with market value, assessed value is seldom a dependable guide.

Your needs. Also irrelevant to the proper asking price for your property is the amount of money you must take out of it. You may require $40,000 net in order to buy your next home. That fact may influence your decision to sell or not to sell–you cannot move unless you have the $40,000–but it is not the basis for pricing your present home.

Your problems are not the buyer's concern. The public is looking at various houses and comparing prices. Supply and demand, operating in the open market, will set the value for your house. Your home can be priced properly only if it is considered in competition with other property.

Emotion. You cannot charge for sentiment, for the fact that your daughter took her first steps on the patio and your son had a clubhouse behind the garage. Your emotions can lead to serious mistakes in setting the asking price.

In the case of divorce, for example, emotions can wreak havoc with price. If one party is impatient to leave town, and the other isn't getting the money anyway, a buyer is likely to pick up a bargain.

Dramatic family changes may produce sellers who just want to turn their backs on the whole situation. Still, you should aim for a sale at fair market value, without letting emotions influence your listing price.

Factors That Count

These are the factors that you should consider.

Urgency of the sale. You will reduce your asking price in proportion to your need for a quick sale. If foreclosure threatens, offer a bargain price right from the start. If you must leave the house vacant, first add up what it would cost you to carry it for three or four extra months–mortgage payments, insurance, taxes, utilities, and lost income from the equity you will have tied up in the house. You might be better off listing below market value rather than incurring those expenses and in the end selling at a lower price anyway.

Competition. If few homes are for sale in your desirable location, yours can be marked up a bit for scarcity. If, on the other hand, a local corporation recently moved out of town and the market is flooded with houses in your price range, you will have to discount to find a buyer. Your agent can tell you whether there is, at the moment, a buyer's or seller's market. If you are selling on your own, find out about local unemployment figures; they are a good guide.

Special financing. If your home has a large FHA or VA loan that can be assumed at a rate below today's levels, your mortgage is probably the most valuable part of the property. The house is likely to bring a premium from a buyer willing to exchange a higher total price for savings in interest payments in the years ahead. Much the same is true, in a difficult mortgage market, if you are willing to hold the loan yourself.

Finding Those Comps

Comparable sales are the key to proper pricing. Nothing matters as much as *comps,* which are completed transactions as similar to yours as possible. The homes selected for comparison should be physically nearby, for no single factor determines value more surely than location. The sales should also be as recent as six months or less; two-year-old sales have almost no meaning in today's volatile market. And they should be close in style, square footage, property size, condition, and age to your property–the closer the better.

Your agent can furnish figures on comparables; at least three are recommended, and if six close comps are available, so much the better. Pay little attention to neighborhood scuttlebutt; sellers exaggerate the amount received and buyers minimize the price paid.

An agent will probably not offer you a free appraisal. Experts feel that if it's free, it isn't an appraisal. Instead, you will receive a *comparative market analysis.* This computation lists several recent nearby sales, notes how long each stayed on the market, how close the asking price was to the eventual sales figure, and then compares the houses with yours. The process is a simple version of the market approach, the technique most often employed for formal residential appraisals. Figure 6.1 shows a sample comparative analysis form.

Besides considering the comparative market analysis, you should study a complete list of homes currently on the market in your area. Buyers will be choosing homes to view from that group. Consider your property through their eyes and judge how your asking price compares–whether it would attract you before you knew the property.

You should also be studying classified ads for houses in your area, as well as Internet sites like Realtor.com, to build a general background on the current market. A comparison of the average price of comparable sales with the average asking prices of similar homes not yet sold can give you an idea of how much bargaining seems to be built-in. Community custom varies in this matter. Your agent may have a computer printout of past sales, with asking prices and sale prices listed for easy comparison.

Bargaining practices vary with individual preferences. Some sellers detest bargaining and list at a rock-bottom price that is firm. Others tack on a few thousand dollars just to see if they'll be lucky. Nevertheless, you can often find a discernible trend, giving you a clue to what the average buyer might expect. You may find sale prices from 5 to 10 percent below listing prices.

Remember that owning real estate means having control of it, and that includes setting your asking price. Your agent may be eager to persuade you to set a reasonable price or, on the other hand, may try to avoid making any recommendation. In the end, the decision is entirely yours.

FIGURE 6.1
Comparative Market Analysis

Competitive Market Analysis

Date ______ Comparative Market Analysis for ______ Sugg. list price $ ______

Address	Style	Const	Age	No. of Rms	No. of Bdrms	No. of Baths	Gar	Fplc	Pool	C/A	Size Prop	Assess Value	Taxes	Comments & Extras	Fair Market Value

1. SIMILAR HOMES RECENTLY SOLD: These tell us what people are willing to pay . . . for this kind of home . . . in this area . . . at this time.

															Closed Price	Date	Adj. Price

2. SIMILAR HOMES FOR SALE NOW: These tell us what we are competing against. Buyers will compare your home against these homes.

															Askg Price	Days on Mkt.

3. EXPIRED LISTINGS–SIMILAR HOMES UNSOLD FOR 90 DAYS OR MORE: These illustrate the problems of overpricing.

PROBLEMS OF OVERPRICING: A. HARD to get salespeople excited. B. HARD to get people to make an offer. C. HARD to get good buyers to look. D. HARD to get financing.

SOURCE: John E. Cyr and Joan M. Sobeck, *Real Estate Brokerage: A Success Guide* (Chicago: Real Estate Education Company, 1992), p. 244.

Expenses of Selling

Know the definition of *equity:* the amount of money you will realize if you sell your home at fair market value and pay all the liens (claims) against it. Equity is often the sales price of the house minus the amount owed on the mortgage.

Although you cannot set your list price on the basis of the amount of money you need to receive, it is wise to estimate what you may net and what your selling expenses may be as you price the house.

Depending on your financing and the buyer's, state law, and other factors, your costs of selling are likely to be these:

- *Commission.* This is technically earned when you reach agreement with the buyer, but usually paid at final transfer of title.
- *Points* (see Chapter 10). Your agent can orient you on points, taking into account the current mortgage market.
- *Adjustments.* You may owe the buyer for unpaid property taxes or be owed money for fuel oil left in the tank. Items like these will be adjusted at time of closing.
- *Fees.* These may include a lawyer's fee, title insurance, escrow, or title company charges. Your main responsibility is to prove clear and marketable title.
- *Transfer taxes.* In some states, this item must be paid by the seller, no matter how other costs are shared.
- *Inspections.* Depending on local custom, you may be expected to pay for code inspections, a termite check, or a land survey.
- *Special assessments.* If, for example, your property is being assessed because of new sidewalks or similar neighborhood improvements, you might be asked to pay this lien in a lump sum at closing.
- *Present liens.* This includes your mortgage and other claims or judgments of record against the property.
- *Required repairs.* Your agent can help judge whether the FHA, VA, or a lending institution will require that you make specific repairs or bring your home up to code. Consider this matter when you set your price.

- *Prepayment penalty.* Your present conventional mortgage, if paid before its due date, may involve a prepayment penalty.
- *Unexpected credits.* You may receive monies at closing that you don't anticipate. The fuel oil is an example. In some states, property taxes are paid in advance, and adjustments may result in a sizable refund to you. Prepaid insurance should also be refunded. You may have established an escrow account at your lending institution, with money collected in advance for tax and insurance expenses you will no longer owe. This sum will be returned to you.

If You Price Too High

At any given time, there is a large pool of buyers in the market for a home. The current group of buyers constitutes your best prospects. It will take approximately three months to replace them with an equal number of newcomers to the market.

If your house is overpriced, you will lose the advantage of this ready group of buyers. Brokers know the amount of activity you receive the first few weeks of your listing period indicates whether your home is priced properly. Homebuyers are accustomed to comparing properties and may refuse even to view yours if it is overpriced. You and your agent may know that you will sell for $20,000 less, but buyers don't know. Fiduciary duty prohibits your agent from telling them this or advertising the fact. So your overpriced property receives little attention.

Surveys show that the longer a house is on the market, the greater is the discount from listing price when it finally sells. The buying public eventually sets an accurate price. The overpriced house lingers on the market, requiring a price adjustment before it attracts a buyer.

"We can always come down" is a phrase agents don't enjoy hearing. It implies a slow start, wasted advertisements, unpleasant discussions with the homeowner, and eventually, a shopworn property. Knowledgeable buyers ask how long a house has been on the market and why it hasn't sold. Even when the agent explains that only the price was wrong, buyers may remain suspicious.

If you have your heart set on trying a high price "just to see," first work out a written plan to drop the price at intervals: If the house hasn't attracted enough attention in two weeks, the price will be cut to a certain level. If you haven't had an offer within a month, you will lower it again. Make sure that you will be down to estimated market value within six weeks. Such a commitment at the beginning ensures a logical handling of the problem.

Remember also that overpricing your home can invite trouble. If you refuse to budge from your own opinion of your homes' value, be prepared to offer your own fact sheet to an appraiser (for any buyer who must obtain financing). Enhancements or improvements may have been construed as adding more value to your home than is justified. The appraiser need not pay attention to your opinions, using established criteria over which you will have no control. You and the buyer may have agreed that the house is worth $195,000. But if the appraiser doesn't agree, you have a problem. The mortgage loan will be offered on a lower figure, and the buyer may not be able (or willing) to complete the purchase.

If Your House Is Underpriced

The first serious consequence of underpricing, of course, is that you will lose money. Even the most experienced agent is fooled, occasionally, when a house that seemed properly priced suddenly turns out to be a "hot" listing.

What are the signs? One is an immediate rush of calls from other offices either to your agent asking how to show the property or directly to you requesting appointments. Another sure sign is a jam-packed open house. Prospects are piled up in the living room, waiting their turn to see the property, while your agent phones the office for reinforcements.

Whether using an agent or selling on your own, you may receive several purchase offers immediately if you have underpriced. Experienced agents may advise prospective buyers to offer more than the asking price, so that if their proposal is presented at the same time as several others, it stands a good chance of acceptance. A bidding war may sound exciting on the surface, but may also result in headaches and withdrawn offers all around. Your agent will know how to handle multiple offers, so that you can consider them all at the same time, if possible.

If such a situation develops, consult your attorney or the office broker. If it appears that a mistake has been made in the asking price; can you now refuse a full-price offer? Can you raise your list price? Obtain professional advice as quickly as you can.

In the absence of any offers, it is possible to raise your asking price immediately. Your agent or lawyer will know the procedure, although it is seldom used.

The $10,000 Barrier

One final point to be considered in pricing your property is the $10,000 barrier. There is very little difference in market reaction between a house priced at $147,000 and one priced at $149,000, but a great difference between houses priced at $149,000 and $151,000. If you are wavering over a few extra thousand and the higher figure will take you just above $150,000, remember that you are automatically cutting out of your buying public all those who told their agents, "Don't show us anything over $150,000." You could be eliminating the best prospects for your home. Use the tactic new homebuilders and car dealerships do. Consider $149,990 instead. It is just as useful in attracting buyers as $149,000 would be.

Professional Appraisals

Although most sellers rely on their agent's comparative market analysis figures, watch out for the few who will quote almost any price to secure your listing. Others may recommend a low price, hoping for a quick and easy sale. A few feel that they have no right to recommend any price on a property for which they may earn a commission.

The money invested in a professional appraisal may be worth spending in the beginning, or later if you and the agent are stymied as to the proper price. There are different types of appraisals, however, so be careful to tell the appraiser that you are interested in an appraisal for sales purposes, and not one for refinancing or insurance use.

SELLER'S TIP

To avoid pricing your property too high or too low, and to find its closest fair market value, obtain:

- A professional appraisal
- A comparative market analysis, with sales information on several similar homes in your area
- Several brokers' informal recommendations

An appraisal can be a valuable bargaining tool during contract negotiations with your buyer. Although it is simply an estimate–albeit an informed, skilled one–the buyer usually accepts it as an impartial, almost scientific proof of value, as indeed the courts do.

Selling on Your Own

Those who don't use a broker are usually advised to pay a few hundred dollars for a complete written appraisal done by a professional appraiser with a designation, appraiser's license, or certification–someone with special study and qualification. (Make it clear that you need only a simple written report; you don't want to pay for a 30-page dissertation with floor plans and photographs of the neighborhood.) You have little to gain from selling your house in one day because you've priced it too low.

Can you ask real estate brokers for free advice on the matter? Yes and no.

It's patently unfair to mislead an agent by asking for a market analysis on the pretense that you plan to list the property. But what if you were up-front about it? You might call several firms, explain that you intend to try marketing the house yourself, and ask whether they are willing to confer with you on that understanding.

Even an oral off-hand opinion will require an hour's preparation time on the agent's part, and another hour traveling to your home and inspecting it. Understandably, some brokers will refuse to donate their time and expertise to your project.

Others, though, may be perfectly willing to provide the service, hoping to make a friend in the process. It is not unheard of for confident, but helpful brokers to even lend out FSBO signs for your use in the hopes of getting your listing if and when that happens. Some brokers believe that nine out of ten FSBOs eventually do list, and they're glad for a chance to meet you and try to sell their services.

CHAPTER

7

Preparing Your House to Sell

Consider what happens to a used car when it is traded in at a dealership. Almost the minute the deal is made, the car is whisked away for a thorough detail job, mechanical inspection, and repairs so that the dealer can sell it for top dollar. Somehow, the next buyer ends up believing that the spotless interior means that the car has been immaculately maintained for all of its 93,999 miles.

Just as a few hundred dollars can reap, perhaps, thousands more for a car, your home deserves a detail job in preparation for hitting the real estate market.

What can you do to show it to best advantage? Start by asking your agent for suggestions. Better yet, walk through some model homes and see some of the more inexpensive touches professional furnishers and decorators use that make a huge difference to potential homebuyers.

If you are selling on your own, call in a brutally honest friend. You want someone who will view your house with a fresh eye. After all, you may have learned to live with that broken front step, perhaps even having stopped noticing it altogether. But anyone else approaching your home will notice it instantly. You can go over the house and grounds yourself with the checklist in Figure 7.1.

FIGURE 7.1

House and Grounds Preparation Checklist

	Needs Work	When to Do
Exterior	______	______
Cut grass (shovel snow)	______	______
Mend fence, gate, steps	______	______
Install house numbers	______	______
Plant annual flowers	______	______
Pick up toys, tools, etc.	______	______
Move camper, old car	______	______
Trim shrubs	______	______
Edge lawns	______	______
Seal blacktop driveway	______	______
Close garage door	______	______
Store trash cans	______	______
Wash windows	______	______
Entrance		
Tighten handrail	______	______
Replace light bulbs	______	______
Mend doorbell	______	______
Buy new doormat	______	______
Mend screen	______	______
Remove pawprints and fingerprints	______	______
Paint threshold	______	______
Polish brass	______	______
Front hall		
Clean out closet	______	______
Remove clutter	______	______
Add a plant, fresh flowers	______	______
Living room		
Remove crowded pieces	______	______
Pack away distracting items	______	______
Clean out fireplace ashes, lay fire	______	______
Shampoo carpet	______	______
Repaint stained ceiling	______	______

FIGURE 7.1
House and Grounds Preparation Checklist (Continued)

	Needs Work	When to Do
Kitchen	______	______
Clean stove and oven	______	______
Clear counters	______	______
Scrub sink	______	______
Remove fingerprints	______	______
Replace faucet washers	______	______
Starch curtains	______	______
Add a plant	______	______
Bathroom		
Replace shower curtain	______	______
Freshen grout around tub	______	______
Change toilet seat	______	______
Remove personal items	______	______
Bring in a plant	______	______
Clean (repaint) medicine cabinet	______	______
Buy new towels	______	______
Remove tub mat	______	______
Bedrooms		
Store personal items	______	______
Remove valuables	______	______
Clear dressers	______	______
Clean out closet	______	______
Add live plant	______	______
Remove excess furniture	______	______
Attic, basement		
Clear stairs	______	______
Check light bulbs	______	______
Vacuum floors	______	______
Dust away cobwebs	______	______
Straighten stored items	______	______
Garage		
Hose down floor	______	______
Tidy stored items	______	______
Keep doors closed	______	______
Replace light bulbs	______	______

What you are looking for is advice on which features can be inexpensively improved and which may be left alone. You can spend little or no money and still enhance your property markedly. Attend first to all those items that require no expense.

Exterior Work

Prospective buyers will probably park across the street–that is where the agent will usually guide them. Sit there in your own car and see how the house strikes you. Remember that your property will never get a second chance to make a first impression. Is the lawn as nearly perfect as possible, or could it benefit from a little fertilizer? Are the bushes trimmed? Is your garage door closed? One detail can make a great difference. Of course, it's too late to landscape, but a few showy, in-season annuals can add sparkle to your front lawn at small expense.

Your fences and gates should be in good repair, possibly repainted. Rusty toys and moldering shopping guides must be picked up. Downspouts and gutters should be firmly attached; house numbers need checking also. Don't forget your driveway; remove unsightly oil stains and fill in small cracks. An old car, pick-up truck, or a camper that lives in your driveway may need another home for the interim.

SELLER'S TIP

- Your property will never get a second chance to make a first impression. Details can make a great difference.

No matter how attached you may be to your flamingos, wooden whirligigs, decorative eagles, and artificial flowers, all such items are a matter of personal taste. Your exterior will look more spacious and serene without them; store them in your garage for the duration.

Not the most pleasant of views, trashcans should be kept neatly concealed.

You already have enough assignments for a full Saturday's work, and you haven't arrived at the front door yet!

The Main Entrance

Stand at your front door where the buyer will stand, and look around. Are the light and the doorbell in working order? Make sure that your screen door or storm door is in good condition and the muddy pawprints beside the door have been scrubbed. Any glass panels or cut glass in the door should sparkle, as should every window in the house. Even if you don't paint any other part of the house, consider touching up the front entrance. A bit of paint can do wonders for a worn threshold. If your door handle is old, loose, or its brass is hopelessly tarnished, decide for yourself what effect the investment in a new one may have on a potential buyer.

Your front hall or entry foyer should be free of clutter. The usual line-up of shoes, kids' backpacks, and entry tables full of pocket change and car keys will have to be eliminated. A vase of (fresh) flowers is a welcoming touch. In the front-hall closet, remove out-of-season clothing and dead storage. All your closets will look larger if they are orderly and uncrowded.

The Living Room

Lay a fire in the fireplace, consider whether the carpets could benefit from a steam-cleaning, remove unnecessary pieces of large furniture and store them somewhere. Even though you cherish them, consider removing personal possessions such as trophies, artificial flowers, family pictures, political and religious items. Most living rooms can be improved if two-thirds of their distracting accessories are taken out. You want a room that the buyers can picture themselves in, with plenty of space for their own items. Excess belongings can be packed away; after all, you will be doing that when you move, anyway. Pack-rat homeowners have been known to strip a crowded house of half their possessions on the advice of their agent, and rent a self-storage unit for a few months.

Although there is no hard-and-fast rule about repainting your home's interior, you must attend to cracks and water stains on walls or ceilings. The stain may go back five years to the time when your teenager let the tub overflow. Even if you try to explain it, the buyer will remain dubious about your plumbing system. Simply repaint the ceiling and remember to disclose on an eventual contract that there was some damage, but it was repaired. You must not cover your problems in an attempt to hide them, but neither do you owe the buyer a complete explanation of your teenager's age-appropriate lapses in judgement.

As for small cracks in walls or ceilings, they may have been there for decades, but some buyers will be sure that they indicate danger of imminent collapse. Cracked window panes leave an impression that the house has been neglected; attend to them before anyone views the property. And if your home has dual-paned glass, replace the ones where condensation may have appeared between the panes, giving a cloudy, wet view. Some window manufacturers give lifetime guarantees and will replace them for free.

The Kitchen

Kitchens and bathrooms traditionally sell houses. It seldom pays to remodel in anticipation of selling, unless your kitchen is terribly out of sync with what other homeowners in your neighborhood have done with theirs. (If your kitchen is truly a relic, while every one else's look like pictures from a Home Depot ad, adjust your asking price accordingly.) You can, however, check a number of items. Leaky faucets must be repaired and stains bleached out of the sink. To show off your expanse of kitchen counters, remove most items, leaving only one or two decorative pieces or basic countertop appliances.

Even if your stove is not included in the sale, someone will be sure to open the oven, so keep it spotless. A greasy oven is a real turn-off, and the impression it conveys will extend to the rest of the house. Glass doors on oven, toaster oven, or microwave should be polished.

In insect-prone areas, keep extermination up-to-date. Remove sticky fingerprints everywhere. If you want to invest a small amount of money, try bright, inexpensive curtains or window toppers, or dress up your cupboards with attractive knobs.

The Baths

Looking at other people's bathrooms can be unappealing; make it as easy as possible. Take a good look at your shower curtain; a stained one can be replaced with a sparkling, inexpensive new one in a solid, neutral color. White is always a good choice. If you have a sliding glass tub enclosures, get rid of hard water stains and shine up the doors and hardware. Consider replacing a chipped toilet seat as well. Bring in a potted plant for your vanity top. Remove tub mats, and put away all make-up, dental appliances, shaving needs, and toiletries.

Check grout around your tub and shower. If necessary, bleach or strip and re-grout areas that have begun to look like science experiments. Buy a set of solid-colored towels and washcloths to be set out at the last minute before the house is shown.

This is a good time to clean out the medicine chest. If made of wood, the inside can be painted with a few minutes' effort. And if it is metal and mirrored, use your all-purpose spray cleaner on it to make it sparkle.

The Bedrooms

In bedrooms, straighten out closet clutter, remove large or crowded pieces of furniture if possible, put out your best comforters or bedspreads. Again, make sure that the windows are spotless. Clear off dresser tops except for the bare necessities, and stash away as many toys as possible in children's rooms. If you have a teenager, you may have some family discord over the removal of posters and photos, but cut a deal for a new CD or two to make up for their boring surroundings.

Throughout the House

Throughout the entire house, replace burnt-out light bulbs. Wash doorknobs and light switches. Check staircase treads and tighten railings. Make it easy for house hunters to use your attic and basement stairs, which should be free of clutter. Thoroughly dust and polish banisters and stair risers to a shine.

If you are not a plant person, consider borrowing some particularly full and healthy ones from friends. Just a few plants or trees, judiciously spotted around the house, add warmth and color.

If your home has a basement, hose down the floor there as well as the floor in the garage. Your electric box may be inspected, so clean off cobwebs and dust.

Spending Money

Except in rare instances, it is unwise to invest much cash in improving a house that is going on the market. It is usually impossible to recoup the outlay by raising your price. Eliminate major improvements from your plans, unless your house is drastically out of date for the rest of the neighborhood.

If you are prepared to spend some money on a fix-up, your best investment–after soap–is probably paint. Take a tip from the merchandisers of new model homes: paint every room the same color to make the house look larger. A light, neutral shade is the best choice. This is not the time to strive for spectacular results, for you want to harmonize with almost anyone's furniture. Don't forget to paint the insides of closets as well.

One get-the-most-for-your-money item is resealing a blacktop driveway to give the outside of the house a crisp, clean appearance. Adding some concrete mow strips around the front flower beds can make your front yard look like a model home's. Ambitious homeowners may go on from there to sand and refinish wood floors, or install new bathroom fixtures, such as towel bars or faucets. (By the time some homeowners make changes like these, their house looks so good that they feel a bit melancholy about parting with it.)

If your house features what appraisers tactfully call casual housekeeping, your agent is in a delicate situation. The broker knows that time and again, such a house remains on the market for months, and eventually sells for thousands of dollars under its real value. But suggestions that a house needs cleaning and tidying are difficult to put politely.

SELLER'S TIP

To improve the appearance of your home for showing to prospective buyers, best results come from:

- Achieving an attractive, well-maintained front view for that crucial first impression
- Cleaning, especially in the kitchen and bathrooms
- Removing clutter and personal items for greater spaciousness
- Painting where needed to improve visual appeal

Take seriously, therefore, any suggestion by your broker that you consider a professional cleaning service. If you have doubts about your housekeeping, ask your agent or that brutally honest friend whether a professional job is indicated.

Final Preparations

As you look forward to the first showing of your home, gather your fact sheets, copies of the listing material (your agent may provide a professionally prepared flyer), and past utility bills. If you have pictures of the back lawn when it was blanketed with snow, or the front lawn with the cherry trees in blossom, display them prominently so that prospects can appreciate the beauty of your home in every season.

Advertising

One of the agent's first tasks is to create advertising for your property. You may be asked to help, or to suggest phrases. It can be useful to mention your own reasons for buying the house. If your home is fairly new and you still have the builder's brochure, your agent will be delighted to use elements of it in his or her advertising or fliers.

If you are placing your own advertisements, you may be shocked when the first bills come in. Remember that long ads are not better than short ones. Buyers do not respond to lists that simply catalog the house's features, and they may even skip over long ads. They read the bewildering variety of offerings not to select, but to eliminate houses. Too much information may include the one fact that turns them off. Leave them something to inquire about.

An inexpensive and sometimes free medium for owner advertising is various sites on the World Wide Web. Some to take a look at are Owners.com, fsboconnection, and FSBO.net. In Blanche Evan's book, *Homesurfing.net* (Dearborn), the author addresses the proliferation of Web sites designed specifically for FSBOs, but finds that owners generally lack the sophistication, knowledge of inviting marketing verbiage, and consistent photos to show off their listings properly. In addition, potential homebuyers surfing the Net cannot seem to find enough nearby homes within the same Web site with which to compare the FSBOs. This tends to make home cyber-shoppers eventually give up and move on to MLS-type, professional real estate sites like Realtor.com, where thousands of homes appear.

Your ad should include location, number of bedrooms and baths, price, and one or two picture-making phrases. "For Sale By

Owner" is always an attention-getter; your initial ad could be "First Ad Today" or "New on Market."

Be sure your ad doesn't include anything that implies a preference for buyers based on race, religion, or other classes protected by fair housing laws as listed in Chapter 5. Phrases like "near St. Simon's church" or "suitable for elderly couple" can be considered violations.

If you do sell through an agent, the chances of the right buyer calling on your particular ad are remote. In the end, your buyer will probably have first contacted the broker about another property. Although advertising represents the largest item in the broker's budget, it accounts for only one-third of sales. Most sales come from referrals or other contacts, For Sale signs, and the firm's backlog of purchasers.

Using the Internet

Web sites come and go with amazing frequency, but by the early 2000s, a few had established track records and seemed profitable enough to stick around. One is Realtor.com, which aims at listing every property offered by REALTORS® across the country. Others include HomeAdvisor.com and HomeSeekers.com. Local newspapers may sell online classified ads, local brokers often establish their own Web pages, and online regional Multiple Listing Services are found in many areas.

Many real estate brokers these days are armed with laptop and palm-sized computers, enabling them to access online listing information from virtually anywhere at any time, when in the past they may have traveled with tome-like listing books in their back seats.

The Internet Real Estate Directory <www.ired.com> lists thousands of links. HomeStore.com, Inman.com, and Realty Times.com carry excellent news, advice, and information about the national real estate market with links provided to all kinds of interesting and helpful places.

CHAPTER

8

Showing Your Home

Put some cookies in the oven, send the kids and the dog to the neighbor's, and set the stereo on low, easy listening music. Buyers are on their way!

Selling on Your Own

People who knock on your door after noticing your For Sale By Owner sign should be told to phone you for an appointment and handed a marketing flyer. When you receive a call, ask for the caller's own phone number "so I can call you back and confirm." This provides a certain amount of identification ahead of time, for safety's sake. You'll want to ask several qualifying questions before making a decision to invite prospects over.

The advance appointment gives you time to prepare your home and to arrange for another adult to be in the house with you if you wish.

When you give prospects directions to your house, consider the most attractive approach. No law says that you must direct them past the town dump if the route through the park works just as well.

Right after your house goes on the market, watch out for bargain hunters on the prowl for unsophisticated FSBOs. They will be less interested in the house itself than in finding out whether you will sell with no down payment and whether you will carry financing (discussed in Chapter 10). Such buyers often cannot qualify for bank loans because they have poor credit or insufficient income.

Before you place your first advertisement, you will have calculated the amount of cash and income a buyer would need to qualify for a mortgage loan on your property (again, see Chapter 10). You will not, therefore, invite in everyone who inquires. Apply the same standards to every caller to make sure you observe human rights law. You have a right to ask name, phone number, and present address, and whether they rent or have another house to sell. You may also ask about employment and income. They may, of course, refuse to answer. Then you'll have to play it by ear.

It's not a bad idea to have a local mortgage loan consultant make up a financing flyer for your home, giving sample loan scenarios based on your asking price. He or she will appreciate the extra marketing exposure, and your buyers will have some ready information on whether they can afford the payments on your home. You may even work out an arrangement for any prospective buyers to call this mortgage lender for a prequalification by phone, and for the lender to call you with feedback before going further.

See Figure 8.1 for a handy list of things to do when selling on your own.

If You're Using an Agent

If the broker has a prospect waiting in the wings for property like yours, arrangements for the first showing may be made as soon as you sign the listing. In areas where there is a comprehensive Multiple Listing Service, you can expect to hear from other brokers soon after your properly priced house goes on the market.

Advance Notice

Agents always try to arrange appointments or leave phone messages that they will be coming by around a certain time. If they are setting up several houses for the buyer, they might say, "We'll be over between two and three o'clock," rather than promising to

FIGURE 8.1
Checklist for Selling on Your Own

- ❑ Retain a lawyer who specializes in real estate.
- ❑ Visit open houses in your neighborhood for three weeks.
- ❑ Clip classified ads for houses in your neighborhood.
- ❑ Phone agents for information on ads you clipped.
- ❑ Interview at least three local brokers (see Chapter 3). Be frank about "not wanting to list yet."
- ❑ Polish your home to show it at its best (see Chapter 7).
- ❑ Ask your lawyer for a blank copy of a typical purchase offer.
- ❑ Prepare fact sheets on your property.
- ❑ Prepare a lawn sign.
- ❑ Place your classified ad. Buyers need to know neighborhood, style of house, number of rooms and bedrooms, and price or price range (and baths and garages, if more than one). Keep the ad short.
- ❑ Never answer "How much would you take?" directly.
- ❑ Ask serious prospects to bring you a credit report.
- ❑ When you receive an oral offer you like, ask your lawyer to prepare a contract acceptable to both parties.
- ❑ Follow the buyer's mortgage application process, and check at least once a week—or have your lawyer do so—to see how it's going.

ring the bell at 2:30 PM. If you have arranged for lockbox ease in showing your home, you'll need only vacate for that period.

Don't hold out for too much advance notice. You could be eliminating one of the most promising prospects, the transferred employee who is in town for a few hours, needs to find a place today, and wants to come right over. Try to say yes. After all, it will take the salesperson half an hour to drive over, and you can accomplish a great number of last-minute spiff-ups in the interim. Make the house as freely available as possible.

Even if you have left a key with the listing office or have consented to a lockbox so that the house can be shown while you are at work, most agents will still phone ahead to see if anyone is at home. It is customary for them at least to leave a message on your voicemail or answering machine. To prepare for these visits, you'll have to see that the place is tidy before you leave each day. In the event someone does enter, you should find a business card left behind, ideally with the time of the visit noted on it.

No Advance Notice

Even with a broker's sign out front, people may simply knock on your door asking if they may see the house. Tell them pleasantly that it is being shown only by the office whose telephone number is on the sign outside. Do not admit any strangers; you retained an agent to avoid just such situations. Chances are slim that random inquirers are really qualified to buy. If, on the other hand, they are good prospects, they should receive professional treatment from the beginning. A slight difficulty in getting into the house will only make it more desirable.

Once in a while, an agent may ring your doorbell without phoning in advance. It's not uncommon to get a cell phone call from an agent who is sitting in the car right in front of your house, asking permission to show waiting clients through.

If possible, welcome them. The broker knows what the clients can afford and what they seek; if the agent thinks it's worth the trouble, it probably is. You can gain a few minutes to tidy up by suggesting that they inspect the exterior first, or having them wait in the car a bit longer.

Prospects who enter a house this way are already half sold. They are grateful for your cooperation, and the sense of discovery and unplanned adventure in such a showing often results in an offer.

Preparing for an Open House

Your home may also be marketed through holding one or several prearranged open house events. The first type of open house you may experience is not for the buying public itself. Often, your broker's or agent's own office associates will tour your house as well as other new listings on the same weekday afternoon, so that they may consider it for current or future clients. If so, agents love nothing more than an assortment of cookies or fresh fruit left for them on the kitchen countertop for their day of touring, and may just remember your house first when speaking to their prospects.

The first weekend your home is officially on the market is generally the best time for the first open house, so that potential buyers or agents at the peak of their initial interest may tour your home without the formality of an appointment.

You—or your agent—advertise the open house and put out signs inviting all comers to visit during specified hours. It's helpful if the open house takes place when there are other ones in the neighborhood, usually on Saturdays or Sundays. Some areas restrict signs; in other areas balloons, flags, and streamers lend a festive atmosphere.

After all the preparation, you will be longing to see the fun. If you have an agent, though, you'll probably be asked to leave before the open house starts. Should you decide that you couldn't bear to go away, visit a neighbor so you can see what happens.

Unless your house is strikingly underpriced, don't expect hordes of visitors. And remember that fewer than 1 house in 20 is sold through an open house.

The agent is experienced in handling visitors and will probably insist that they identify themselves and sign in. For the agent, it's an opportunity to meet buyers. If you run the open house yourself, always ask people to sign in, and ask for identification. If you have several prospects at once, ask them to wait in the living room or, in good weather, outside, while you escort one couple at a time through the house.

The neighbors who have always been curious about you or your house will probably show up at the first open house, perhaps saying that they are considering selling theirs and just want to compare. It is wise to welcome them and even to have invited them. Neighbors may have friends or relatives who have always wanted to live nearby. An agent, of course, has an extra motive for being cordial, hoping to produce a successful sale and to be remembered when it's time to list the next house on the street.

Set for Seduction

After all the preparation you've put in during the past few weeks, what more can you do to show your house at its best?

Plenty–whether for an open house or a private showing. Go through the house and raise every window shade and blind. Draw the drapes back from those spotless windows. A bright house looks larger and more cheerful. If you've ever noticed model homes windows, you'll see that they lack blinds, obscuring drapery, and even screens, permitting as much light inside to show off the home's interior.

Turn on lights from top to bottom, even in the daytime. Those same model homes exude extra charm from shaded lamps and sparkling chandeliers. Buyers shouldn't have to grope for the pull-cord in the gloomy corner of the basement, and they should find your attic stairs illuminated and welcoming.

Your house can appeal to all five senses as much as it can to rational inspection. Consider the sound level. Stop your dishwasher or clothes dryer in mid-cycle and check for other noisy appliances. If you want to leave your stereo set on, play neutral, easy-listening music softly. If your pool has a waterfall included in its design, turn it on. You are trying, after all, to set up a seduction scene.

The beds are made, of course, with your best spreads or comforters, and every room is as tidy as possible. Toilet seats are down, and those new towels have replaced the family ones. This doesn't mean that there should be no signs of life–if you have fine linen and china, a beautifully set table adds appeal.

Homeowners have been known to put a cake in the oven every time a prospect was on the way, or to simmer a cinnamon stick for a few minutes. If, on the other hand, you have a heavy smoker in your home, empty ashtrays and spray air freshener at the last moment. These days, agents report that some buyers won't even enter a house if they can tell the owner smokes.

On any day that isn't sweltering, start a fire to dramatize your open hearth. If you regard a wood fire as a nuisance, buy pressed logs. One will burn alone and add a cozy glow throughout an afternoon's open house, leaving very little ash. And viewers won't have to wonder if the fireplace works.

Time to Clear Out

No matter how charming your children and pets are, getting them out of the house during showings is a must. Set up an emergency routine. On two minutes' notice, your kids should be able to corral Rover, put him on a leash, turn off the television, and dash out the back door for sanctuary in a neighbor's kitchen.

It's important that the house be as empty as possible and free from distractions. House hunting is confusing and tiring work. The buyers are probably looking at several places within a few hours, trying to fix each in their minds. Ideally, they like to wander and explore, trying the place on for size, perhaps pretending it's already theirs.

Selling Techniques

If you are showing the house yourself, learn to do it professionally. Study the description below of the broker's standard techniques. You may wish to use a last-minute checklist before your buyers arrive, whether selling on your own or using a broker (see Figure 8.2).

If You Have an Agent

Falling in love with a house is like falling in love with a person, and three's a crowd. Your role is to be pleasant and unobtrusive, if not downright unavailable. This spares your feelings and the buyers'.

It's difficult to watch strangers go through your house. You might be surprised by the strength of your emotional reaction to

FIGURE 8.2
Last Minute Checklist

- ❑ Kids out
- ❑ Pets out
- ❑ Dishwasher, television off
- ❑ Window shades up (daytime)
- ❑ Drapes pulled back (daytime)
- ❑ Fire started
- ❑ Cinnamon simmered or gingerbread in the oven
- ❑ Lights on throughout
- ❑ Clean towels
- ❑ Empty, scoured sink
- ❑ Fact sheets available
- ❑ Guest book for sign-in
- ❑ Garage door closed
- ❑ Beds made
- ❑ Soft music
- ❑ Utility bills handy

a random word of criticism. You would probably be upset by the buyers who never get farther than your front hall, or who whiz through in one minute flat. The agent is used to it and knows that if buyers are searching for an eat-in kitchen or downstairs master bedroom, they look for that first, cross your house off the list if it isn't there, and save their energy for the next house.

With you watching, prospects are inhibited about opening closets, trying out windows, stroking the banister, and performing all those get-acquainted gestures that are the house-hunting equivalent of kicking the tires and slamming the doors of a new car.

Of course, if you are showing the house yourself, you need to monitor prospects unobtrusively just for security reasons.

Here They Come, There You Go

And so, buyers are on their way over, you've given the house its last-minute sparkle, and you peek out the windows as they pull up.

They're probably traveling in one car; this gives the broker more control and opportunity for conversation. It's customary to park across the street for a good view of your property. You may think that they are taking an unreasonably long time to reach the front door. Remember that in good weather, many brokers make it a practice to show the outside first, building suspense for the house itself.

If your house has lockbox showing capability, disappear before lookers arrive. If not, and you happen to be home, greet the buyers with a smile, wait to be introduced and then excuse yourself. "Don't bother with the lights; I'll take care of them later. If you need me, I'll be next door." There is a proper time for you to reappear, but consider first the reasons why you shouldn't hang around.

Let the Broker Show the House

Potential buyers are reluctant to voice objections with you standing by. They can speak frankly to the broker, who knows whether the house might fit their needs and how to respond.

"That den is so tiny."

"Yes," agrees the broker, who would never contradict a valid observation. "You did say you were looking for a home office, though. I suppose it could be down on this floor."

"You know, it might just do. Ben, come and look at this little room." When they start showing the house to each other, the wise broker fades into the background.

Although you know your home, the agent knows these buyers. They've already looked at several properties today, they are remarkably suspicious about plumbing problems, they want a neighborhood full of kids, and they need a long dining-room wall for an heirloom breakfront.

An eager homeseller, full of nervous chatter, can blunder in several ways with these people. Proud of the new paint job, you might point out that the living room ceiling was just redone to get rid of an old stain from the time when your absent-minded teenager . . . . You'd never realize the needless anxiety this stirs up in some buyers.

If they ask about children in the neighborhood, you might voice your own attitude and reply, "They never bother us; you wouldn't know there were any around." And the buyers might conclude, perhaps wrongly, that your street lacks just the playmates they had hoped to find for their children.

As for that dining room, the broker won't say a single word while the buyers stand spellbound in the doorway, mentally placing their furniture against the long wall. If you stick around while a skilled broker shows your house, you may become nervous listening to the silence. Although the broker may not say much, he or she is listening very hard. Don't expect a stream of patter and salesmanship. A good broker uses skill and expertise to match buyer and house, and then lets the place sell itself, putting in a few deft words where they will do the most good.

The agent tries never to argue, and fades away discreetly when it becomes obvious that husband and wife need to confer in private. Such moments arrive as buyers begin to feel they may have found the right house, but neither can voice that conviction until they have compared notes. Your house showing is likely to involve a great deal of silence, which can be unnerving to you as a homeowner.

Another problem, if you join the group, is the simple matter of space. It's easy for stairways and halls to become crowded. The broker knows better than to enter small bedrooms with prospects.

If it's obvious that they might be really interested in your home, the broker may suggest that they go back through it once more, on their own. If they say "yes, we'd like to," you may be close to a sale.

When You Reappear

If you've been over at the neighbor's house and now realize that these prospects have been in the house a long time (20 minutes or more), it may be helpful for you to put in an appearance.

The broker wants to begin and end the viewing in the most pleasant room: the living room (with the log burning on the hearth), the kitchen (with the cookies cooling on the counter), or the family room (with the soft music wafting through to the hallways). This is a good place for you to be discovered, sitting at your ease, and prepared to answer questions. If the buyers are serious, they'll accept your invitation to sit down and chat.

You have valuable information for them: the distance to the nearest supermarket, the time the school bus comes, how far it is to the library or the tennis club.

Remember that you must tell the truth about your property. Don't vouch for facts you're not sure of. They could come back to haunt you later. Refer troublesome questions back to the listing agent, who has probably heard them all before.

It will help in future negotiations if you and the buyers like one another, but you may notice some nervousness on the part of the broker if you become too informative at this point. The broker expects to act as a buffer between buyers and sellers.

Topics to Avoid

Don't answer any questions about price. The correct answer to "Would you take $162,000?" is "We'll consider any written offers that come through our agent" (or, with no agent, "through our lawyer"). You should have asked your lawyer for a blank contract, which you can offer to a buyer who doesn't seem to know what to do next.

If you hear, "We need to move in by September; are you going to be out by then?" you might reply, "I'm sure we could work out the details."

This is also a poor time to discuss the sale of furniture or appliances. It's destructive to get hung up on small matters before the main event. If you've listed your stove and refrigerator as "negotiable" and are now asked if you'd leave them, say "That depends."

The unspoken words here are "That depends on how close you come to our list price." To a question about whether you'd sell the pool table or the home theater system, a good response is "We thought we'd decide after the sale of the house is settled."

SELLER'S TIP

When a prospective buyer seems to like your home, wait for a written offer before:

- Answering any questions about price
- Discussing negotiable property such as curtains or appliances
- Agreeing on a date to vacate

Get a Report

If you were away from home while the house was being shown, you can request that the broker call back later to report. Remember that the prospects may have looked at several houses. If they decide to put in a purchase offer on one of the others, the agent may be busy handling the details of that offer.

You can still ask for a call when the broker is free, to learn what the reaction was to your home. Request a frank report and do it each time you realize your home has been shown; you'll have valuable information on how your asking price strikes the buying public or suggestions on ways to enhance your home's appeal further.

Or perhaps you'll hear the real estate broker's ultimate compliment, "Your place shows well." And then, "They want to think it over. I may be getting in touch with your listing agent with an offer."

CHAPTER

9

Negotiating Your Sales Contract

The word *broker* derives from an old Middle English word for *go-between,* and nowhere is this more evident than when the agent brings you and your buyer to what is legally known as a *meeting of the minds.* A successful agent develops valuable skills in negotiation, and a new salesperson will call upon the broker's experience in this matter. With both parties under stress, tact and diplomacy are called into action. The broker knows enough of law and finance to make suggestions for dealing with difficulties. In the end, your salesperson derives the most satisfaction from a "win-win" situation, in which both parties feel they have achieved their goals and made a good deal.

With no broker involved, you must deal face-to-face with the would-be buyer. Always remember that oral agreements for the sale of real estate are not binding. The buyer could offer you $180,000 cash in front of five witnesses; you could shake hands on the deal and even accept a $10,000 deposit. And the buyer could still back out of the deal the next day and demand return of the deposit. As far as the law is concerned, there was no contract.

The statute of frauds demands that certain contracts be made in writing to be legally enforceable, and one of those is any contract for the sale of real property.

This makes negotiation particularly delicate, for you will only give yourself away if you engage in too much oral dickering.

Your Preparations

Study the sample contract to purchase shown in Figure 9.1 to familiarize yourself with typical provisions–but *don't* try to use it. Obtain a contract suitable to your area from your broker, lawyer, or legal bookstore. If your agency uses one specially designed form for its transactions, try to obtain samples of other standard contracts used in your area.

Local custom dictates the manner in which the offer to purchase will be made. The form may be called an agreement to buy and sell, a binder receipt and option, an agreement to purchase, a sales contract, or an offer and acceptance. Study it ahead of time so that when an offer comes in, you will be familiar with the standard provisions and can concentrate on the specific terms being offered.

It is helpful, also, if you familiarize yourself with the financing options open to potential buyers of your home. Chapter 10 discusses some alternatives. Because you will be asked to make decisions based upon the buyers' plans for financing, be conversant with their choices. Your salesperson will have information on current financing opportunities.

Some of your strongest offers will be those from buyers who have prepared themselves to purchase a home by having obtained a lender's prequalification letter. They may have even gone further, by procuring a full preapproval (they are completely loan-approved, pending a property address) for a home up to a specific price. These buyers will (understandably) not reveal what their price ceiling is, but will be in a better bargaining position compared to others who did not bother to take this step.

Presentation of the Offer

If you are using an agent, you will probably hear first by telephone that a written offer has come in on your property. Because offers must be presented immediately, you might even be notified while you are out of town and need to get yourself to a nearby fax machine to receive it.

Most homeowners react by asking immediately how much the buyers are prepared to pay. The agent, however, has learned to

FIGURE 9.1 Real Estate Sales Contract

REALTOR®

EQUAL HOUSING OPPORTUNITY

PURCHASE AND SALE CONTRACT FOR RESIDENTIAL PROPERTY

Plain English Form published by and only for use of members of the Greater Rochester Association of Realtors, Inc. and the Monroe County Bar Association.

COMMISSIONS OR FEES FOR THE REAL ESTATE SERVICES TO BE PROVIDED ARE NEGOTIABLE BETWEEN REALTOR AND CLIENT.

When Signed, This Document Becomes A Binding Contract. Buyer or Seller May Wish To Consult Their Own Attorney.

TO: ______________________________ (Seller) FROM: ______________________________ (Buyer)

OFFER TO PURCHASE

Buyer offers to purchase the property described below from Seller on the following terms:

1. PROPERTY DESCRIPTION.

Property known as No. ______________________ in the (Town) (City) (Village) of ______________________, State of New York, also known as Tax No. ______________________ including all buildings and any other improvements and all rights which the Seller has in or with the property.

Approximate Lot Size: ______________________. (Check if applicable) [ ] As described in more detail in the attached description.

Description of Buildings on Property: ______________________

2. OTHER ITEMS INCLUDED IN PURCHASE. The following items, if any, now in or on the property are included in this purchase and sale. All heating, plumbing, septic and private water systems, lighting fixtures, flowers, shrubs, trees, window shades and blinds, curtain and traverse rods, storm windows, storm doors, screens, awnings, TV antennae, water softeners, sump pumps, window boxes, mail box, tool shed, fences, underground pet containment fencing with control devices, wall-to-wall carpeting and runners, exhaust fans, hoods, garbage disposal, electric garage door opener and remote control devices, intercom equipment, humidifier, security systems, smoke detectors, all fireplace screens and enclosures, swimming pool and all related equipment and accessories, and the following, if built-in: cabinets, mirrors, stoves, ovens, dishwashers, trash compactors, shelving and air conditioning (except window units). Buyer agrees to accept these items in their present conditions. Other items to be included in the purchase and sale are:

____

[ ] Seller represents to the best of Seller's knowledge that any heating, plumbing, air conditioning, electrical systems and included appliances are presently in good working order, except for

____

Items not included are: ______________________.

Seller represents that he has good title to all of the above items to be transferred to Buyer, and will deliver a Bill of Sale for the same at closing.

3. PRICE: AMOUNT AND HOW IT WILL BE PAID: The purchase price is ______________________ Dollars $ ______________, Buyer shall receive credit at closing for any deposit made hereunder. The balance of the purchase price shall be paid as follows: (Check and complete applicable provisions.)

[ ] (a) Seller agrees to pay a loan fee of ________% of the mortgage amount.

[ ] (b) All in cash, or certified check at closing.

[ ] (c) By Buyer assuming and agreeing to pay according to its terms, the principal balance of the mortgage in the approximate amount of $ ______________ held by ______________________, provided that the mortgage is assumable without the holder's approval. Buyer understands that the mortgage bears interest at the rate of ________% per year and the monthly payments are $ ______________ which includes principal, interest, taxes and insurance (strike out any item not included in payment), with the last payment due on approximately ______________ 19/20______. Buyer agrees to pay the balance of the purchase price over the amount of the assumed mortgage in cash or certified check at closing. Buyer understands that principal balance may be lower at time of closing because of monthly payments made after this contract is signed. If the mortgage to be assumed provides for graduated or balloon payments, then a copy of the original bond and mortgage shall be furnished to Buyer's attorney for approval within ten days after acceptance of this offer.

[ ] (d) By Buyer delivering a purchase money bond and mortgage to Seller at closing. This purchase money bond and mortgage shall be in the amount of $ ______________, shall be amortized over a term of ________ years and all due and payable in ________ years from the date of closing, shall bear interest at the rate of ________% per year, and shall be paid in monthly installments of $ ______________, including principal and interest. The mortgage shall contain the statutory clauses as to payment, insurance, acceleration on default of thirty days, taxes, assessments, and water rates and also shall provide for late charges of 2% of any monthly payment which is not paid within 15 days after it is due and for recovery of reasonable attorney's fees if the mortgage is foreclosed.

The mortgage shall allow Buyer to prepay all or part of the mortgage without penalty at any time but shall also provide that the mortgage be paid in full if Buyer sells the property, unless Seller consents in writing to assumption of the mortgage debt. The balance of the purchase price will be paid at closing in cash, or certified check.

FIGURE 9.1 Real Estate Sales Contract (Continued)

4. CONTINGENCIES. Buyer makes this offer subject to the following contingencies. If any of these contingencies is not satisfied by the dates specified, then either Buyer or Seller may cancel this contract by written notice to the other. (Check and complete applicable provisions.)

[ ] (a) **Mortgage Contingency.** This offer subject to Buyer obtaining and accepting a ______________ mortgage loan commitment in an amount not to exceed ______________ at an interest rate not to exceed ______%, for a term of ______ years. Buyer shall immediately apply for this loan and shall have until ______________ to obtain and accept a written mortgage commitment. The conditions of any such mortgage commitment shall not be deemed contingencies of this contract but shall be the sole responsibility of Buyer. If the loan commitment requires repairs, replacements, or improvements to be made or painting to be done, before closing, then Seller shall do the work and install the materials and improvements needed or have the same done, at Seller's expense. However, if the cost of doing so exceeds $______________, Seller shall not be obligated to have such work done, and Buyer will be allowed either to receive credit at closing for the amount recited above and incur any necessary expenses to comply with the loan commitment requirements, or to cancel this contract by written notice to Seller, and any deposit shall be returned to Buyer. Issuance and acceptance by the Buyer of a written mortgage commitment shall be deemed a waiver and satisfaction of this contingency.

[ ] (b) **Mortgage Assumption Contingency.** This offer is subject to Buyer obtaining permission to assume the existing mortgage loan balance referred to above in (3c) by ______ 19______. If the mortgage holder requires that the interest rate be increased for such approval to be given, Buyer agrees to assume the mortgage at such rate as long as it does not exceed ______% at the time of the commitment. [ ]Buyer agrees to obtain a release of Seller's liability and to pay any assumption or release of liability fees.

[ ] (c) **Sale Contract Contingency.** This offer is subject to Buyer obtaining a contract for the sale of Buyer's property located at ______________ no later than ______________, 199______. Unless and until Buyer has removed this sale contingency in writing, if Seller receives another acceptable purchase offer, Seller may notify Buyer in writing that Seller wants to accept the other offer and Buyer will then have ______________ days to remove this sale contingency by written notice to the Seller. If Buyer does not remove this sale contingency after receiving notice from Seller, Buyer's rights under this contract shall end, and Seller shall be free to accept the other purchase offer and Buyer's deposit shall be returned. Buyer may not remove this sale contingency if Buyer's mortgage loan commitment requires the sale and/or transfer of this property as a condition of the mortgage loan funding, unless Buyer has a contract for the sale of this property which is not then subject to any unsatisfied contingencies.

[ ] (d) **Transfer of Title Contingency.** This offer is contingent upon the transfer of title to Buyer's property located at ______________ no later than ______________, 199______. [ ] Buyer represents that Buyer has entered into a contract for sale of Buyer's property which is now subject to the following contingencies: [ ] None; [ ] Mortgage; [ ] Assumption of Mortgage; [ ] Sale of Property; [ ] Transfer of Title; [ ] Attorney Approval; and/or [ ] Other______________. Unless and until Buyer has obtained a contract for sale of Buyer's property which is not subject to any unsatisfied contingencies, and has so notified the Seller in writing, if Seller receives another acceptable purchase offer, Seller may notify Buyer in writing that Seller wants to accept the other offer and Buyer will then have ______________ days to remove this transfer of title contingency by written notice to the Seller. If Buyer does not remove this transfer of title contingency after receiving notice from Seller, Buyer's rights under this contract shall end, and Seller shall be free to accept the other purchase offer and Buyer's deposit shall be returned. Buyer may not remove this transfer of title contingency if Buyer's mortgage loan commitment requires the sale and transfer of this property as a condition of the mortgage loan funding, unless Buyer has a contract for sale of this property which is not then subject to any unsatisfied contingencies.

[ ] (e) **Attorney Approval.** This contract is subject to the written approval of attorneys for Buyer and Seller within ______________ days from date of acceptance (the "Approval Period"). If either attorney makes written objection to the contract within the Approval Period, and such objection is not cured by written approval by both attorneys and all of the parties within the Approval Period, then either Buyer or Seller may cancel this contract by written notice to the other and any deposit shall be returned to the Buyer.

[ ] (f) **Waiver of Attorney Approval.** This offer is not subject to the Buyer's attorney approval.

[ ] (g) **Other Contingencies.** ______________________________

____

5. Closing Date and Place. Transfer of title shall take place at the ______________ County Clerk's Office or at the offices of Buyer's lender on or before ______________, 19______.

6. Buyer's Possession of Property.

[ ] Buyer shall have possession of the property on the day of closing, in broom clean condition, with all keys to the property delivered to Buyer at closing.

[ ] Seller shall have the right to retain possession for______________ days after closing at the cost of $______________ per day, plus utilities. At possession, the property shall be broom clean and all keys shall be delivered to Buyer.

7. Title Documents. Seller shall provide the following documents in connection with the sale:

A. Deed. Seller will deliver to Buyer at closing a properly signed and notarized Warranty Deed with lien covenant (or Executor's Deed, Administrator's Deed or Trustee's Deed, if Seller holds title as such).

GRAR 3/94

B. Abstract, Bankruptcy and Tax Searches, and Instrument Survey Map. Seller will furnish and pay for and deliver to Buyer or Buyer's attorney at least 15 days prior to the date of closing, fully guaranteed tax, title and United States Court Searches dated or redated after the date of this contract with a local tax certificate for Village, or City taxes, if any, and an instrument survey map dated or redated after the date of this contract. Seller will pay for the map or redated map and for continuing such searches to and including the day of closing. Any survey map shall be prepared or redated and certified to meet the standards and requirements of Buyer's mortgage lender and of the Monroe County Bar Association.

FIGURE 9.1 Real Estate Sales Contract (Continued)

8. Marketability of Title. The deed and other documents delivered by Seller shall be sufficient to convey good marketable title in fee simple, to the property free and clear of all liens and encumbrances. However, Buyer agrees to accept title to the property subject to restrictive covenants of record common to the tract or subdivision of which the property is a part, provided these restictions have not been violated, or if they have been violated, that the time for anyone to complain of the violations has expired. Buyer also agrees to accept title to the property subject to public utility easements along lot lines as long as those easements do not interfere with any buildings now on the property or with any improvements Buyer may construct in compliance with all present restrictive covenants of record and zoning and building codes applicable to the Property. Seller agrees to furnish a smoke alarm affidavit at closing and to cooperate in executing any documents required by federal or state laws for transfer of title to residential property.

9. Objections to Title. If Buyer raises a valid written objection to Seller's title which means that the title to the property is unmarketable, Seller may cancel this contract by giving prompt written notice of cancellation to Buyer. Buyer's deposit shall be returned immediately, and if Buyer makes a written request for it, Seller shall reimburse Buyer for the reasonable cost of having the title examined. However, if Seller gives notice within 5 days that Seller will cure the problem prior to the closing date, or if the title objection is insurable and Buyer is willing to accept insurable title, then this contract shall continue in force until the closing date, subject to the Seller performing as promised and/or providing insurable title at Seller's expense. If Seller fails to cure the problem within such time, Buyer will not be obligated to purchase the property and Buyer's deposit shall be returned together with reimbursement for the reasonable cost of having the title examined.

10. Recording Costs, Mortgage Tax, Transfer Tax and Closing Adjustments. Seller will pay the real property transfer tax and special additional mortgage recording tax, if applicable. Buyer will pay mortgage assumption charges, if any, and will pay for recording the deed and the mortgage, and for mortgage tax. The following, as applicable, will be prorated and adjusted between Seller and Buyer as of the date of closing: current taxes computed on a fiscal year basis, excluding any delinquent items, interest and penalties; rent payments; fuel oil on the premises; water charges; pure water charges; sewer charges; mortgage interest; current common charges or assessments; prepaid F.H.A. Mortgage Insurance Premium (M.I.P.) of approximately $_______________, with the exact amount to be calculated at closing in accordance with F.H.A. formulae. Any F.H.A. insurance premium which is not prepaid, but rather paid monthly, shall be adjusted at closing. If there is a water meter at the property, Seller shall furnish an actual reading to a date not more than thirty (30) days before the closing date set forth in this contract. At closing the water charges and any sewer rent shall be apportioned on the basis of such actual reading.

11. Zoning. Seller represents that the property is in full compliance with all zoning or building ordinances for use as a ____.
If applicable laws require it, the Seller will furnish at or before closing, a Certificate of Occupancy for the property, dated within ninety (90) days of the closing, with Seller completing the work and installing the materials and improvements needed to obtain Certificate of Occupancy. However, if the cost of obtaining a Certificate of Occupancy exceeds $ _______________________, Seller shall not be obligated to have such work done, and Buyer will be allowed either to receive credit at closing for the amount recited above, and incur the necessary expenses to obtain the Certificate of Occupancy, or to cancel this contract by written notice to Seller, and any deposit shall be returned to Buyer.

12. Risk of Loss. Risk of loss or damage to the property by fire or other casualty until transfer of title shall be assumed by the Seller. If damage to the property by fire or such other casualty occurs prior to transfer, Buyer may cancel this contract without any further liability to Seller and Buyer's deposit is to be returned. If Buyer does not cancel but elects to close, then Seller shall transfer to Buyer any insurance proceeds, or Seller's claim to insurance proceeds payable for such damage.

13. Condition of Property. Buyer agrees to purchase the property "as is" except as provided in paragraph 2, subject to reasonable use, wear, tear, and natural deterioration between now and the time of closing. However, this paragraph shall not relieve Seller from furnishing a Certificate of Occupancy as called for in paragraph 11, if applicable. Buyer shall have the right, after reasonable notice to Seller, to inspect the property within 48 hours before the time of closing.

14. Services. Seller represents that property is serviced by: ________ Public Water, ________ Public Sewers, ________ Septic System, ________ Private Well.

15. Deposit to Listing Broker. Buyer (has deposited) (will deposit upon acceptance) $_______________________ in the form of a _______________________
with _______________________(Escrow Agent) at _______________________(bank), which deposit is to become part of the purchase price or returned if not accepted or if Buyer's contract thereafter fails to close for any reason not the fault of the Buyer. If Buyer fails to complete Buyer's part of this contract, Seller is allowed to retain the deposit to be applied to Seller's damages, and may also pursue other legal rights Seller has against the Buyer, including a lawsuit for any real estate brokerage commission paid by the Seller.

16. Real Estate Broker.
[ ] The parties agree that _______________________________________ brought about this purchase and sale.

[ ] It is understood and agreed by both Buyer and Seller that no broker secured this contract.

17. Life of Offer. This offer shall expire on_______________________, 19______, at _____________ .m.

18. Responsibility of Persons Under This Contract; Assignability. If more than one person signs this contract as Buyer, each person and any party who takes over that person's legal position will be responsible for keeping the promises made by Buyer in this contract. If more than one person signs this contract as Seller, each person or any party who takes over that person's legal position, will be fully responsible for keeping the promises made by Seller. However, this contract is personal to the parties and may not be assigned by either without the other's consent.

19. Entire Contract. This contract when signed by both Buyer and Seller will be the record of the complete agreement between the Buyer and Seller concerning the purchase and sale of the property. No verbal agreements or promises will be binding.

20. Notices. All notices under this contract shall be deemed delivered upon receipt. Any notices relating to this contract may be given by the attorneys for the parties.

21. Addenda. The following Addenda are incorporated into this contract:
[ ] All Parties Agreement [ ] Services [ ] Engineer's Inspection [ ] Mediation [ ] Electric Availability [ ] Utility Surcharge [ ] Lead Warning [ ] Other: _______________

FIGURE 9.1 Real Estate Sales Contract (Continued)

Dated: ______________________ BUYER ______________________

Witness: ______________________ BUYER ______________________

[ ] ACCEPTANCE OF OFFER BY SELLER [ ] COUNTER OFFER BY SELLER

Seller certifies that Seller owns the property and has the power to sell the property. Seller accepts the offer and agrees to sell on the terms and conditions above set forth.

[ ] Waiver of Seller's attorney approval. This offer is not subject to Seller's attorney approval.

Dated: ______________________ SELLER ______________________

Witness: ______________________ SELLER ______________________

ADMINISTRATIVE INFORMATION

Buyer: ______________________

Social Security Number: ______________________

Address: ______________________

______________________ Zip: ______________________

Phone: (H) ______________________ (B) ______________________

Attorney: ______________________

Address: ______________________

Phone:(B) ______________________ (FAX) ______________________

Selling Broker: ______________________

Address: ______________________

Phone: ______________________ Broker Code: ______________________

Selling Agent: ______________________ Phone:(H) ______________________

Selling Agent I.D. # ______________________ FAX ______________________

Seller: ______________________

Social Security Number: ______________________

GRAR MLS # ______________________

Address: ______________________

______________________ Zip: ______________________

Phone:(H) ______________________ (B) ______________________

Attorney: ______________________

Address: ______________________

Phone:(B) ______________________ (FAX) ______________________

Listing Broker: ______________________

Address: ______________________

Phone: ______________________ Broker Code: ______________________

Listing Agent: ______________________ Phone:(H) ______________________

Listing Agent I.D. # ______________________ FAX ______________________ field such questions. Revealing the purchase price over the telephone, without discussing accompanying matters, is considered a poor practice. You will probably be asked to set a time for face-to-face presentation of the offer. Some brokers ask a secretary to set up the appointment, heading off your direct request for information. You will be asked to name a time when all owners of the property can be present.

When you have listed your house with one member of a multiple listing system and the offer is secured by another office, local custom governs the procedure. The offer may be turned over to your listing agent for presentation. In other areas, the selling office may contact you directly. Or your listing agent may be notified and asked to set up the appointment for the selling broker. In any event, you may request that your original agent attend the meeting for presentation of the offer. The buyers will probably not be present.

Bear in mind that your agent, although duty-bound to find you the best deal, is naturally eager to sell the house through his or her own office and thus retain the whole commission. When an offer comes in, ask whether any other offers are in preparation elsewhere or rumored to be in the offing.

If several offers come in within a day or two, it is best to consider all of them at the same time. The one first signed by would-be buyers does not have precedence. As long as you have not acted on any offer, you are free to consider all of them and to respond to whichever one you choose.

If you are selling on your own, it's best to ask for time to consider a written offer in privacy. A day or two is not unreasonable, and will give you time to consult a fee-for-services broker or your attorney and formulate a response.

Price

You may have done some research on the probability of receiving your full asking price. Except in the hottest of real estate markets, brokers believe one transaction in ten goes through at the full list price; the proportion may well be different in your area. Among factors that may limit the price offered are the cost of comparable properties now on the market, the buyers' knowledge of recent similar sales, and—often most important—the buyers' ability to pay. Bear in mind that although you and the buyers can agree on any price, there may be hazards ahead if they cannot carry a proposed mortgage loan, or if the lender makes an unfavorable appraisal of your home's value.

Terms

The buyers will detail the terms on which they plan to buy the property. Before you take your house off the market on their behalf, you'll want some assurance that the transaction is likely to conclude successfully.

If you receive an all-cash offer, ask the broker, attorney, or buyers themselves about their ability to come up with that amount of money, and the source of the funds. Although this might appear to be none of your business, you will be making a decision based upon their ability to fulfill their obligations.

If the buyers want to take over your present mortgage, your mortgage holder can advise you of any complications. Ask for an explanation of contingent liability.

A buyer's new loan on the property may find you being asked to pay points to a lending institution. This subject is discussed at length in Chapter 10.

You may be asked to carry the loan (hold the mortgage yourself). Before agreeing to such an arrangement, read carefully the section on *purchase-money mortgages* in Chapter 10. You can make your response conditional: "We accept the offer, subject to verification of employment and income and a satisfactory credit report within 10 days. . ."

Contingencies

Often the buyers will make their offer subject to certain conditions of the sale, referred to as *contingencies.* This means that they promise to buy the property, but only if:

- They are able to secure an FHA mortgage loan in the amount of $140,000 with interest at a certain percent.
- Their present home is sold.

- The employer with which they came into town to interview hires them by a certain date.
- A spouse approves the house.
- There is a satisfactory home inspector's report.

Other contingencies (the purchase of a house can be contingent on just about anything) can be written into an offer. To protect yourself, each contingency should be accompanied by a time limit. The inspector's report can usually be obtained within three days; so might the spouse's approval. You will not run much of a risk if you accept and take your house off the market for a few days.

The stipulation that financing must be obtained is understandable. In fact, most real estate contracts are contingent upon financing approval if not written for cash. You can request that the buyers promise prompt application to a lending institution and even require written approval within a certain number of days, because lenders can procure quicker answers these days than ever before. The contract may even stipulate that they will apply to three lending institutions, if necessary, and under the guidance of your agent. Again, make sure everything is in writing within the contract itself.

When the contingency is for the sale of the buyers' present property, judgment is called for on your part. Some sellers simply refuse all contingent offers of this type. Others find them reasonable, because the buyers will need the money from their sale to buy your house.

When you accept a contingent offer, you are trading worry about the sale of your own property for worry about the sale of someone else's, over which you have no control. You have a right to investigate how likely the other house is to sell and whether it is being listed at a reasonable price. You can even insert into your contract provisions about this matter.

The terms of an offer—whether it is a clean, all-cash deal or one that involves accepting a contingency—often affect the sales price eventually agreed upon. If you are going to wait for the sale of the buyers' house, you have some justification for sticking to a higher price in return for the uncertainty.

In any event, make sure that any offer contingent upon the sale of the buyers' present property includes an *escape clause,* sometimes called a *kick-out.* This provision allows you to continue showing your home. If you receive another offer that you want to accept, you notify the first buyers that they must remove their contingency within a few days or withdraw. Either they agree to buy your home by the specified date come what may, or they must void the contract and drop out of the picture, allowing you to negotiate with your new purchaser.

Local custom suggests the exact terms of the escape clause. You might allow a period of one month in which the buyers can be secure in their contract; after that, if their own home hasn't sold, they could be bumped by another offer. Usually you promise the first buyers a period up to five business days in which to make their decision if an escape clause is invoked, but in some areas it can be as short as what is called a "72-hour first right of refusal."

Personal Property

The purchase contract should detail all of the gray-area items mentioned at the time of listing: play equipment, custom-sized area rugs, garage storage cabinets, workshop benches, and, in general, all fixtures that you will leave with the property. In addition, you may agree to include items of personal property such as kitchen appliances, washer and dryer, or matching drapery.

The contract should also mention those items you will remove. Oral agreement is not a sufficient guarantee against misunderstandings later.

Earnest Money

Your buyers will be asked to put a deposit into the hands of the broker or an attorney to prove that their intentions are serious and to serve as a source of damages should they back out for no good reason. You can expect to see their safeguards written into the contract. It may state that their deposit will be returned if the lender's appraisal comes in below the purchase price, if you renege for no good reason, or if they fail to receive their mortgage commitment, for example. You can request a similar provision: that their deposit is in jeopardy if they do not act in good faith.

The deposit is not a legal requirement for the contract. If the cash for their purchase is coming from the sale of their present home, the buyers may be unable to deposit earnest money or may be reluctant to do so. You should not accept an offer, however, unless it is accompanied by some sort of deposit. The money signifies that the buyers mean business.

Local custom varies, and the buyers may have been told that 6 percent or even 10 percent is standard. They may well come up with less.

Pay attention to the form of the deposit. The buyers may be out-of-towners who do not keep large sums in a checking account; have they promised to make the check good as soon as they get back home? A promissory note is of little value in this matter, and a cash deposit of $500 is often more useful than a note for $5,000. Deposits may also be increased later, with the initial amount accompanying the offer, and one or two more similar amounts deposited during a specified time frame, or as the bigger contingencies are removed. The broker is legally liable to you for any representation about the earnest money, because you are basing your decisions upon what you are told.

Buyers may be understandably reluctant to hand a deposit directly to a seller. Where agents are involved, the money is usually kept in the broker's escrow account. If there is no agent, suggest that the money be held by your attorney, or failing that, by the buyers' attorney or an escrow company.

If your home was built before 1978, the EPA requires that before the contract can become binding, the buyer of your property be given 10 days in which to conduct an inspection for lead paint hazards. If the buyer agrees, however, that time can be shortened or eliminated. If lead paint hazards are found, you cannot be required to remedy the situation, but the buyer need not go through with the purchase. An addendum outlining the requirement and acknowledging the prospective buyer's receipt of a lead paint information booklet should be part of the purchase contract. The booklet, which can be found in Appendix D at the back of this book, may be reproduced without permission.

FIGURE 9.2
Responsibility for Costs

Buyer	Seller	
☐	☐	Survey
☐	☐	Points
☐	☐	Title insurance
☐	☐	Pest inspection
☐	☐	Recording fees
☐	☐	Transfer fees
☐	☐	Escrow or closing fees
☐	☐	Title search
☐	☐	Bank's attorney
☐	☐	Broker's commission

Other Provisions

The purchase contract will contain details on those items that must be apportioned between you and the buyer at closing: water bills, property taxes, and the like. It stipulates the type of deed you must deliver, which party bears responsibility for loss resulting from fire before the time of closing, the procedure if a cloud on the title is found, and many other matters intended to head off disagreements as the transaction progresses. Figure 9.2 lists these and other costs for which the contract should specify which party will be responsible.

A closing date will be specified. Unless the legal clause "time is of the essence" is included, the closing date mentioned is merely a target and might come and go with the contract still continuing in effect. It is especially crucial to specify a hard, fast closing date if you need the proceeds of this home to purchase another by a certain date. It is reasonable, however, to leave a cushion between closing and buyer occupancy, stated in terms such as "closing plus two days" to coordinate moves. If agreed to, this means that you may stay up to two extra days, paying a nominal daily rent before having to move out.

In most areas, possession of the property is usually given on the date of settlement. It rarely becomes necessary to let the buyers move in ahead of time or for you to remain after closing. If the buyer moves in as a tenant, you should take certain precautions, which are discussed in Chapter 11. Try to avoid such an arrangement. If you plan to stay on after closing, you may be asked to pay a daily rent and even to deposit a sum into escrow to ensure that you will eventually move out as agreed. Like all other arrangements, these should be written into the original sales contract.

To safeguard yourself, you may wish to include certain limitations in the contract. Perhaps you will make repairs, if they are required by a lending institution, only up to a certain dollar amount. You may want to limit the number of points you pay. If appliances are included in the sale, you will want to transfer them "as is" where state law permits.

Figure 9.3 lists some, but not all, of the protections you need from a written contract.

Your Response

The offer you receive will probably contain a time limit, "This offer is good until Saturday noon. . . ." In most states, the buyers are free to withdraw their offer before you have accepted it. If they do not, and if you accept before Saturday noon, then you have a firm purchase contract, binding upon both parties. Not responding to an offer usually deems the deal dead.

You have three possible responses to the offer: yes, no, and maybe.

FIGURE 9.3
Sample Contract Provisions Checklist

Date: ____________________

Buyer: ____________________

YES	NO	
❑	❑	Approval by your attorney before contract becomes firm?
❑	❑	Items you want to remove from the property (lighting fixtures, etc.)?
❑	❑	Escape clause (kick-out) if the offer is contingent upon the sale of buyer's present home?
❑	❑	Assurance that the buyer will apply for mortgage loan in timely fashion?
❑	❑	Time limit for buyer to obtain mortgage commitment?
❑	❑	Dollar limit on repairs you may be required to make?
❑	❑	Reimbursement for property taxes you may have prepaid, heating oil in your tank, and the like?
❑	❑	Return of money in your escrow account with your lender (if mortgage being assumed)?
❑	❑	"Assumption of," not "taking title subject to" your present mortgage, if it is to be turned over to the buyer?
❑	❑	Substantial "good faith" earnest money deposit?
❑	❑	Forfeiture of earnest money if buyer withdraws for no good reason?
❑	❑	Specific target date for closing?

Yes

"Yes" is an acceptance of the offer as it stands, without any alteration. If yours is a state where attorneys are integral players in real estate transactions, you can write above your signature the words, "subject to the approval by my attorney" (or any other third party you deem knowledgeable). In this case, your lawyer, friend, or discount broker must later approve the wording and provisions of the contract. If he or she does not, you may void the contract, or both parties may agree to amend it.

You may have arranged beforehand to telephone this third party while you are considering the purchase offer. If the offer is on a standard form with which the broker or lawyer is familiar, a few minutes may suffice to go over the specific terms detailed so that you can receive counsel by phone.

Alternatively, you can take the contract for a lawyer's review before you accept it. Keep two precautions in mind. First, many attorneys will not counsel you on price, a matter that they consider out of their field of expertise. And second, there is always the possibility that you have a nit-picking lawyer, unaccustomed to real estate transactions, who may delay and fuss around until you lose a favorable offer. In the end, you must make your own decision, taking into account the advice of both agent and attorney.

No

You can always refuse an offer completely. Once you have rejected it, you cannot change your mind, even five minutes later, and get it back. Suppose, for example, that the offer is good until Saturday at noon. On Friday night you reject it. You cannot then change your mind on Saturday morning and accept it. If you did, you would have to ask the buyers whether they would like to reinstate their offer. This is difficult, however, because, in the emotion of home buying, the buyers may have already deemed your house "not meant to be," and have refocused their efforts on other homes or even other areas.

Because you know that an underpriced house sells quickly, you may be skeptical of a good offer that comes in promptly. It is only human to argue that, "If I received an offer for $200,000 after only one week, what might I get by waiting a while longer?" The true bargain, however, is usually snapped up within a day or two. After a week, you can assume that the market is operating normally. Experience has shown that the first offer is often the best one. Because a new home on the market is exposed to a large group of potential buyers, your best offer is likely to come from that group. Be cautious, then, about rejecting a first offer just on principle. Agents find little comfort in saying, "I told you so," if you are waiting vainly three months later to equal that first proposal.

Maybe

Better than a simple refusal is a *counteroffer.* With a counteroffer, you agree to accept the buyers' proposal if a few changes are made.

Again, you run the risk of losing your buyers. You have not accepted their proposal, and they are now free to accept or reject yours. A counteroffer, though, with its possibility for reaching eventual agreement, is better than an outright rejection.

While a counteroffer is pending, your house is more or less tied up. Make the counteroffer good for only a short time, perhaps a day or two.

If your house has turned out to be a hot property and you anticipate other offers within the next few days, you may prefer not to be bound by a written counteroffer. "Tell them to come back $10,000 higher and I'll consider it," you might say informally, without committing yourself.

Inexperienced negotiators sometimes assume that the proper procedure is for the buyer to start with a low offer and for the seller to counter somewhat under the asking price, depending on a series of counter-counteroffers to bring them eventually to a price halfway between. In practice, however, too many counters usually kill a transaction. The parties lose sight of the main goal—reaching an agreement—as emotions rise and the process becomes a test of wills.

Your buyers are well advised to make their first offer as high as they are prepared to go, and you to make any counteroffer close to the price you would take. If you are determined to stand pat on your asking price, consider the buyers' pride and offer a token reduction–perhaps a few hundred dollars–to signal your goodwill. Offer to throw in the refrigerator or the trash compactor. These could be items that the buyers do not particularly want, but they provide a way for the buyers to save face while accepting your price. At least, they may reason, their low offer was not wasted, for it won some concessions.

During price negotiations, it is essential to remember your objective. You may insist on the last few dollars as a matter of principle, completely overlooking the fact that when you set your original asking price, that extra thousand was tacked on "just to see." Resolve before you start that you will not lose a deal over a few thousand dollars.

SELLER'S TIP

On considering your response to a purchase offer, keep in mind that:

- The first offer received after placing your property on the market is often the best.
- It is better to respond with a counteroffer rather than to reject an unsatisfactory offer.

A counteroffer may concern itself with matters other than price. You might, for example, "accept all terms and conditions except that purchase price shall be $175,900"; "accept all terms and conditions except that date of closing shall be June 30"; or request that an escape clause be added to the contingency regarding the sale of the buyers' present property. Any terms discussed earlier in this chapter can be added to your counteroffer. Special circumstances may suggest other provisions. As long as both parties agree and the matter is not illegal, almost anything can be written into your contract. For unusual provisions, your attorney or the buyers' should supply the wording.

Signatures

Do not be surprised if the agent is not willing to leave an offer with you overnight or drop it at your broker's office. The agent's experience is that the transaction proceeds best when he or she retains possession of the original contract. Unsigned duplicates can, of course, be left with you or retained by your agent. As soon as you and the buyers have signed a final acceptance, all parties will receive duplicates of the signed originals.

It is not essential for all buyers to sign the offer, but all sellers must. In some states, various provisions dictate that a spouse sign, even if not an owner of record.

When you and the buyers have signed an exact acceptance of all terms, the contract is binding and the broker has theoretically earned the commission.

Role of the Backup

You are well within your rights to entertain backup offers on your property. In hot real estate markets or in areas where any listing is big news, this is actually the more prudent way to go. Perhaps you sign a firm contract with Buyer A, only to find Buyer B beating down your door on the next day. Buyer B is willing to do anything to own your house, and will wait around in hopes that A's transaction somehow falls through. You can then accept an offer from B "subject to the nonperformance of existing contract with A." Buyer A, of course, has a firm contract with you and will probably be the next owner. But if anything goes wrong with that transaction, you can then obtain a release from A and sell to B, with the price and the terms already agreed upon in your backup contract. You are in an enviable position.

Even more enviable is a market in which *bidding wars* take place, where homes are listed at an already somewhat inflated-sounding price, but actually sell for higher. As in an auction, bids begin coming in, leaving the seller to sit back and decide just which offer contains the most desirable price and terms. This is rare, however, and no one envies the real estate appraiser who must try to justify these artificially created values.

Offers across the Land

Long distance offers and closings are no longer the formidable prospects they once were. Title companies and attorneys' offices are able to transmit many documents electronically for a New Yorker's purchase of a home in California or vice versa.

Your broker or agent is well acquainted with how this may be accomplished, with the initial offer and counteroffers done by fax.

Electronic closings have now become possible through the magic and increased security of the Internet. Federal approval has been obtained for electronic signatures, making the equation even simpler. Some feel real estate transactions will be totally paperless in the future.

CHAPTER

10

Your Buyer's Financing

You may think that financing is the buyer's concern, but it is of vital importance to you. How will you respond to these questions?

- "Are you willing to consider an FHA offer?"
- "Will you hold the mortgage yourself for high interest and a five-year balloon?"
- "Can I take over your VA loan if I'm not a veteran?"
- "Would you drop your price $15,000 for all cash?"

Preparing to judge the buyer's financing proposal requires homework on your part. Become familiar with the possibilities. Ask a mortgage consultant for a briefing on the current alternatives. Find out about new and innovative loan programs as they become available locally. Some lenders are more than pleased to provide a spreadsheet or flier for you to give to prospective buyers, showing several possible lending scenarios for your particular home in exchange for the marketing exposure they receive.

There is no single best financing plan out there. More than a hundred different mortgage plans are available from lending institutions in almost any given area. Each of these plans is there because it fits a certain situation best—buyer's need, seller's convenience, type of property.

Asking, "What's the best mortgage around right now?" is like walking into a drugstore and asking, "What's the best medicine you have?"

A broker, working with a customer, develops a financing strategy for that buyer within the first few minutes of conversation. Recent bankruptcy? Better search for an assumable mortgage. Two young professionals with gradually increasing incomes? Suggest an adjustable-rate mortgage starting them out with the lowest possible monthly payments. A small business owner just getting established? Find a portfolio lender who is more generous with its loan program guidelines.

Is the Buyer Capable?

If you are using a real estate broker, your agent will perform a cursory prequalification on the buyer, if this has not already been done by the buyer's agent or by a loan consultant ahead of time. The process involves an analysis of income, debts, assets, credit scores, and available cash to determine whether the buyer is financially capable of purchasing your home.

If you are selling on your own, you need the same assurance before you accept an offer and take your home off the market. The buyer who is serious should not mind being asked to get a loan prequalification, or even a full preapproval, before you make a firm commitment to sell. If you are confident that the buyer will check out favorably with a lender, you may begin to negotiate, but with the stipulation that the offer be contingent upon the buyer's preapproval by an agreed-upon date. One of the seller's worst mistakes is tying up the house for months, only to find that the prospective buyer is financially unable to complete the purchase. The more you know about prospective buyers, the more likely you are to have a problem-free sale.

All-Cash Buyers

Most agents can count on one hand the number of contracts they have written involving all-cash purchases.

Advantages. The advantages to you in an all-cash sale include:

- You will receive your money immediately.
- The closing date may be set for your convenience, because no mortgage commitment need be obtained.
- With no contingencies for obtaining financing, you can count on a firm sale and make your plans with confidence.
- An appraisal will not be necessary.
- No inspections will be required by any institution

Disadvantages. Possible negatives include:

- For income tax or personal reasons, you may prefer not to receive all proceeds immediately.
- Aware of the value of an all-cash sale, the buyer may expect a price concession in return. (Consider giving it!)

Before accepting an all-cash offer, though, insist upon proof that the money is available (a gift letter from a grandmother isn't really proof, and expected money from an inheritance is somewhat risky). A current bank statement or proof through an attorney or an accountant of where the funds will be drawn should suffice. Insist upon a substantial deposit, with written provision that it will be forfeited if the buyer is unable to perform.

Assuming Your Loan

If your mortgage is assumable by the next owner of the house, the mortgage will fall into one of two categories: freely assumable or assumable with lender approval.

Freely Assumable Mortgages

These include all FHA loans placed before December 15, 1989, and all VA loans placed before March 1, 1988 (more about new rules for FHAs and VAs placed after those dates in a moment). If your mortgage is presently one of these types, any buyer may take it, along with the house, with no change in interest rate or term. The buyers need not prove that they can qualify to carry the loan. The lending institution has no say in the matter. All that is necessary is your assent. The buyers pay the difference in cash at time of closing, or they may request that you hold a second mortgage–more on that later. Suppose, for example, that you own a $100,000 house with a VA loan on which you presently owe $85,000. The buyers (who need not be veterans) can take the loan along with the house, paying you the remaining $15,000 in cash.

Advantages. Your advantages include:

- No points are due, you receive your money immediately, the sale is firm, and the closing date need not be subject to a lender's convenience.
- Your house is easily sold, for a large number of buyers are looking for such mortgages and can afford the down payment. Your VA or FHA loan, which may have a lower interest rate than is currently available, may be the most valuable thing about your house.
- You may command a premium for your property. The fortunate buyers have few closing costs to pay, save on mortgage or appraisal fees, and need not have a lender inspection. The buyers may be willing to pay something extra for the savings anticipated over the years from a low interest rate.

Disadvantages. Here are a couple of drawbacks to consider.

- Think carefully before allowing an assumption if the buyer wants you to carry a second mortgage for most or all of the remaining purchase price. Observe the procedures listed in the Purchase-Money Mortgages section later in this chapter. It is particularly risky if the buyers have no cash of their own in the property; they'd have little to lose if things got bad and they decided to leave the key in the mailbox and just walk away.
- One other drawback to allowing a mortgage assumption is that you may retain contingent liability. If the mortgage were foreclosed and the property could not be sold for sufficient money to clear the debt, the lender, FHA or VA, could eventually require you to make up the deficiency.

> This possibility becomes more remote with every passing day, however, as the debt is reduced and if the dollar value of the house increases. Caution is indicated, though, in a neighborhood that is deteriorating or an area that is economically depressed.

There is a procedure under which the new borrower, if willing, can prove qualifications and release the seller from further liability. If the seller is to be released, the buyer who assumes an older VA loan must be a veteran with an entitlement.

FHA and VA Mortgages Assumable with Lender Approval

For FHA loans made after December 15, 1989, and VA mortgages placed after March 1, 1988, the buyer assuming the loan must prove financial qualification to the satisfaction of the lending institution. The original borrower would have no further liability.

If the buyer assuming a newer FHA loan is not able or willing to prove qualification, a simple credit check and appraisal of the property may be substituted, and the seller retains liability for five years. After that time, if mortgage payments are current, the original borrower is no longer liable.

Mortgages Assumable with Lender Approval

Conventional loans, those not backed by the FHA or VA, are usually not assumable. The majority must be paid off when the property is sold.

But a third category of loans exists–those assumable with the lender's approval. Many adjustable-rate mortgages (ARMs) fall into this group; so do new FHA and VA loans.

If your present mortgage is of this type, your buyer can apply to the lender to assume your loan. The new borrower must supply sufficient qualifications to carry the debt and, in the case of an ARM, the interest rate may be adjusted. Closing costs are less than those required for placing a new loan.

Conventional mortgages vary in this matter and in other provisions. If yours is being assumed, your lender can tell you whether you run any risks.

Secondary Mortgage Market

When every bank in town sets the same limits on some of their loans, chances are that these loan guidelines are set by the secondary mortgage market. Many lenders make loans and then turn around and sell them (packaged with many other mortgages) to big investors in the secondary mortgage market. The largest buyer in this field is Fannie Mae (FNMA), the Federal National Mortgage Association. When Fannie Mae announces that it will buy a certain type of mortgage, lending institutions listen.

Portfolio Loans

If you or the buyer has a situation that doesn't meet the standards of the secondary market, search for a local lender making portfolio loans. These are traditional mortgages, in which the bank (or savings and loan institution) lends its own money, collects and keeps the payments, and retains the mortgage in its own portfolio. Because such loans don't have to meet the nationwide standards of the secondary market, lenders can be more flexible. An antique house that doesn't meet current building standards or a self-employed buyer with unusual qualifications might well need a portfolio loan.

Points

The payment of points when a new mortgage loan is made compensates the lender for an interest rate that does not reflect the true cost of the money. Each point is 1 percent of the loan being placed. It is due as a one-time, lump-sum payment, usually at the time of transfer of title. Points may be financed under *some* programs, making the rate effectively higher. If buyers wish to pay more, rather than less up-front money, they may also *buy down* their own interest rate. Read on a bit further about seller-paid buydowns.

If your buyer is looking for a $100,000 mortgage, and the lending institution demands two points, then $2,000 is due.

When interest rates fluctuate daily, lending institutions prefer to change the number of points charged rather than constantly alter the interest rates on mortgages. The number of points charged thus may vary from one lender to another and from one week to another. Keeping track of the local situation is one of a broker's major concerns.

If $2,000 is due in points before your buyer can place a $100,000 mortgage, who pays this sum? The answer depends on what is negotiated in your sales contract. If you are committed to paying points, make sure that the buyers consider your interests when they choose their lender.

In times of high interest rates, which might make it difficult for your buyers to qualify for the proposed mortgage loan, you may be asked to participate in a seller-paid buydown. A lending institution offers you the opportunity of paying extra points; in return, your buyers can place their loan at a lower interest rate. Although this process reduces your proceeds from the house, it may enable the buyers to purchase.

Although points represent up-front interest payments, they are subject to varying treatment by the Internal Revenue Service. Your buyer can deduct immediately, in the year they are paid, all points on a mortgage to buy a residence, even those you pay.

Most important to you: Points paid by the seller are not deductible, but merely a cost of selling. They may reduce your capital gain, but if you're using one of the special homesellers' tax breaks (see Chapter 13), that may not matter.

This factor may be significant when you are working out a sales contract; points (if the buyer has the extra money to pay them) don't cost the buyer as much as they cost you, because the points represent an income tax deduction for the buyer.

Conventional Mortgages

Conventional loans are those transactions negotiated between borrower and lender with no government backing. If the buyer puts less than 10 or 20 percent down, a conventional loan may require the borrower to purchase *private mortgage insurance*

SELLER'S TIP

When negotiating a contract with the buyer, keep in mind that the payment of points:

- Reduces your capital gain from the sale of the property
- Gives the buyer an income tax deduction

(PMI) to protect the lender in case of default. Buyers must qualify for PMI payments on top of their normal monthly payment of principal, interest, taxes, and insurance. Any loan requiring PMI will probably require an impound account, making PITI (principal, interest, taxes, and insurance) and PMI payable on a prorated basis each month.

New legislation allows discontinuing PMI on request when equity reaches 20 percent, and mandates dropping it automatically when equity reaches 22 percent. Equity is based on the original appraisal at the time of purchase, or a new appraisal, whichever is lower. This legislation applies only to mortgages placed after January 1, 2000.

Advantages. If the buyer secures a conventional loan, your advantages include the following.

- The application process is less complicated than it is with FHA or VA, and the time between application and mortgage commitment may be shorter.
- The lender is more concerned with the security of the loan than with the condition of the house, so you are less likely to be asked to make repairs than with FHA- or VA-backed mortgages.

Disadvantages. Drawbacks to conventional loans, from your point of view, include:

- In a difficult mortgage market, down payment requirements and interest rates may rise to impractically high levels, effectively shutting out many of your potential buyers.
- The bank will base its loan on the value reported by its own appraiser.

Depending on how expensive homes are in your area, the highest loan amounts are referred to as *jumbo* loans, and are usually offered at a slightly higher interest rate. Jumbos are any loan that exceeds conventional loan limits. You may find that your buyers will try to stay within conventional-rate limits, putting more money down to avoid having to take out a jumbo loan.

Adjustable-Rate Mortgages (ARMs)

As interest rates rise, more buyers opt for adjustable-rate mortgages; when rates fall, buyers favor fixed-rate loans. Even in a great fixed-rate market, ARMs are offered routinely to buyers who cannot qualify for fixed rates, or for those who don't plan to stay in the property for long. Adjustables involve a vocabulary that may be entirely new to you if you haven't shopped for a loan lately.

Adjustment period. This a set period during which the interest rate may be changed to keep pace with the current levels. Most buyers choose loans that are adjusted yearly; three-year and five-year periods are also common.

Index. Rates will be adjusted up or down according to an index, most commonly based on the monthly average of Treasury securities (called MTA). Other indexes used by institutional (portfolio) lenders currently include the Cost of Savings or Cost of Funds indexes (COSI or COFI). Mortgage brokers and bankers may use the international LIBOR (London Interbank Offered Rate) index.

Margin. The lender will add an agreed-upon margin to the index, perhaps 2 or 3 percent. If T-bills were selling at 7 percent, the loan with a 2-percent margin would be repaid at 9 percent.

Cap. Most ARMs contain caps, or limitations on how far the rate can rise or fall at each adjustment.

Lifetime cap (ceiling). ARMs generally contain a certain limit beyond which the interest rate cannot rise. A 5-percent cap is commonly offered; the ARM that started at an 6-percent rate could never go beyond 11 percent.

Convertibility. This provision allows the borrower to choose, at some time or times during the life of the loan, to change to a fixed-rate loan. Convertible loans may start at slightly higher rates in return for this privilege, or—of concern to you as seller if you are paying the points—an extra point may be charged. This feature usually requires the borrower to have made on-time mortgage payments up to and including the period of convertibility.

PMI. Private mortgage insurance, which indemnifies the lender against default, is generally placed on all conventional loans where the down payment equals less than 20 percent. Because of the lender's increased risk in such a high loan-to-value (LTV) ratio, there is an extra premium placed on top of the buyer's principal, interest, taxes, and insurance (PITI). PMI approvals are separate from mortgage underwriting approvals, because the insurance is carried by an outside company. It is possible for borrowers to be approved for a mortgage loan pending PMI approval, and then fail to qualify for the extra payment each month, forcing the buyers either to put more money down to eliminate the necessity for PMI, or to bow out of the deal completely.

FHA and VA Mortgages

Advantages. Here are just a few advantages to buyers and/or sellers for FHA and VA mortgages.

- These loans, government insured or guaranteed, are oriented to the borrower's benefit.
- A number of special FHA programs are available with little or no down payment. VA loans can be made with no down payment.
- If your house falls within the price limits for these loans, you will have a wide pool of buyers. The low down-payment provisions and fixed interest rate, as well as the fact that all of these mortgages are assumable with lender's approval if the house is later resold, make FHA and VA loans attractive to buyers.

Disadvantages. Your disadvantages as a seller are these.

- Because the money comes from local lenders, these loans may not be available in all areas, and the top loan amount, particularly in the case of FHA, is of limited use in high-price areas.
- More paperwork and occasionally a longer wait for mortgage commitment are involved. The house and the buyers must sometimes be approved by both the local lender and by a government agency.
- A stringent inspection of the property is conducted, and specific repairs may be requested before the mortgage is granted. In most cases, repairs must be paid for by the seller. You always have the option, though, of refusing to make repairs and voiding the contract. Your contract can state that you will make repairs only up to a given dollar amount.

If you have a solid buyer who is short of cash and your home is within an applicable price range, both FHA and VA lenders will allow you to pay some of the buyer's closing costs. Indeed, the VA will even allow a generous seller to pay all the buyer's costs, prepaid taxes, points–the works. With VA mortgages requiring no down payment, a lucky veteran could theoretically get in with no cash outlay at all. Why would a seller agree to such an arrangement? To get the house sold.

Other military service-based loans may be available to veterans in various states.

FmHA Loans

In some rural areas, the Farmers Home Administration (FmHA), a division of the U.S. Department of Agriculture, makes direct loans to buyers. Strict income limits are set, usually in low- to middle-income brackets, and monthly payments are tailored to the borrower's income. You might find a buyer who plans to use FmHA if you are located in an area with fewer than 10,000 residents and your home is of modest size and price. One drawback is that the source of loans can be cut off when available funds are depleted for the fiscal quarter-year.

Some Creative Programs

Also available are combination type-loans, such as the 80-15-5, which can eliminate the need for PMI if the buyer qualifies according to its guidelines. In programs such as this, the buyer would take an 80 percent first mortgage, a 15 percent institutional money second mortgage, requiring only 5 percent of their own funds for a down payment. Lenders can play with these numbers, making it into an 80-10-10 for example–whatever is desirable or possible for the buyer in terms of ratios and qualifying criteria. Some creative mortgage consultants know just how to make all the puzzle pieces fit.

Your area may also offer some local bond program mortgages, which have income limitations, but can work well for lower-income buyers. Local lenders may be able to give you information on these programs.

Purchase-Money Mortgages

Although any loan used for buying real estate is strictly called a *purchase-money mortgage,* the term is often employed for seller financing, those transactions in which you are asked to take back, or carry, the loan yourself. These arrangements are possible, of course, only when you do not need your proceeds immediately for the purchase of another home.

You may lend money on a first mortgage, the buyers' primary loan on the property. Or you may carry a second mortgage, lending the buyers some of the down payment needed to assume your first mortgage.

When times get rough in the mortgage market, you may receive proposals for *creative financing,* a term that denotes all sorts of ingenious devices for making a detour around regular mortgage arrangements.

One possibility is a land contract, or contract for deed. With this arrangement, you retain title to the property until the buyers have made all their mortgage payments to you. Or a land contract may be in effect only until the buyers have paid enough to constitute an acceptable down payment, at which time you turn over title (give them a deed).

Often a purchase-money mortgage involves a balloon arrangement. You may not be willing to wait 30 years for your money, yet the buyer cannot afford the large monthly payments necessary to retire the debt in five years. Payments are therefore set as if the mortgage were indeed for a 30-year period. At the end of five years, however, the entire remaining debt becomes due and payable; that large lump-sum payment is the balloon. The understanding is that either you will renew the loan or the buyer will be able, by that time, to refinance with an outside lender. With the average family moving every five years, the house may have changed hands and the debt been paid off anyway.

Advantages. If you can afford to wait for your money, the advantages of holding a mortgage yourself include:

- Your house is more easily sold in a difficult mortgage period.

- You may have income tax advantages if you receive your money over a period of years.
- You may be able to hold out for a higher sales price, because you are doing the buyers a favor.
- A house that cannot pass a lender's inspection can be sold this way with fewer complications.
- You will not owe points to a lender.

Disadvantages. Drawbacks are summarized simply: Will the buyers meet their responsibilities, or will you find yourself with the house–and a host of problems–back on your hands?

Precautions. If you consider becoming the lender for your own home, a number of precautions are in order.

First, make sure that you receive a down payment large enough to cover the expenses of selling, the ready cash you need from the property, and as much more as possible. A large down payment represents safety for you, because it means that if you ever have to foreclose, the debt may be covered by the sale of the property. A large down payment also serves to separate strong buyers from weak ones.

Next, insist on an analysis of the borrowers' financial position in much the same way that a regular lending institution would do. Your broker can obtain a credit report on the buyers or you may insist that the buyers provide you with a lender's preliminary assessment. It is essential that it be a satisfactory one, indicating that they meet their financial obligations on time. Any compromise on this point is unwise.

Analyze the buyers' present debts and income to ensure that they are not getting in over their heads. Look for job stability and prospects of advancement.

You may be asked to take a second mortgage, lending the buyers some of the money needed to assume your present loan. Second mortgages usually carry higher interest rates than first mortgages. Later, if you prefer your money in one lump sum, you can sell the second mortgage at a discount to an investor. The size of the discount may surprise you, though.

The second mortgage carries a higher degree of risk. In case of foreclosure, the property would be sold and the proceeds used to pay off unpaid taxes and the first mortgage, before you received payment on your second mortgage. There might be insufficient funds, in that case, to cover your loan. Again, your best protection is a large down payment.

Lease Options

A lease option is basically a rental agreement with an option to buy. It commits you to sell the property for a given amount of money at any time within a stated term (other provisions may apply). If the tenants decide not to exercise their option to purchase, they commonly remain on the property as simple tenants and may forfeit the money they put up in a lump-sum payment for the option.

Lease options are usually structured with this lump-sum payment up front, to be placed in the owner's trust account or in an escrow account, which may be used later as a partial down payment should the tenants decide to exercise the option to buy. The tenants may also pay you a specified monthly amount above and beyond the customary rent, contributing towards that fund. If you have not already agreed upon the eventual price of the house, you may both agree to have an appraisal (or the best of two) performed to establish the market value at the time your tenants are ready to formally purchase the home. At the conclusion of the option term you have both established, your tenants may be in a position to obtain outside financing or you may decide to carry financing.

From the seller's point of view, a lease option can be a fine device for securing good tenants who will consider the property their own and take good care of it. The arrangement could, however, result in no sale at all—or a forced sale you don't really want. You'd need to keep option contributions separate during the term, so that your tenants might later use them towards their purchase, if they choose to buy.

FIGURE 10.1
Calculating Buyer's Monthly Payment

A. Payment to amortize $1,000 (from Appendix A)	$________
B. Times number of thousands borrowed	× ________
C. Monthly payment for principal and interest	$________

For the payment of a loan of $74,500 at 10 percent for 25 years:

- Find the monthly payment necessary to amortize $1,000. According to the chart in Appendix A, the figure is $9.0870.
- Multiply this by the number of thousands being borrowed: $9.087 × 74.5 = $676.9815.
- Round off to whole cents. The $676.98 amount represents the monthly payment necessary for principal and interest to retire a loan of $74,500 at 10 percent over a period of 25 years.

Qualifying Ratios

See Figure 10.1 for directions on calculating buyer's monthly payment and Figure 10.2 for calculating balloon payments. If you are asked to hold a mortgage yourself, you may find Figure 10.3 helpful in calculating the income you might expect from your buyers.

If you are selling on your own, it is wise to determine at the start how much income a buyer will need to qualify for your home. How much they will need to borrow, of course, depends on how much they can put down. There's no way you can guess the amount of cash your eventual buyers will have on hand, but it's safe to say that most buyers borrow as much as possible. Loans commonly run from 80 percent to, in the case of a VA loan, 100 percent of the value of your home.

FIGURE 10.2
Calculating Balloon Payments

Perhaps, with the loan in the example in Figure 10.1, you and the buyers have set the payment as if it were going to run on a 25-year schedule, but you have agreed that at the end of 10 years the entire remaining amount will become due and payable. What will that amount be?

Appendix B contains the factors needed to calculate the amount. The chart for 10 percent interest on a 25-year loan shows that after 10 years have elapsed, the remaining balance is .902 (90.2 percent) of the original loan.

A. Amount of original loan	$________
A. Multiply by factor from Appendix B	× ________
B. Remaining principal balance	$________

In the example given, the remaining balance, the large final payment at the end of 10 years, is $74,500 × .846 (84.6%), or $63,027. Almost 85 percent of the original loan is still due.

Lending institutions judge borrowers by using qualifying ratios (often dictated by secondary lenders such as Fannie Mae). When a ratio of 28/36 is quoted, it means:

- Borrowers can spend up to 28 percent of their gross monthly income for mortgage payments (principal, interest, one-twelfth of yearly property taxes and homeowners insurance–or PITI).
- They may spend up to 36 percent of monthly income, including other installment (debt) payments (auto loans, for example).

Every borrower's situation is different, of course. More or less cash available for a down payment makes a difference, and so does other indebtedness (car loans, revolving credit, student loans). And by the time your borrower actually receives the loan, interest rates may have changed markedly.

FIGURE 10.3
Calculating Buyer's Needed Income

Estimate of fair market value:	$ ________ (A)
90 percent of value (assumes a 10 percent down payment)	$ ________ (B)
Current average interest rate ____ percent	
Monthly payment to carry amount on line B (use factors in Appendix A)	$ ________ (C)
One-twelfth yearly property taxes	$ ________ (D)
One-twelfth annual insurance cost	$ ________ (E)
Monthly mortgage payment (add lines C, D, and E)	$ ________ (F)

Multiply this amount by 52 to find a rough estimate of the annual income required for the proposed mortgage loan.

See Figure 10.3 for an approximation of the annual income the buyer needs to buy your house.

Credit Scoring

Buyers of your home now have the ability to obtain quick low-cost or no-cost credit reports on themselves, either by contacting credit bureaus directly (TRW, Equifax, and Trans-Union are the three most often used by lenders) or on the World Wide Web at FreeCreditReports.com.

Credit scoring is something that, up until about four years ago, had little to do with mortgage lending. When lenders traditionally reviewed the credit worthiness of a borrower, an underwriter used to make a somewhat subjective decision based on a person's past payment history. Then lenders began to notice a correlation between credit scores and mortgage delinquencies, so today they use credit scores.

The first such system was called FICO (originated by Fair Isaac & Company). On a scale of 365 to 840, a FICO score of, for instance 585, carries with it more than 2 to 1 odds that an account will go delinquent. One of 700 would tell a lender that the chances were only 1 in 288 that the buyer would fail to make timely mortgage payments.

Lower scores don't necessarily kick a buyer out of qualifying range. VA and FHA guidelines are generally more lenient, as well as some portfolios lenders' product guidelines. And there are always *subprime* lenders who offer higher interest rate loans for the credit-score impaired.

CHAPTER

11

In the Tunnel

"We've sold our house!"

When can you joyfully spread the news to your friends? Is it the day someone first expresses an intention to buy? The time when you reach written agreement on price and terms? After all of the contingencies have been removed? Or the final settlement session, when the money and the front-door key change hands?

Although most transactions do proceed smoothly from contract to eventual transfer of title, you, the agent, and the buyers all have responsibilities while the sale is "in the tunnel." All of you can help ensure the successful outcome of your mutual plans.

The Agent's Responsibilities

Your broker or lawyer will furnish duplicate originals of the final purchase agreement, which has now become a binding contract to you, the buyer, the lending institution, and the escrow agent or other parties involved.

When a new mortgage is being placed, the agent should make him or herself available to assist your buyer with lender recommendations. If the buyers have already been prequalified or approved by their own lender, the certificate of preapproval or letter of prequalification should already be in your or your agent's hands. If no agent is involved, you should check to see that prompt application is being made (your purchase agreement should already have given a date for this to be accomplished).

Unless you already know that the deposit is safely tucked into an escrow account, you are entitled to a report on its progress. If you are not notified when the check clears or the promissory note is made good, do not hesitate to inquire.

Merely finding a buyer for the property will not ensure a successful sale. You and your agent must be on top of the mortgage application process. You'll want to hear as soon as possible that the buyers' credit checked out well and the house appraised at a satisfactory figure. A status check should be performed weekly, or the lender should be asked to fax the status of the loan periodically.

You may hear about snags in the paperwork: the verification of employment form has not been returned, or a required inspection has not been documented. It may be necessary to arrange appointments for an appraiser, a home inspector, a termite inspector, or a surveyor.

SELLER'S TIP

Between the time of signing a sales agreement with the buyer and closing, keep informed about:

- Deposit of earnest money in an escrow account
- The buyer's progress in obtaining financing
- Any problems that need to be resolved before closing

You and the Buyers

Remember that buyers often are jittery, worrying about whether they made the right decision. A malady known as *buyer's remorse* can set in during this period. You are also facing change and upheaval. It may be advisable to talk with the buyers through your broker if he or she recommends it. Any contact you have should be cordial and reassuring, but also limited and noncommittal. Many queries are best answered, "I'm not sure; you'll have to speak with our agent," or "The broker probably knows about it."

Your buyers may have seen your house for half an hour at most, on only one occasion. It is understandable that they desire a closer inspection. They may want to measure for curtains, show the place to their parents, or take some pictures or video. If there is a broker, he or she should accompany them to handle sudden doubts that may arise. You have a binding contract, but the sale will go more smoothly with buyers who are eager to complete the transaction once their doubts are laid to rest.

At this point, you may want to let the buyers know which appliances or furniture you will be selling. Keep your negotiations friendly.

Buyers Moving In

Lawyers agree that it is a poor idea to allow the buyers to move in before the house is recorded in their name. If circumstances dictate such an arrangement, discuss the matter thoroughly with an attorney. Among points to be considered in a moving-in agreement are:

- The buyers must first have their formal, documented loan approval.
- A high security deposit must be established. Some sellers require that all of the cash the buyers will need at closing be deposited.
- The buyers promise not to make any changes in the property until they legally own it.

- Rent might be set at a higher rate than the prospective mortgage payments so that there will be an incentive to go to settlement on time.
- A written agreement should promise that the buyers will accept everything "as is" on the day they move in. Who pays for subsequent repairs should be settled in advance.
- Buyers should have homeowners insurance in place with a special interim rider agreement, fully releasing you from liability ("hold harmless") for their belongings and their safety.
- Your accountant can advise whether the rental period jeopardizes your special tax treatment for profit on the sale of one's own home.

If you have already moved from the property and it's nearly closing time, you may consider permitting a "garage rental" giving buyers keys to your empty garage for the storage of their furniture and belongings until the close of escrow, but effectively locking them out from the home's interior. A daily rental rate should be established, and all of the stipulations listed above should apply.

Along the Way

Your buyers must act in good faith to fulfill any conditions outlined in the purchase contract. If a new loan is being sought, they must make an application promptly at a lending institution appropriate to the financing planned, and must cooperate in securing the necessary papers.

If the purchasers must sell their present home, you may have specified in the contract that they will list it immediately in the open market. Seldom will you have control, however, over the price they ask for the property or how they answer purchase offers they receive. Should you accept an offer contingent on another sale, be careful you don't set yourself up for a domino effect. If your contingent buyers also accept a contingent offer on their own home, when fallout occurs (their buyer falls out, so your transaction becomes compromised), it's like taking a can from the bottom of a stacked display, with everything on top of it crashing down in the process. You may already have specified in the purchase agreement that your buyers cannot also accept offers contingent on the sale of their home just to avoid this.

The contract will contain your agreements about which party will arrange and pay for termite inspection, a survey, an engineer's report, and such matters. Usually these responsibilities are established by community custom. During the waiting period, the buyer, seller, escrow agent, or attorneys where applicable will attend to these items.

Flood insurance must be purchased by the buyers, if the lender requires it as a condition for lending money on the house. If the property is in a designated flood plain, borrowers can sometimes avoid flood insurance if a survey shows that the building is above the 100-year flood mark. The lender will ask them to prove that they are placing adequate hazard insurance on the property. They must arrange this before closing.

Seller's Problems

You may be informed, to your surprise, that the roofer with whom you quarreled last fall has filed a mechanic's lien that encumbers your title to the house. To clear this lien, pay it off. Your escrow officer or attorney may be willing to convey the good news to the contractor; the worker may be so delighted at the prospect of payment that a compromise sum is agreed upon. If you prefer to challenge the lien, you can release it by posting a bond pending adjudication.

Other liens (unpaid taxes, personal judgments) against your house must be cleared.

A title search may disclose unexpected claims against the property by your former spouse or by long-ago heirs of a previous owner. A simple quitclaim deed may be used in such cases. By signing this deed, the person involved waives any rights he or she might have without laying claim to the property.

If you are caught between two homes and won't receive the proceeds from the old one in time to close on the new, a specific type of short-term loan is possible. Banks call such interim financing a *swing loan, bridge loan,* or *turnaround.* Your broker, attorney, or lender can help you investigate this.

Appraisal and Repair of Property

If a new mortgage loan is being sought, two hurdles must be cleared before title to a house is transferred. The house must be appraised at the agreed-upon sales price, and it must meet the lender's standards for condition.

In some areas, particularly if the house is a multiple dwelling, repairs may be required before transfer of title. When a new FHA or VA loan is being placed, the buyer pays for an appraisal and inspection. The report may stipulate specific repairs needed before the mortgage can be placed. The FHA standards deal primarily with the health and safety of the occupants and preservation of the structure. If your exterior paint is shabby, it need not be redone. If, however, bare wood is in evidence, a paint job will be required to preserve the material. Redecorating will not be required on the interior, but a handrail for the basement steps might be requested.

You are not bound to make these repairs unless specified in your contract. If you choose not to, you may void the contract and start looking for another buyer. This means, of course, that you are back to square one, with the additional handicap of not wanting to consider any further FHA or VA offers.

It is usually better to proceed with the repairs specified. With certain programs, the buyer may volunteer to assist; with others, you must do the work yourself. If you cannot afford the repairs, ask your broker's help in finding a worker who will wait until the day of transfer for payment.

If the house isn't appraised favorably, the lending institution will refuse to base its loan on the sales price. With FHA or VA contracts, your buyers have the option of dropping out at this point. They may be so upset that they will do just that. Often, though, the problem is solved by renegotiation. You might drop your price to the amount of the appraisal, or the buyers might agree to make a larger down payment. Often a compromise is worked out, with each party giving up something.

Buyers' Problems

If your purchasers plan to obtain a new mortgage loan and have not already been preapproved for the amount necessary to purchase your home, the progress of their application is of great importance. You can expect the broker to monitor the process, and the attorney for either party may also check up from time to time.

The application process consists mainly of packaging various documents that will affect the lender's decision, such as the buyers' credit scores, explained in Chapter 10.

The buyers' income will either be verified by their employers or the lender will merely require paycheck stubs and W-2s, because documentation requirements for many lenders have lessened drastically in recent years. If your buyer is self-employed, the lender will also require a profit-and-loss statement, usually prepared and certified by an accountant.

An unpleasant surprise may turn up at this point. Forgotten or unknown judgments against the buyers may surface, even as they might in your own records. These are not fatal to the application. The buyer can clear them by paying them off.

More serious is the discovery that the prospective purchasers have been less than frank about their credit history. A bankruptcy they "forgot" to mention, or several large debts presently outstanding, can seriously threaten their chances for the loan.

If such problems develop, you have a right to be notified, for time is money in your situation. If there is a chance that the transaction might fall through, you should be told at once. Your broker can assess the chances of failure.

You can always put your house back on the market, subject to nonperformance of the existing contract. This enables you to start searching for another buyer immediately, pending the outcome of the present problem.

It is, of course, a serious step and should be considered only when the outlook becomes bleak. As mentioned earlier, much of this can be avoided if your broker insists on a verified loan prequalification or full-fledged loan preapproval as a condition of the contract by a date early in the escrow process.

The Deal That Fails

If your transaction falls apart, your broker's help will be essential in advising you of your rights or responsibilities. Should you back out for no legally acceptable reason, you may be liable for damages, and even for a type of suit—unique to real estate—that calls for specific performance. The concept of specific performance arises from the fact that each property is different and that money damages may not adequately compensate the buyer who insists on purchasing your specific house.

Even if the buyers are agreeable to dropping their claims, remember that your real estate broker, having performed the services for which he or she was retained, may be entitled to full commission. Depending on circumstances, the broker may press a claim for the commission, or may waive it in favor of your goodwill and the hope of future business.

If the buyer backs out with no adequate reason, you may be entitled to damages, and your broker may be entitled to a commission, for which you are liable. Your broker or lawyer will know whether legal action is indicated. To avoid a lawsuit, the buyer often abandons the earnest money deposit. Sometimes that sum is then divided between seller and broker.

Occasionally, a transaction falls apart with no one at fault. Certain conditions in the contract may be impossible to fulfill, the buyers may fail to secure the mortgage loan, or you may be unable to provide marketable title. In such a case, the purchase contract may specify that the buyers are to receive full return of their deposit.

CHAPTER

12

The Day of Reckoning

In your area the process may be called *settlement, transfer, closing escrow,* or *passing papers.* It may be held in the county courthouse, the lending institution, a title company, a real estate office, or an attorney's office. No matter what terminology is used, it's the fruit of everyone's labors and the time when the transfer of ownership finally takes place.

What does a typical settlement look like? In one city, buyers, sellers, attorneys, brokers, and a paralegal from the lending institution may gather around a long table. In another area, there may not be a meeting at all; details are handled by mail, courier, or electronically through an escrow company. In no aspect of real estate does local custom vary more.

Whatever the practice, however, the skeleton of the transaction remains the same:

1. The seller proves marketable title.
2. The buyer pays for the property.
3. The seller delivers the deed.

If new financing is involved, settlement includes the signing and delivery of a bond and mortgage or, in some states, a trust deed.

The *deed* is a bill of sale for real estate. You do not want to sign and deliver the deed until you receive your money. The buyers, on the other hand, cannot pay you until they receive their mortgage loan. The lender will not turn over the money without receiving a mortgage. But the buyers cannot sign a mortgage until they own the property. It is obvious that the various transactions must take place at one time and in precise order.

If it is customary in your area for the seller to attend the closing and you are unable to do so, arrangements can be made for you to sign the deed ahead of time; this one act is your major contribution to the ceremonies. In many eastern states, it is at this point that front-door keys may also be handed over. In other areas, buyers must wait to hear that they are "on record" (the deed has been entered into the public records) before getting the keys, garage door openers, and security codes for the house.

The Settlement or Closing Date

As soon as the purchasers have secured a firm mortgage commitment, the person in charge of the closing can arrange a date suitable to all parties. Additional paperwork may be required; escrow companies or attorneys must set up times for their roles, and your moving plans and the buyers' must be considered and coordinated.

If your contract stipulated a targeted closing date, and that day comes and goes, the contract may still be in force. Sometimes, a definite, "essential" time has been agreed to by both buyer and seller, forcing the issue.

In states where escrow and title companies are used, the closing process can take more than one day. A buyer can sign the loan documents, if already prepared and waiting at the escrow office, any time during the month. When the time for closing arrives, the lender will wire the funds and the buyer may then submit the remaining down payment and closing costs (this is usually done after a final walk-through). All parties then wait for the *funding* to take place, which can usually take anywhere from 24 to 48 hours. A final title report tells everyone that the property is free of *clouds on title,* and the buyer is able to take clear possession. An escrow officer or title officer then physically stands in line at the county recorder's office and waits to record the deed. After this is accomplished, a cheery voice notifies the buyer by telephone that the purchase is "on record."

Preliminary Preparations

You have held your garage sale, notified the post office and magazine publishers, talked with the telephone company, secured a mover, and finished your packing. Now what?

Plan on leaving the house in broom-clean condition; if not spotless, it should be neat at least. Broom-clean condition assumes that piles of old newspapers have been removed, the refrigerator is empty, trash has been removed or left in a tidy fashion, and floors have received one final sweeping.

Most buyers request a walk-through of the house, and many agents write this into the purchase agreement, so that there is no misunderstanding. In some areas, this takes place within a day or two of closing; in others, on the date of possession. This is a reasonable and prudent step. The buyers want to check for newly broken windowpanes, make sure that you are leaving the workshop bench you promised, and uncover any last-minute problems before closing, rather than afterward. As usual, it is helpful if they are accompanied by the broker, with your participation limited to a few cordial bits of information or advice about the property.

If possible, leave all warranties for recently purchased appliances or systems; if the house is less than ten years old, leave the builder's warranty agreement as well, because in most states, homes carry a ten-year structural warranty. Leave manufacturers' instructions for your home's appliances and systems (heating, air conditioning, security, etc.) for the subsequent buyers' use.

Call your utility companies and arrange for final readings of your meters. If your heating system uses fuel oil, it may be practical to arrange for the tank to be filled completely so that you will know how much you are leaving behind. You can pay this bill and settle with the buyers at closing for the full tank.

Make a last minute check of the fine print on your purchase contract to see that you have kept your promises regarding items such as fireplace equipment, smoke alarms, and play equipment.

SELLER'S TIP

If you are required to attend the closing:

- Get final utility readings
- Leave the house in clean condition
- Check the purchase contract to make sure you have complied with all agreements
- Leave behind any in-force warranty for the house, appliances, or systems for the new owners

In states where sellers attend the closing, they usually take with them all door keys, security alarm codes, and remote controls for garage doors. In newer areas, in condos, or for co-op apartments, where secure group mailboxes are used, mailbox keys are also handed over.

Adjustments at Closing

You and the buyers have a number of financial details to settle. Property taxes will undoubtedly be adjusted. In some areas, taxes are paid in advance. In this case, if you met your last bill, you have paid for the year ahead. If you are closing at, for example, the end of the fourth month, the buyers will receive a house with taxes paid for the year, and they should reimburse you for the eight months to come.

In other areas, property taxes are paid in arrears, as opposed to in advance. The bill for the current year will not be due for eight months. Because you have lived in the house for four months, you should pay a sum equaling four months' taxes to the new owners, who will later pay for the full year.

In the same way, you will adjust water or sewer charges.

If there are tenants, you should turn over any security deposits and advance rents to the new owners, who will return these monies to the tenants when they vacate the house.

If the buyers are assuming your mortgage, interest payments will be adjusted so that you pay for the days that you owned the house. The new owners will have to meet the next bill, which will cover the present month's interest.

Your present mortgage payments may include monthly charges for tax or insurance fees. Your lender sets up an escrow or reserve account to collect these funds for later disbursal. If the mortgage is being paid off, rather than assumed, you will receive the balance of this account directly from the lender. Otherwise, the new owners will reimburse you for monies in this account, which remains with the mortgage.

Figure 12.1 shows a sample RESPA (Real Estate Settlement Procedures Act) settlement form.

You may be asked for a bill of sale on furniture or appliances being left with the property.

The escrow officer or the attorneys for both parties explain and justify figures for all these adjustments that appear on the closing statement.

A sample completed closing statement is shown in Figure 12.2.

Seller's Costs

Some closing costs are negotiable between seller and buyer, although the last minute is not the time for haggling. Other costs are yours and may include:

- *Liens and claims against your property.* Before the purchasers will take title, they usually insist that you clear up unpaid taxes, your present mortgage, home improvement loans, mechanics' liens, judgments, and any other liens on record.
- *Unpaid special assessments.* In the absence of any other agreement, you may be expected to pay in one lump sum special charges levied against your area for new sidewalks, street lighting, or other improvements.

FIGURE 12.1 Sample RESPA Settlement Form

A. **Settlement Statement**

U.S. Department of Housing and Urban Development

OMB Approval No. 2502-0265

B. Type of Loan			
1. ☐ FHA 2. ☐ FmHA 3. ☐ Conv. Unins. 4. ☐ VA 5. ☐ Conv. Ins.	6. File Number:	7. Loan Number:	8. Mortgage Insurance Case Number:

C. Note: This form is furnished to give you a statement of actual settlement costs. Amounts paid to and by the settlement agent are shown. Items marked "(p.o.c.)" were paid outside the closing; they are shown here for informational purposes and are not included in the totals.

D. Name & Address of Borrower:	E. Name & Address of Seller:	F. Name & Address of Lender:

G. Property Location:	H. Settlement Agent:	
	Place of Settlement:	I. Settlement Date:

J. Summary of Borrower's Transaction		K. Summary of Seller's Transaction	
100. Gross Amount Due From Borrower		**400. Gross Amount Due To Seller**	
101. Contract sales price		401. Contract sales price	
102. Personal property		402. Personal property	
103. Settlement charges to borrower (line 1400)		403.	
104.		404.	
105.		405.	
Adjustments for items paid by seller in advance		**Adjustments for items paid by seller in advance**	
106. City/town taxes to		406. City/town taxes to	
107. County taxes to		407. County taxes to	
108. Assessments to		408. Assessments to	
109.		409.	
110.		410.	
111.		411.	
112.		412.	
120. Gross Amount Due From Borrower		**420. Gross Amount Due To Seller**	

FIGURE 12.1 Sample RESPA Settlement Form (Continued)

200. Amounts Paid By Or In Behalf Of Borrower		**500. Reductions In Amount Due To Seller**	
201. Deposit or earnest money		501. Excess deposit (see instructions)	
202. Principal amount of new loan(s)		502. Settlement charges to seller (line 1400)	
203. Existing loan(s) taken subject to		503. Existing loan(s) taken subject to	
204.		504. Payoff of first mortgage loan	
205.		505. Payoff of second mortgage loan	
206.		506.	
207.		507.	
208.		508.	
209.		509.	
Adjustments for items unpaid by seller		**Adjustments for items unpaid by seller**	
210. City/town taxes to		510. City/town taxes to	
211. County taxes to		511. County taxes to	
212. Assessments to		512. Assessments to	
213.		513.	
214.		514.	
215.		515.	
216.		516.	
217.		517.	
218.		518.	
219.		519.	
220. Total Paid By/For Borrower		**520. Total Reduction Amount Due Seller**	
300. Cash At Settlement From/To Borrower		**600. Cash At Settlement To/From Seller**	
301. Gross Amount due from borrower (line 120)		601. Gross amount due to seller (line 420)	
302. Less amounts paid by/for borrower (line 220)	( )	602. Less reductions in amt. due seller (line 520)	( )
303. Cash ☐ **From** ☐ **To Borrower**		**603. Cash** ☐ **To** ☐ **From Seller**	

L. Settlement Charges

700. Total Sales/Broker's Commission based on price $ @ % =	Paid From Borrowers Funds at Settlement	Paid From Seller's Funds at Settlement
Division of Commission (line 700) as follows:		
701. $ to		
702. $ to		
703. Commission paid at Settlement		
704.		
800. Items Payable In Connection With Loan		
801. Loan Origination Fee %		
802. Loan Discount %		
803. Appraisal Fee to		
804. Credit Report to		
805. Lender's Inspection Fee		
806. Mortgage Insurance Application Fee to		
807. Assumption Fee		
808.		
809.		
810.		
811.		

FIGURE 12.1 Sample RESPA Settlement Form (Continued)

900. Items Required By Lender To Be Paid In Advance				
901. Interest from to	@$	/day		
902. Mortgage Insurance Premium for		months to		
903. Hazard Insurance Premium for		years to		
904.		years to		
905.				
1000. Reserves Deposited With Lender				
1001. Hazard insurance	months@$	per month		
1002. Mortgage insurance	months@$	per month		
1003. City property taxes	months@$	per month		
1004. County property taxes	months@$	per month		
1005. Annual assessments	months@$	per month		
1006.	months@$	per month		
1007.	months@$	per month		
1008.	months@$	per month		
1100. Title Charges				
1101. Settlement or closing fee	to			
1102. Abstract or title search	to			
1103. Title examination	to			
1104. Title insurance binder	to			
1105. Document preparation	to			
1106. Notary fees	to			
1107. Attorney's fees	to			
(includes above items numbers:		)		
1108. Title insurance	to			
(includes above items numbers:		)		
1109. Lender's coverage	$			
1110. Owner's coverage	$			
1111.				
1112.				
1113.				
1200. Government Recording and Transfer Charges				
1201. Recording fees: Deed $	; Mortgage $	; Releases $		
1202. City/county tax/stamps: Deed $	; Mortgage $			
1203. State tax/stamps: Deed $	; Mortgage $			
1204.				
1205.				
1300. Additional Settlement Charges				
1301. Survey to				
1302. Pest inspection to				
1303.				
1304.				
1305.				
1400. Total Settlement Charges (enter on lines 103, Section J and 502, Section K)				

FIGURE 12.2 Sample Seller's Closing Statement

SELLER'S CREDITS

Sale Price $ 89,500.00

ADJUSTMENT OF TAXES

School Tax	to	Amount $ 1,176.35	Adj. 10	mos. 18	days	$ 1,039.16
City/School Tax	to	Amount $	Adj.	mos.	days	$
County Tax	19__	Amount $ 309.06	Adj. 4	mos. 18	days	$ 118.52
Village Tax	to	Amount $	Adj.	mos.	days	$
City Tax Embellishments		Amount $	Adj.	mos.	days	$

Total Seller's Credits $ 90,657.68

PURCHASER'S CREDITS

Deposit with Nothnagle $ 500.00

~~(Assumed)~~ (New) Mortgage with seller $ 40,000.00

12% interest, 15 years, payments $

$480.07, beginning $

$

Total Purchaser's Credits $ 40,500.00

Cash (Rec'd) ~~(Paid)~~ at Closing $ 50,157.68

EXPENSES OF PURCHASER

Mortgage Tax	$
Recording Mortgage	$
Recording Deed	$
ESCROWS:	
___ mos. insurance	$
___ mos. school tax	$
___ mos. county tax	$
___ mos. village tax	$
PMI FHA Insurance	$
Total:	$
Bank Attorney Fee	$
Points	$
Title Insurance	$
Interest	$
	$
	$
Legal Fee	$
Total	$
Cash Paid to Seller:	$
Plus Purchaser's Expenses:	$
Total Disbursed:	$

EXPENSES OF SELLER

Title Search Fee	$ 220.00
Transfer Tax on Deed	$ 358.00
Filing of Gains Tax Affidavit	$ 1.00
Discharge Recording Fee	$
Mortgage Tax	$ 100.00
Surveyor's Fees	$
Points	$
Mortgage Payoff	$
Real Estate Commission	$ 487.00
Water Escrow	$
19 school tax	$ 1,182.14
Federal Express	$ 14.00
	$
	$
Legal Fee	$ 550.00
Total	$ 7,295.14
Cash Received:	$ 50,157.68
Less Seller's Expenses:	$ 7,295.14
Net Proceeds:	$ 42,862.54

- *Transfer tax.* In some states or districts, a tax is due when property is transferred, and you may find a legal provision that this one expense be paid by the seller.
- *Attorney or escrow agent.* Escrow and title fees, and who pays them, will be spelled out on your closing papers. If an attorney was used, this is when his or her fee is paid.
- *Survey, title insurance, termite inspection.* Again based on custom, the contract you sign dictates whether you or the buyer will pay.
- *Prepayment penalty.* You may owe a penalty fee to the lender if your conventional loan is being paid off before its due date. State laws have been whittling away at these charges, however.

Carrying the Mortgage

If you will be holding a first or second mortgage or a land contract yourself, your attorney can draw up the document. If the buyer offers to pay for preparing the mortgage, be sure to have your own lawyer approve or amend it. In most states, the mortgage you receive consists of two parts: a note or bond (personal promise to pay back the loan) and the mortgage or trust deed, which is a claim against the property if the promises made in the bond are not kept.

Just as the buyer is advised to have the deed put on record immediately, so should you see that the mortgage is promptly entered into the public records. Most escrow companies automatically perform this task. This will give you priority, ahead of later claims on the property, if there is trouble in the future.

Actual Transfer of Title

When you or your escrow officer are in possession of the buyer's funding check (it should be in the form of a cashier's check, money order, or verified wired funds, by the way), you are ready to turn your property over to the new owner. As the seller, you sign the deed. It may take one of several forms, depending on the situation, state law, and local custom.

- A *quitclaim deed* simply transfers any rights you may have in the property.
- A *special warranty deed* (or bargain and sale deed with covenants) transfers your rights and promises that you have in no undisclosed way encumbered the property.
- A *full warranty deed* further guarantees the buyer's protection againstlaims raised by any other parties.

Because the transfer of title gives the new owner your rights in the real estate, you are called the *grantor.* Often, only the grantor signs the deed. Title to the property transfers at the moment you place the deed into the hands of the *grantee.* "Signed, sealed, and delivered" is the old phrase, and at the moment of physical delivery and acceptance of the deed, the property is no longer yours.

CHAPTER

13

Moving and Tax Considerations

Letting People Know

One of your first assignments when you move is to collect a stack of change-of-address cards from the post office. You'll want to notify everyone in your address book, including the following individuals and offices:

- Accountant
- Attorney
- Credit card companies
- Church clubs and organizations
- Dentist
- Insurance company
- Internet Service Provider (ISP)
- Magazine subscriptions
- Physician
- Social Security Administration
- Stockbroker
- Voter registration

The post office will forward first-class mail for one year, but if you want parcels and publications forwarded you must agree to pay additional postage.

Be sure the buyer of your home has your new address and, if you know it, your new phone number, so that any mail that gets lost in the shuffle can be sent on to you promptly.

Tying Up Loose Ends

When you have a firm moving date, ask for final readings on gas, water, and electric meters. Check whether you have any deposits that should be refunded. Refunds may also be due on your security deposit if you're renting, prepaid cable TV service, and the renters or homeowners insurance you'll be canceling.

SELLER'S TIP

When you move, you may have refunds coming from:

- Utility and security deposits
- Unused renters or homeowners insurance
- Prepaid cable or other service

Notify anyone who calls at your home regularly: diaper service, pool or water softener servicers, pest controllers, trash collector, housekeeper, or gardener.

Return library books, pick up dry cleaning, and empty lockers.

If you're changing towns, find out about the transfer of medical and school records.

Running Your Garage Sale

Remember that most moving companies charge by the hundred pounds. If you have some idea how much that might be, you can decide which things are worth taking and which might be more cheaply replaced. If you're up to your ears in kids, work, or packing and need help, professional organizers (in the Yellow Pages under "Organizing Services and Systems, Household and Business" or on the Internet <www.napo.net>) provide an excellent service to relocating homeowners by helping them weed out the items they may not have touched for several years. They are also experts at helping you pack in an efficient and organized manner. The unneeded items can be sold at a garage sale, placed at a consignment shop, or donated to charity.

SELLER'S TIP

If you hold a garage sale:

- Be prepared for "pickers" who arrive early.
- Save receipts for articles donated to charity.
- Arrange ahead of time for a charity to pick up bags or boxes of unsold items the next day.

When you've advertised your garage sale, be prepared for antique seekers and garage sale enthusiasts who will knock on your door an hour before you're ready. It's best to price everything the night before, leaving little to be done the next morning. When you're asked if you'll take less, say that whatever is left will sell at half-price at the end of the sale. If you donate the leftovers to charity, ask for a receipt to back up your income tax deduction.

If You Move Yourself

Truck rental agencies have information to help you estimate what size truck or trailer you'll need. You can rent a hand-truck or dolly, furniture pads, and straps, and buy cartons specifically made for packing. Your rental can be round-trip or one-way. Be sure to ask about drop-off locations.

Though moving companies seldom accept credit cards, truck rental companies often will. Remember that in addition to the daily charges, you'll have costs for gasoline and tolls.

Be sure to check with your insurance company to see whether you need any additional insurance coverage to supplement the rental agency's own policy, or in addition to any insurance carried by the professional movers you may hire.

Hiring a Professional Mover

The more packing you do yourself, the more you save. The moving company can sell you cartons of uniform size intended for china, clothing, and other items. Or you can ask for sturdy cartons at local liquor stores and larger ones from computer stores.

The mover should furnish first a nonbinding estimate and service order, listing the items to be moved. Expect to pay extra for packing and unpacking, disassembly and assembly, moving items up or down stairs at either location, and any large item like a piano. (Some concerned homeowners hire a separate piano-moving company entirely, because safely moving a heavy musical instrument, especially a grand piano, takes a specialized type of dolly and moving process.) The final contract you sign should match the estimate and service order; double-check it.

The final weight of your shipment will be determined by having the truck weighed empty and again after it is loaded. Be prepared to make payment in cash or certified check when the movers arrive at the new location, because it is doubtful they will unload otherwise. (If the bill is more than 10 percent over the estimate, you are entitled to 30 days in which to make up the overage.)

Be sure to hand-carry jewelry, a portable file of important documents, medications, and a suitcase for each family member. A cooler with some perishable foods you can't bear to waste can come in handy for the trip, or even to unpack immediately upon arriving at your next home. Take along a box containing a hammer, screwdriver, cleaning supplies and rags, extension cords, paper plates and cups, plastic utensils, saucepan, coffee maker and coffee, snacks, toothbrushes, soap, and towels.

SELLER'S TIP

When you move, carry with you:

- Medications
- Perishable foods that can withstand the trip
- Jewelry
- Important papers
- Cash or certified check for the movers

Income Tax and Moving Expenses

Your new job (or transfer) must be at least 50 miles farther from your old home than the old job was for your moving expenses to qualify as tax deductible. (If you had no previous job, the new employment must be at least 50 miles from your old home to qualify.) In addition, the new employment must be full time.

You can deduct everything you spend for:

- Packing, crating, and transporting household goods and personal effects
- Mileage for one trip only, the move for yourself and members of your household
- Tolls and parking fees
- Storing and insuring goods, if necessary, for 30 days
- Disconnecting and connecting utilities
- Shipping your car or pets
- Transportation and lodging for yourself and your household (but not meals) while en route to your new home

In contrast to older IRS regulations, which once allowed you to deduct house-hunting trips, the new rules cover only the final one-way trip.

Tax Considerations

Homeseller's Tax Advantages

A great tax break is available for the treatment of profit realized on the sale of your home, known to the IRS as your principal residence. In general, this is considered to be the place where you reside most of the time. It may be a mobile home or a houseboat, a cooperative or condominium apartment. If you own one home, but live in another that you rent, your principal residence is the rented house, and no special tax treatment would apply to the sale of the house you own.

If you would owe no federal tax, your sale should not be reported to the IRS and you need not mention it on your tax return.

Selling at a Loss

If you sell your own home (or a vacation home you don't rent out) at a loss, no deduction is allowed on your income tax return. You may not claim a capital loss. The rules, of course, are different for business or rental property, which qualify for capital gain or loss treatment in the ordinary way, on Schedule D.

Computing Your Cost Basis

The first step in calculating your profit is to determine your cost basis. To the original price of your home, add certain closing costs and the money you have spent on improvements over the years. Improvements are permanent additions to the value of your property; repairs and redecorating don't count. A new roof or furnace counts as an improvement; fixing the old ones would be considered repairs and do not add to your cost basis.

If you built your house yourself, you may not include as part of the cost basis the value of your labor, or any friend's labor that you did not pay for. If you received the house as a gift, your cost basis is generally the giver's cost basis. If you inherited the house,

SELLER'S TIP

When you calculate the adjusted cost basis of your home be sure to include:

- Original cost
- Money spent on permanent improvements
- Legal costs of buying and selling

you use a stepped-up basis, usually the value of the property when the former owner died.

Items you must subtract from cost basis include:

1. Any losses you may have deducted on income tax returns for fire or other cause
2. Money you received in return for easements
3. Energy improvement credits you may have claimed
4. Depreciation you may have claimed when all or part of your home was formerly used for home office or as a rental

Use Figure 13.1 to calculate your adjusted cost basis, and Figure 13.2 to calculate your gain. Notice that when computing your profit (capital gain), the IRS is not interested in any mortgage you may have to pay off on the property. What counts are cost basis, sales price, and costs of selling.

Special Tax Break

When you sell your home, you can take advantage of a delightful law that allows up to $500,000 profit for joint filers ($250,000 for a single homeowner) free of any federal income tax ever. The exclusion from capital gains tax, which went into effect for sales after May 7, 1997, can even cover previous, postponed tax on earlier home sales under the more complex laws in effect before that date.

FIGURE 13.1

Calculating Your Adjusted Cost Basis

Add:	Purchase price of your home	$________
	Attorney fees when you bought	________
	Tax assessments for street or sidewalks	________
	Amounts spent for:	
	Fences	________
	Paving (not maintaining) driveway	________
	Wall-to-wall carpeting	________
	Permanent fixtures	________
	New roof or furnace	________
	Finishing basement or attic	________
	Adding new bath	________
	New (not repaired) plumbing	________
	New wiring	________
	Extensive remodeling	________
	Building an addition	________
	Insulation	________
	Storm windows and screens	________
	Permanent landscaping	________
	Other ____________________	________
	____________________	________
	Total of above items	$________
Subtract:	Losses (fire, etc.) deducted on income tax returns	________
	Amount received for easements, etc.	________
	Depreciation claimed in past years	________
	Deferred profit on previous residence(s)	________
Adjusted Cost Basis		$________

FIGURE 13.2

Calculating Your Gain

To compute the amount of your profit (known to the IRS as your *capital gain*), subtract adjusted cost basis from the sales price. You may also subtract certain costs of selling. Last-minute fix-up costs are not deductible at this point. Any prepayment penalty on a mortgage you pay off may be deductible as prepaid interest elsewhere on your income tax return.

Calculating Your Profit

Sales Price	$______
Subtract cost basis	______
Subtract expenses paid by seller:	______
Real estate commissions	______
Legal fees	______
Advertising expenses	______
Points paid to your buyer's lender	______
Title insurance	______
Survey	______
Transfer taxes and closing costs	______
Adjusted Sales Price	$______

This free lunch on the IRS is available to homesellers of any age, and you can do this more than once in your lifetime–theoretically as often as every two years. (There is even an exception to the two-year limit, if a quick move is needed because of a job change or illness.)

You must have owned and occupied the property as your main home for at least two of the five years before the sale. If only one spouse is the owner, the couple is still entitled to as much as

SELLER'S TIP

The new liberal tax laws allow tax-free profit:

- Up to $500,000 per couple ($250,000 for a single seller)
- For sellers of any age
- As often as every two years

$500,000 tax-free profit on the sale, but both must have occupied the property for the required two years.

A vacation home or rental property could later be converted into your own main home, if you lived there permanently for at least two years after leaving your previous home. Consult an accountant, though, about possible recapture of depreciation previously taken on rental property.

For real estate being sold that is not your main residence (vacation homes, vacant land, rental property), capital gains laws apply.

- *Capital gains.* Your profit is classified as short-term or long-term capital gains, depending on how long you have owned the house. The holding period for long-term gains tax treatment is 12 months. Tax rates are no higher than 20 percent (10 percent for those in the lowest tax brackets). Assets held for less than a year are taxed as ordinary income. Depreciation previously claimed on income property is recaptured at 25 percent.
- *Installment treatment.* If you carry financing for all or part of the purchase price (hold a mortgage with the buyers paying you monthly), you will owe tax on your profit year by year, as you collect it, unless that profit is covered by one of the homeseller's tax breaks.

Miscellaneous Provisions

If you are using part of your property for a farm, a home office, rental apartment, or other business property, your sale is treated, for tax purposes, as two separate transactions. The chance to defer taxes will apply to that percentage of the real estate considered to be your residence. The balance of your proceeds will be taxed as if you had sold business property.

For homeowners of any age, then, and in almost every case, tax on the profit from the sale of one's home can be excluded from tax permanently.

Seniors who took advantage, years ago, of the once-in-a-lifetime exclusion of up to $125,000 gain on a sale are now entitled to use the new, more liberal tax treatment on a future sale or sales as well.

Giving Your House to the Kids

If you sell your home to your children, or transfer title in any way that does not involve the open market, you have a transaction that may be ruled "not at arm's length." Before you take any such action, discuss with an attorney the income or estate tax consequences. The IRS has definite ideas about the interest you might charge your children if you carried a mortgage for them.

The gift of one's homestead to a son or daughter may mean that the elderly parent loses favorable property tax treatment, becomes liable for payment of state gift tax, or faces an unexpected problem in the event of a child's divorce or bankruptcy. In certain circumstances, it is more prudent for children to wait to inherit property than to receive it as a gift. The disposition of real estate should be considered in the wider framework of estate planning, and professional guidance is essential.

Afterword

If You Are Pleased with an Agent

If you are pleased with the service you received from your real estate broker, there are several ways to show it. Agents are used to taking clients out to lunch or dinner; it's a real thrill when you proffer the invitation instead. Any small token—a bottle of wine, a plant for the office—will be a welcome surprise. Your agent will proudly show an invitation to your housewarming back at the office.

It is remarkable how few satisfied clients take the trouble to write to a real estate office. A letter addressed to your salesperson's supervising broker will be read aloud at a sales meeting, posted on a bulletin board, and treasured by the agent involved.

Particularly gratifying to any agent are future referrals. The standard answer to, "What can I do to repay your extra care?" is a cheerful, "Just send me a client!"

APPENDIX

A

Monthly Payment Tables

Your monthly mortgage payment will include interest on the amount borrowed, plus a bit more intended to whittle down the principal still owed. As the loan is gradually paid, less interest is owed, and a larger portion of each payment can go toward principal.

The following tables cover loan terms of 1 to 40 years, with interest rates between 2 percent and 19 percent.

To find your mortgage payment:

1. Search the left-hand column until you find the interest rate on your loan.
2. Search the top line for the number of years you will be making payments.
3. Follow the percentage line across and the "number of years" column down until the two intersect. The figure indicated is the monthly dollar amount necessary to amortize (pay off) a loan of $1,000 in the given time, at the given rate of interest.

   Example: If a 10 percent loan has a term of 25 years, the two lines intersect at 9.0870. This means that $9.087 a month, for 25 years, would pay off a loan of $1,000 at 10 percent interest.

4. Multiply the figure indicated by the number of thousands being borrowed. This gives you the monthly payment necessary to amortize the entire loan.

   Example: If, in the example given with step 3, the loan amount is $74,500, this represents 74.5 thousands. Multiplying $9.087 by 74.5 gives you $676.9816, which would be rounded off to a monthly payment of $676.98.

The figure you have found represents principal and interest only; if a lending institution requires escrow for taxes and insurance, one-twelfth of those costs must be added to arrive at the PITI payment.

MONTHLY PAYMENT TO AMORTIZE A LOAN OF $1,000

Term of Loan

Interest Rate	1 Year	2 Years	3 Years	4 Years	5 Years	6 Years	7 Years	8 Years
2.000%	84.2389	42.5403	28.6426	21.6951	17.5278	14.7504	12.7674	11.2809
2.125%	84.2956	42.5952	28.6972	21.7497	17.5825	14.8054	12.8226	11.3364
2.250%	84.3524	42.6502	28.7518	21.8044	17.6373	14.8605	12.8780	11.3920
2.375%	84.4093	42.7053	28.8066	21.8592	17.6923	14.9157	12.9335	11.4478
2.500%	84.4661	42.7604	28.8614	21.9140	17.7474	14.9710	12.9892	11.5038
2.625%	84.5230	42.8155	28.9162	21.9690	17.8025	15.0265	13.0450	11.5600
2.750%	84.5799	42.8707	28.9712	22.0240	17.8578	15.0821	13.1009	11.6164
2.875%	84.6368	42.9259	29.0262	22.0791	17.9132	15.1378	13.1570	11.6729
3.000%	84.6937	42.9812	29.0812	22.1343	17.9687	15.1937	13.2133	11.7296
3.125%	84.7506	43.0365	29.1363	22.1896	18.0243	15.2497	13.2697	11.7864
3.250%	84.8076	43.0919	29.1915	22.2450	18.0800	15.3058	13.3263	11.8435
3.375%	84.8646	43.1473	29.2468	22.3005	18.1358	15.3620	13.3830	11.9007
3.500%	84.9216	43.2027	29.3021	22.3560	18.1917	15.4184	13.4399	11.9581
3.625%	84.9787	43.2582	29.3575	22.4116	18.2478	15.4749	13.4969	12.0156
3.750%	85.0357	43.3137	29.4129	22.4674	18.3039	15.5315	13.5540	12.0733
3.875%	85.0928	43.3693	29.4684	22.5232	18.3602	15.5883	13.6113	12.1312
4.000%	85.1499	43.4249	29.5240	22.5791	18.4165	15.6452	13.6688	12.1893
4.125%	85.2070	43.4806	29.5796	22.6350	18.4730	15.7022	13.7264	12.2475
4.250%	85.2642	43.5363	29.6353	22.6911	18.5296	15.7593	13.7842	12.3059
4.375%	85.3213	43.5920	29.6911	22.7472	18.5862	15.8166	13.8421	12.3645
4.500%	85.3785	43.6478	29.7469	22.8035	18.6430	15.8740	13.9002	12.4232
4.625%	85.4357	43.7036	29.8028	22.8598	18.6999	15.9316	13.9584	12.4822
4.750%	85.4930	43.7595	29.8588	22.9162	18.7569	15.9892	14.0167	12.5412
4.875%	85.5502	43.8154	29.9148	22.9727	18.8140	16.0470	14.0752	12.6005
5.000%	85.6075	43.8714	29.9709	23.0293	18.8712	16.1049	14.1339	12.6599
5.125%	85.6648	43.9274	30.0271	23.0860	18.9286	16.1630	14.1927	12.7195
5.250%	85.7221	43.9834	30.0833	23.1427	18.9860	16.2212	14.2517	12.7793
5.375%	85.7794	44.0395	30.1396	23.1996	19.0435	16.2795	14.3108	12.8392
5.500%	85.8368	44.0957	30.1959	23.2565	19.1012	16.3379	14.3700	12.8993
5.625%	85.8942	44.1518	30.2523	23.3135	19.1589	16.3964	14.4294	12.9596
5.750%	85.9516	44.2080	30.3088	23.3706	19.2168	16.4551	14.4890	13.0200
5.875%	86.0090	44.2643	30.3653	23.4278	19.2747	16.5139	14.5487	13.0807
6.000%	86.0664	44.3206	30.4219	23.4850	19.3328	16.5729	14.6086	13.1414
6.125%	86.1239	44.3770	30.4786	23.5424	19.3910	16.6320	14.6686	13.2024
6.250%	86.1814	44.4333	30.5353	23.5998	19.4493	16.6912	14.7287	13.2635
6.375%	86.2389	44.4898	30.5921	23.6573	19.5077	16.7505	14.7890	13.3248
6.500%	86.2964	44.5463	30.6490	23.7150	19.5661	16.8099	14.8494	13.3862
6.625%	86.3540	44.6028	30.7059	23.7726	19.6248	16.8695	14.9100	13.4479
6.750%	86.4115	44.6593	30.7629	23.8304	19.6835	16.9292	14.9708	13.5096
6.875%	86.4691	44.7159	30.8200	23.8883	19.7423	16.9890	15.0316	13.5716

MONTHLY PAYMENT TO AMORTIZE A LOAN OF $1,000

Term of Loan

Interest Rate	9 Years	10 Years	11 Years	12 Years	13 Years	14 Years	15 Years	16 Years
2.000%	10.1253	9.2013	8.4459	7.8168	7.2850	6.8295	6.4351	6.0903
2.125%	10.1811	9.2574	8.5023	7.8736	7.3420	6.8869	6.4928	6.1484
2.250%	10.2370	9.3137	8.5590	7.9305	7.3994	6.9446	6.5508	6.2068
2.375%	10.2932	9.3703	8.6158	7.9878	7.4570	7.0025	6.6092	6.2655
2.500%	10.3496	9.4270	8.6729	8.0453	7.5149	7.0608	6.6679	6.3246
2.625%	10.4061	9.4839	8.7303	8.1031	7.5730	7.1194	6.7269	6.3840
2.750%	10.4629	9.5411	8.7879	8.1611	7.6315	7.1783	6.7862	6.4438
2.875%	10.5198	9.5985	8.8457	8.2193	7.6902	7.2375	6.8459	6.5039
3.000%	10.5769	9.6561	8.9038	8.2779	7.7492	7.2970	6.9058	6.5643
3.125%	10.6343	9.7139	8.9621	8.3367	7.8085	7.3567	6.9661	6.6251
3.250%	10.6918	9.7719	9.0206	8.3957	7.8680	7.4168	7.0267	6.6862
3.375%	10.7495	9.8301	9.0793	8.4550	7.9279	7.4772	7.0876	6.7477
3.500%	10.8074	9.8886	9.1383	8.5145	7.9880	7.5378	7.1488	6.8095
3.625%	10.8655	9.9472	9.1976	8.5743	8.0484	7.5988	7.2104	6.8716
3.750%	10.9238	10.0061	9.2570	8.6344	8.1090	7.6601	7.2722	6.9340
3.875%	10.9823	10.0652	9.3167	8.6947	8.1700	7.7216	7.3344	6.9968
4.000%	11.0410	10.1245	9.3767	8.7553	8.2312	7.7835	7.3969	7.0600
4.125%	11.0998	10.1840	9.4368	8.8161	8.2926	7.8456	7.4597	7.1234
4.250%	11.1589	10.2438	9.4972	8.8772	8.3544	7.9080	7.5228	7.1872
4.375%	11.2181	10.3037	9.5579	8.9385	8.4164	7.9707	7.5862	7.2513
4.500%	11.2776	10.3638	9.6187	9.0001	8.4787	8.0338	7.6499	7.3158
4.625%	11.3372	10.4242	9.6798	9.0619	8.5413	8.0971	7.7140	7.3805
4.750%	11.3971	10.4848	9.7411	9.1240	8.6041	8.1607	7.7783	7.4456
4.875%	11.4571	10.5456	9.8027	9.1863	8.6672	8.2245	7.8430	7.5111
5.000%	11.5173	10.6066	9.8645	9.2489	8.7306	8.2887	7.9079	7.5768
5.125%	11.5777	10.6678	9.9265	9.3117	8.7942	8.3532	7.9732	7.6429
5.250%	11.6383	10.7292	9.9888	9.3748	8.8582	8.4179	8.0388	7.7093
5.375%	11.6990	10.7908	10.0512	9.4381	8.9223	8.4829	8.1047	7.7760
5.500%	11.7600	10.8526	10.1139	9.5017	8.9868	8.5483	8.1708	7.8430
5.625%	11.8212	10.9147	10.1769	9.5655	9.0515	8.6139	8.2373	7.9104
5.750%	11.8825	10.9769	10.2400	9.6296	9.1165	8.6797	8.3041	7.9781
5.875%	11.9440	11.0394	10.3034	9.6939	9.1817	8.7459	8.3712	8.0461
6.000%	12.0057	11.1021	10.3670	9.7585	9.2472	8.8124	8.4386	8.1144
6.125%	12.0677	11.1649	10.4309	9.8233	9.3130	8.8791	8.5062	8.1830
6.250%	12.1298	11.2280	10.4949	9.8884	9.3790	8.9461	8.5742	8.2519
6.375%	12.1920	11.2913	10.5592	9.9537	9.4453	9.0134	8.6425	8.3212
6.500%	12.2545	11.3548	10.6238	10.0192	9.5119	9.0810	8.7111	8.3908
6.625%	12.3172	11.4185	10.6885	10.0850	9.5787	9.1488	8.7799	8.4606
6.750%	12.3800	11.4824	10.7535	10.1510	9.6458	9.2169	8.8491	8.5308
6.875%	12.4431	11.5465	10.8187	10.2173	9.7131	9.2853	8.9185	8.6013

MONTHLY PAYMENT TO AMORTIZE A LOAN OF $1,000

Term of Loan

Interest Rate	17 Years	18 Years	19 Years	20 Years	21 Years	22 Years	23 Years	24 Years
2.000%	5.7865	5.5167	5.2756	5.0588	4.8630	4.6852	4.5232	4.3748
2.125%	5.8449	5.5754	5.3346	5.1182	4.9228	4.7453	4.5836	4.4356
2.250%	5.9036	5.6345	5.3941	5.1781	4.9830	4.8059	4.6445	4.4969
2.375%	5.9627	5.6940	5.4540	5.2383	5.0436	4.8669	4.7059	4.5587
2.500%	6.0222	5.7539	5.5143	5.2990	5.1047	4.9284	4.7678	4.6209
2.625%	6.0821	5.8142	5.5750	5.3601	5.1662	4.9904	4.8302	4.6837
2.750%	6.1423	5.8748	5.6360	5.4217	5.2282	5.0528	4.8930	4.7470
2.875%	6.2028	5.9358	5.6975	5.4836	5.2906	5.1156	4.9564	4.8108
3.000%	6.2637	5.9972	5.7594	5.5460	5.3534	5.1790	5.0202	4.8751
3.125%	6.3250	6.0590	5.8217	5.6088	5.4167	5.2427	5.0844	4.9399
3.250%	6.3867	6.1212	5.8844	5.6720	5.4804	5.3070	5.1492	5.0051
3.375%	6.4487	6.1837	5.9474	5.7356	5.5446	5.3717	5.2144	5.0709
3.500%	6.5110	6.2466	6.0109	5.7996	5.6092	5.4368	5.2801	5.1371
3.625%	6.5737	6.3099	6.0748	5.8640	5.6742	5.5024	5.3463	5.2039
3.750%	6.6368	6.3736	6.1390	5.9289	5.7396	5.5684	5.4129	5.2711
3.875%	6.7002	6.4376	6.2037	5.9941	5.8055	5.6349	5.4800	5.3387
4.000%	6.7639	6.5020	6.2687	6.0598	5.8718	5.7018	5.5475	5.4069
4.125%	6.8280	6.5667	6.3341	6.1259	5.9385	5.7692	5.6155	5.4755
4.250%	6.8925	6.6319	6.3999	6.1923	6.0056	5.8370	5.6840	5.5446
4.375%	6.9573	6.6974	6.4661	6.2592	6.0732	5.9052	5.7529	5.6142
4.500%	7.0225	6.7632	6.5327	6.3265	6.1412	5.9739	5.8222	5.6842
4.625%	7.0880	6.8295	6.5996	6.3942	6.2096	6.0430	5.8920	5.7547
4.750%	7.1538	6.8961	6.6670	6.4622	6.2784	6.1125	5.9623	5.8257
4.875%	7.2200	6.9630	6.7347	6.5307	6.3476	6.1824	6.0329	5.8971
5.000%	7.2866	7.0303	6.8028	6.5996	6.4172	6.2528	6.1041	5.9690
5.125%	7.3534	7.0980	6.8712	6.6688	6.4872	6.3236	6.1756	6.0413
5.250%	7.4206	7.1660	6.9401	6.7384	6.5576	6.3948	6.2476	6.1140
5.375%	7.4882	7.2344	7.0093	6.8085	6.6285	6.4664	6.3200	6.1872
5.500%	7.5561	7.3032	7.0789	6.8789	6.6997	6.5385	6.3929	6.2609
5.625%	7.6243	7.3723	7.1488	6.9497	6.7713	6.6109	6.4661	6.3350
5.750%	7.6929	7.4417	7.2191	7.0208	6.8434	6.6838	6.5398	6.4095
5.875%	7.7618	7.5115	7.2898	7.0924	6.9158	6.7571	6.6139	6.4844
6.000%	7.8310	7.5816	7.3608	7.1643	6.9886	6.8307	6.6885	6.5598
6.125%	7.9006	7.6521	7.4322	7.2366	7.0618	6.9048	6.7634	6.6356
6.250%	7.9705	7.7229	7.5040	7.3093	7.1353	6.9793	6.8387	6.7118
6.375%	8.0407	7.7941	7.5761	7.3823	7.2093	7.0541	6.9145	6.7884
6.500%	8.1112	7.8656	7.6486	7.4557	7.2836	7.1294	6.9906	6.8654
6.625%	8.1821	7.9375	7.7214	7.5295	7.3583	7.2050	7.0672	6.9429
6.750%	8.2533	8.0096	7.7945	7.6036	7.4334	7.2811	7.1441	7.0207
6.875%	8.3248	8.0822	7.8681	7.6781	7.5089	7.3575	7.2215	7.0990

MONTHLY PAYMENT TO AMORTIZE A LOAN OF $1,000

Term of Loan

Interest Rate	25 Years	26 Years	27 Years	28 Years	29 Years	30 Years	35 Years	40 Years
2.000%	4.2385	4.1130	3.9969	3.8893	3.7893	3.6962	3.3126	3.0283
2.125%	4.2997	4.1744	4.0587	3.9515	3.8518	3.7590	3.3771	3.0944
2.250%	4.3613	4.2364	4.1211	4.0142	3.9149	3.8225	3.4424	3.1614
2.375%	4.4235	4.2990	4.1840	4.0775	3.9786	3.8865	3.5083	3.2292
2.500%	4.4862	4.3621	4.2475	4.1414	4.0429	3.9512	3.5750	3.2978
2.625%	4.5494	4.4257	4.3115	4.2058	4.1078	4.0165	3.6423	3.3671
2.750%	4.6131	4.4899	4.3761	4.2709	4.1732	4.0824	3.7103	3.4373
2.875%	4.6774	4.5546	4.4413	4.3365	4.2393	4.1489	3.7791	3.5082
3.000%	4.7421	4.6198	4.5070	4.4027	4.3059	4.2160	3.8485	3.5798
3.125%	4.8074	4.6856	4.5733	4.4694	4.3732	4.2838	3.9186	3.6523
3.250%	4.8732	4.7519	4.6401	4.5367	4.4410	4.3521	3.9894	3.7254
3.375%	4.9394	4.8187	4.7074	4.6046	4.5094	4.4210	4.0608	3.7993
3.500%	5.0062	4.8860	4.7753	4.6730	4.5783	4.4904	4.1329	3.8739
3.625%	5.0735	4.9539	4.8437	4.7420	4.6478	4.5605	4.2057	3.9492
3.750%	5.1413	5.0222	4.9126	4.8115	4.7179	4.6312	4.2791	4.0253
3.875%	5.2096	5.0911	4.9821	4.8815	4.7885	4.7024	4.3531	4.1020
4.000%	5.2784	5.1605	5.0521	4.9521	4.8597	4.7742	4.4277	4.1794
4.125%	5.3476	5.2304	5.1226	5.0233	4.9315	4.8465	4.5030	4.2575
4.250%	5.4174	5.3008	5.1936	5.0949	5.0038	4.9194	4.5789	4.3362
4.375%	5.4876	5.3717	5.2652	5.1671	5.0766	4.9929	4.6555	4.4156
4.500%	5.5583	5.4430	5.3372	5.2398	5.1499	5.0669	4.7326	4.4956
4.625%	5.6295	5.5149	5.4098	5.3130	5.2238	5.1414	4.8103	4.5763
4.750%	5.7012	5.5873	5.4828	5.3868	5.2982	5.2165	4.8886	4.6576
4.875%	5.7733	5.6601	5.5564	5.4610	5.3732	5.2921	4.9674	4.7395
5.000%	5.8459	5.7334	5.6304	5.5357	5.4486	5.3682	5.0469	4.8220
5.125%	5.9190	5.8072	5.7049	5.6110	5.5246	5.4449	5.1269	4.9050
5.250%	5.9925	5.8815	5.7799	5.6867	5.6010	5.5220	5.2074	4.9887
5.375%	6.0665	5.9562	5.8554	5.7629	5.6780	5.5997	5.2885	5.0729
5.500%	6.1409	6.0314	5.9314	5.8397	5.7554	5.6779	5.3702	5.1577
5.625%	6.2157	6.1071	6.0078	5.9168	5.8334	5.7566	5.4523	5.2430
5.750%	6.2911	6.1832	6.0847	5.9945	5.9118	5.8357	5.5350	5.3289
5.875%	6.3668	6.2598	6.1620	6.0726	5.9907	5.9154	5.6182	5.4153
6.000%	6.4430	6.3368	6.2399	6.1512	6.0700	5.9955	5.7019	5.5021
6.125%	6.5196	6.4142	6.3181	6.2303	6.1499	6.0761	5.7861	5.5895
6.250%	6.5967	6.4921	6.3968	6.3098	6.2302	6.1572	5.8708	5.6774
6.375%	6.6742	6.5704	6.4760	6.3898	6.3109	6.2387	5.9559	5.7657
6.500%	6.7521	6.6492	6.5555	6.4702	6.3921	6.3207	6.0415	5.8546
6.625%	6.8304	6.7284	6.6356	6.5510	6.4738	6.4031	6.1276	5.9438
6.750%	6.9091	6.8079	6.7160	6.6323	6.5558	6.4860	6.2142	6.0336
6.875%	6.9883	6.8880	6.7969	6.7140	6.6384	6.5693	6.3011	6.1237

MONTHLY PAYMENT TO AMORTIZE A LOAN OF $1,000

Term of Loan

Interest Rate	1 Year	2 Years	3 Years	4 Years	5 Years	6 Years	7 Years	8 Years
7.000%	86.5267	44.7726	30.8771	23.9462	19.8012	17.0490	15.0927	13.6337
7.125%	86.5844	44.8293	30.9343	24.0043	19.8602	17.1091	15.1539	13.6960
7.250%	86.6420	44.8860	30.9915	24.0624	19.9194	17.1693	15.2152	13.7585
7.375%	86.6997	44.9428	31.0488	24.1206	19.9786	17.2296	15.2767	13.8211
7.500%	86.7574	44.9996	31.1062	24.1789	20.0379	17.2901	15.3383	13.8839
7.625%	86.8151	45.0565	31.1637	24.2373	20.0974	17.3507	15.4000	13.9468
7.750%	86.8729	45.1134	31.2212	24.2957	20.1570	17.4114	15.4620	14.0099
7.875%	86.9306	45.1703	31.2787	24.3543	20.2166	17.4723	15.5240	14.0732
8.000%	86.9884	45.2273	31.3364	24.4129	20.2764	17.5332	15.5862	14.1367
8.125%	87.0462	45.2843	31.3941	24.4716	20.3363	17.5943	15.6486	14.2003
8.250%	87.1041	45.3414	31.4518	24.5304	20.3963	17.6556	15.7111	14.2641
8.375%	87.1619	45.3985	31.5096	24.5893	20.4563	17.7169	15.7737	14.3280
8.500%	87.2198	45.4557	31.5675	24.6483	20.5165	17.7784	15.8365	14.3921
8.625%	87.2777	45.5129	31.6255	24.7074	20.5768	17.8400	15.8994	14.4564
8.750%	87.3356	45.5701	31.6835	24.7665	20.6372	17.9017	15.9625	14.5208
8.875%	87.3935	45.6274	31.7416	24.8257	20.6977	17.9636	16.0257	14.5854
9.000%	87.4515	45.6847	31.7997	24.8850	20.7584	18.0255	16.0891	14.6502
9.125%	87.5095	45.7421	31.8579	24.9444	20.8191	18.0876	16.1526	14.7151
9.250%	87.5675	45.7995	31.9162	25.0039	20.8799	18.1499	16.2162	14.7802
9.375%	87.6255	45.8570	31.9745	25.0635	20.9408	18.2122	16.2800	14.8455
9.500%	87.6835	45.9145	32.0329	25.1231	21.0019	18.2747	16.3440	14.9109
9.625%	87.7416	45.9720	32.0914	25.1829	21.0630	18.3373	16.4081	14.9765
9.750%	87.7997	46.0296	32.1499	25.2427	21.1242	18.4000	16.4723	15.0422
9.875%	87.8578	46.0873	32.2085	25.3026	21.1856	18.4629	16.5367	15.1081
10.000%	87.9159	46.1449	32.2672	25.3626	21.2470	18.5258	16.6012	15.1742
10.125%	87.9740	46.2026	32.3259	25.4227	21.3086	18.5889	16.6658	15.2404
10.250%	88.0322	46.2604	32.3847	25.4828	21.3703	18.6522	16.7306	15.3068
10.375%	88.0904	46.3182	32.4435	25.5431	21.4320	18.7155	16.7956	15.3733
10.500%	88.1486	46.3760	32.5024	25.6034	21.4939	18.7790	16.8607	15.4400
10.625%	88.2068	46.4339	32.5614	25.6638	21.5559	18.8426	16.9259	15.5069
10.750%	88.2651	46.4919	32.6205	25.7243	21.6180	18.9063	16.9913	15.5739
10.875%	88.3234	46.5498	32.6796	25.7849	21.6801	18.9701	17.0568	15.6411
11.000%	88.3817	46.6078	32.7387	25.8455	21.7424	19.0341	17.1224	15.7084
11.125%	88.4400	46.6659	32.7979	25.9063	21.8048	19.0982	17.1882	15.7759
11.250%	88.4983	46.7240	32.8572	25.9671	21.8673	19.1624	17.2542	15.8436
11.375%	88.5567	46.7821	32.9166	26.0280	21.9299	19.2267	17.3202	15.9114
11.500%	88.6151	46.8403	32.9760	26.0890	21.9926	19.2912	17.3865	15.9794
11.625%	88.6735	46.8985	33.0355	26.1501	22.0554	19.3557	17.4528	16.0475
11.750%	88.7319	46.9568	33.0950	26.2113	22.1183	19.4204	17.5193	16.1158
11.875%	88.7903	47.0151	33.1546	26.2725	22.1813	19.4853	17.5860	16.1842

MONTHLY PAYMENT TO AMORTIZE A LOAN OF $1,000

Term of Loan

Interest Rate	9 Years	10 Years	11 Years	12 Years	13 Years	14 Years	15 Years	16 Years
7.000%	12.5063	11.6108	10.8841	10.2838	9.7807	9.3540	8.9883	8.6721
7.125%	12.5697	11.6754	10.9497	10.3506	9.8486	9.4230	9.0583	8.7432
7.250%	12.6333	11.7401	11.0156	10.4176	9.9167	9.4922	9.1286	8.8146
7.375%	12.6971	11.8050	11.0817	10.4848	9.9851	9.5617	9.1992	8.8863
7.500%	12.7610	11.8702	11.1480	10.5523	10.0537	9.6314	9.2701	8.9583
7.625%	12.8252	11.9355	11.2145	10.6200	10.1226	9.7015	9.3413	9.0306
7.750%	12.8895	12.0011	11.2813	10.6879	10.1917	9.7718	9.4128	9.1032
7.875%	12.9540	12.0668	11.3483	10.7561	10.2611	9.8423	9.4845	9.1761
8.000%	13.0187	12.1328	11.4154	10.8245	10.3307	9.9132	9.5565	9.2493
8.125%	13.0836	12.1989	11.4829	10.8932	10.4006	9.9843	9.6288	9.3227
8.250%	13.1487	12.2653	11.5505	10.9621	10.4708	10.0557	9.7014	9.3965
8.375%	13.2139	12.3318	11.6183	11.0312	10.5412	10.1273	9.7743	9.4706
8.500%	13.2794	12.3986	11.6864	11.1006	10.6118	10.1992	9.8474	9.5449
8.625%	13.3450	12.4655	11.7547	11.1701	10.6827	10.2713	9.9208	9.6195
8.750%	13.4108	12.5327	11.8232	11.2400	10.7538	10.3438	9.9945	9.6945
8.875%	13.4767	12.6000	11.8919	11.3100	10.8252	10.4164	10.0684	9.7697
9.000%	13.5429	12.6676	11.9608	11.3803	10.8968	10.4894	10.1427	9.8452
9.125%	13.6093	12.7353	12.0299	11.4508	10.9687	10.5626	10.2172	9.9209
9.250%	13.6758	12.8033	12.0993	11.5216	11.0408	10.6360	10.2919	9.9970
9.375%	13.7425	12.8714	12.1689	11.5925	11.1131	10.7097	10.3670	10.0733
9.500%	13.8094	12.9398	12.2386	11.6637	11.1857	10.7837	10.4422	10.1499
9.625%	13.8764	13.0083	12.3086	11.7352	11.2586	10.8579	10.5178	10.2268
9.750%	13.9437	13.0770	12.3788	11.8068	11.3316	10.9324	10.5936	10.3039
9.875%	14.0111	13.1460	12.4493	11.8787	11.4049	11.0071	10.6697	10.3813
10.000%	14.0787	13.2151	12.5199	11.9508	11.4785	11.0820	10.7461	10.4590
10.125%	14.1465	13.2844	12.5907	12.0231	11.5523	11.1572	10.8227	10.5370
10.250%	14.2144	13.3539	12.6618	12.0957	11.6263	11.2327	10.8995	10.6152
10.375%	14.2826	13.4236	12.7330	12.1684	11.7005	11.3084	10.9766	10.6937
10.500%	14.3509	13.4935	12.8045	12.2414	11.7750	11.3843	11.0540	10.7724
10.625%	14.4193	13.5636	12.8761	12.3146	11.8497	11.4605	11.1316	10.8514
10.750%	14.4880	13.6339	12.9480	12.3880	11.9247	11.5370	11.2095	10.9307
10.875%	14.5568	13.7043	13.0201	12.4617	11.9999	11.6136	11.2876	11.0102
11.000%	14.6259	13.7750	13.0923	12.5356	12.0753	11.6905	11.3660	11.0900
11.125%	14.6950	13.8459	13.1648	12.6096	12.1509	11.7677	11.4446	11.1700
11.250%	14.7644	13.9169	13.2375	12.6839	12.2268	11.8451	11.5234	11.2503
11.375%	14.8339	13.9881	13.3104	12.7584	12.3029	11.9227	11.6026	11.3309
11.500%	14.9037	14.0595	13.3835	12.8332	12.3792	12.0006	11.6819	11.4116
11.625%	14.9735	14.1312	13.4568	12.9081	12.4557	12.0786	11.7615	11.4927
11.750%	15.0436	14.2029	13.5303	12.9833	12.5325	12.1570	11.8413	11.5740
11.875%	15.1138	14.2749	13.6040	13.0586	12.6095	12.2355	11.9214	11.6555

MONTHLY PAYMENT TO AMORTIZE A LOAN OF $1,000

Term of Loan

Interest Rate	17 Years	18 Years	19 Years	20 Years	21 Years	22 Years	23 Years	24 Years
7.000%	8.3966	8.1550	7.9419	7.7530	7.5847	7.4342	7.2992	7.1776
7.125%	8.4688	8.2282	8.0161	7.8282	7.6609	7.5114	7.3773	7.2566
7.250%	8.5412	8.3017	8.0907	7.9038	7.7375	7.5889	7.4558	7.3361
7.375%	8.6140	8.3756	8.1656	7.9797	7.8144	7.6668	7.5347	7.4159
7.500%	8.6871	8.4497	8.2408	8.0559	7.8917	7.7451	7.6139	7.4960
7.625%	8.7605	8.5242	8.3163	8.1325	7.9693	7.8237	7.6935	7.5766
7.750%	8.8342	8.5990	8.3922	8.2095	8.0473	7.9027	7.7735	7.6576
7.875%	8.9082	8.6742	8.4685	8.2868	8.1256	7.9821	7.8538	7.7389
8.000%	8.9826	8.7496	8.5450	8.3644	8.2043	8.0618	7.9345	7.8205
8.125%	9.0572	8.8254	8.6219	8.4424	8.2833	8.1418	8.0156	7.9026
8.250%	9.1321	8.9015	8.6991	8.5207	8.3627	8.2222	8.0970	7.9850
8.375%	9.2074	8.9779	8.7766	8.5993	8.4424	8.3030	8.1788	8.0677
8.500%	9.2829	9.0546	8.8545	8.6782	8.5224	8.3841	8.2609	8.1508
8.625%	9.3588	9.1316	8.9326	8.7575	8.6028	8.4655	8.3433	8.2343
8.750%	9.4349	9.2089	9.0111	8.8371	8.6834	8.5472	8.4261	8.3181
8.875%	9.5113	9.2865	9.0899	8.9170	8.7645	8.6293	8.5092	8.4022
9.000%	9.5880	9.3644	9.1690	8.9973	8.8458	8.7117	8.5927	8.4866
9.125%	9.6650	9.4427	9.2484	9.0778	8.9275	8.7945	8.6765	8.5714
9.250%	9.7423	9.5212	9.3281	9.1587	9.0094	8.8775	8.7606	8.6566
9.375%	9.8199	9.6000	9.4081	9.2398	9.0917	8.9609	8.8450	8.7420
9.500%	9.8978	9.6791	9.4884	9.3213	9.1743	9.0446	8.9297	8.8277
9.625%	9.9760	9.7585	9.5690	9.4031	9.2573	9.1286	9.0148	8.9138
9.750%	10.0544	9.8382	9.6499	9.4852	9.3405	9.2129	9.1002	9.0002
9.875%	10.1331	9.9182	9.7311	9.5675	9.4240	9.2975	9.1858	9.0869
10.000%	10.2121	9.9984	9.8126	9.6502	9.5078	9.3825	9.2718	9.1739
10.125%	10.2914	10.0790	9.8944	9.7332	9.5919	9.4677	9.3581	9.2612
10.250%	10.3709	10.1598	9.9764	9.8164	9.6763	9.5532	9.4447	9.3488
10.375%	10.4507	10.2409	10.0588	9.9000	9.7610	9.6390	9.5315	9.4366
10.500%	10.5308	10.3223	10.1414	9.9838	9.8460	9.7251	9.6187	9.5248
10.625%	10.6112	10.4039	10.2243	10.0679	9.9312	9.8114	9.7061	9.6133
10.750%	10.6918	10.4858	10.3075	10.1523	10.0168	9.8981	9.7938	9.7020
10.875%	10.7727	10.5680	10.3909	10.2370	10.1026	9.9850	9.8818	9.7910
11.000%	10.8538	10.6505	10.4746	10.3219	10.1887	10.0722	9.9701	9.8803
11.125%	10.9352	10.7332	10.5586	10.4071	10.2751	10.1597	10.0586	9.9698
11.250%	11.0169	10.8162	10.6429	10.4926	10.3617	10.2475	10.1474	10.0596
11.375%	11.0988	10.8994	10.7274	10.5783	10.4486	10.3355	10.2365	10.1497
11.500%	11.1810	10.9830	10.8122	10.6643	10.5358	10.4237	10.3258	10.2400
11.625%	11.2634	11.0667	10.8972	10.7506	10.6232	10.5123	10.4154	10.3306
11.750%	11.3461	11.1507	10.9825	10.8371	10.7109	10.6011	10.5052	10.4214
11.875%	11.4290	11.2350	11.0681	10.9238	10.7988	10.6901	10.5953	10.5125

MONTHLY PAYMENT TO AMORTIZE A LOAN OF $1,000

Term of Loan

Interest Rate	25 Years	26 Years	27 Years	28 Years	29 Years	30 Years	35 Years	40 Years
7.000%	7.0678	6.9684	6.8781	6.7961	6.7213	6.6530	6.3886	6.2143
7.125%	7.1477	7.0492	6.9598	6.8786	6.8047	6.7372	6.4764	6.3053
7.250%	7.2281	7.1304	7.0419	6.9616	6.8884	6.8218	6.5647	6.3967
7.375%	7.3088	7.2121	7.1244	7.0449	6.9726	6.9068	6.6533	6.4885
7.500%	7.3899	7.2941	7.2073	7.1287	7.0572	6.9921	6.7424	6.5807
7.625%	7.4714	7.3765	7.2906	7.2128	7.1422	7.0779	6.8319	6.6733
7.750%	7.5533	7.4593	7.3743	7.2974	7.2276	7.1641	6.9218	6.7662
7.875%	7.6355	7.5424	7.4584	7.3823	7.3133	7.2507	7.0120	6.8595
8.000%	7.7182	7.6260	7.5428	7.4676	7.3995	7.3376	7.1026	6.9531
8.125%	7.8012	7.7099	7.6276	7.5533	7.4860	7.4250	7.1936	7.0471
8.250%	7.8845	7.7942	7.7128	7.6393	7.5729	7.5127	7.2849	7.1414
8.375%	7.9682	7.8788	7.7983	7.7257	7.6601	7.6007	7.3766	7.2360
8.500%	8.0523	7.9638	7.8842	7.8125	7.7477	7.6891	7.4686	7.3309
8.625%	8.1367	8.0491	7.9705	7.8996	7.8357	7.7779	7.5610	7.4262
8.750%	8.2214	8.1348	8.0570	7.9871	7.9240	7.8670	7.6536	7.5217
8.875%	8.3065	8.2209	8.1440	8.0749	8.0126	7.9564	7.7466	7.6175
9.000%	8.3920	8.3072	8.2313	8.1630	8.1016	8.0462	7.8399	7.7136
9.125%	8.4777	8.3939	8.3189	8.2515	8.1909	8.1363	7.9335	7.8100
9.250%	8.5638	8.4810	8.4068	8.3403	8.2805	8.2268	8.0274	7.9066
9.375%	8.6502	8.5683	8.4950	8.4294	8.3705	8.3175	8.1216	8.0035
9.500%	8.7370	8.6560	8.5836	8.5188	8.4607	8.4085	8.2161	8.1006
9.625%	8.8240	8.7440	8.6725	8.6086	8.5513	8.4999	8.3109	8.1980
9.750%	8.9114	8.8323	8.7617	8.6986	8.6421	8.5915	8.4059	8.2956
9.875%	8.9990	8.9209	8.8512	8.7890	8.7333	8.6835	8.5012	8.3934
10.000%	9.0870	9.0098	8.9410	8.8796	8.8248	8.7757	8.5967	8.4915
10.125%	9.1753	9.0990	9.0311	8.9705	8.9165	8.8682	8.6925	8.5897
10.250%	9.2638	9.1885	9.1214	9.0618	9.0085	8.9610	8.7886	8.6882
10.375%	9.3527	9.2782	9.2121	9.1533	9.1008	9.0541	8.8848	8.7868
10.500%	9.4418	9.3683	9.3030	9.2450	9.1934	9.1474	8.9813	8.8857
10.625%	9.5312	9.4586	9.3943	9.3371	9.2862	9.2410	9.0781	8.9847
10.750%	9.6209	9.5492	9.4857	9.4294	9.3793	9.3348	9.1750	9.0840
10.875%	9.7109	9.6401	9.5775	9.5220	9.4727	9.4289	9.2722	9.1834
11.000%	9.8011	9.7313	9.6695	9.6148	9.5663	9.5232	9.3696	9.2829
11.125%	9.8916	9.8227	9.7618	9.7079	9.6601	9.6178	9.4672	9.3827
11.250%	9.9824	9.9143	9.8543	9.8012	9.7542	9.7126	9.5649	9.4826
11.375%	10.0734	10.0063	9.9471	9.8948	9.8486	9.8077	9.6629	9.5826
11.500%	10.1647	10.0984	10.0401	9.9886	9.9431	9.9029	9.7611	9.6828
11.625%	10.2562	10.1909	10.1333	10.0826	10.0379	9.9984	9.8594	9.7832
11.750%	10.3480	10.2835	10.2268	10.1769	10.1329	10.0941	9.9579	9.8836
11.875%	10.4400	10.3764	10.3205	10.2714	10.2281	10.1900	10.0566	9.9843

MONTHLY PAYMENT TO AMORTIZE A LOAN OF $1,000

Term of Loan

Interest Rate	1 Year	2 Years	3 Years	4 Years	5 Years	6 Years	7 Years	8 Years
12.000%	88.8488	47.0735	33.2143	26.3338	22.2444	19.5502	17.6527	16.2528
12.125%	88.9073	47.1319	33.2740	26.3953	22.3077	19.6153	17.7197	16.3216
12.250%	88.9658	47.1903	33.3338	26.4568	22.3710	19.6804	17.7867	16.3905
12.375%	89.0243	47.2488	33.3937	26.5183	22.4344	19.7457	17.8539	16.4596
12.500%	89.0829	47.3073	33.4536	26.5800	22.4979	19.8112	17.9212	16.5288
12.625%	89.1414	47.3659	33.5136	26.6417	22.5616	19.8767	17.9887	16.5982
12.750%	89.2000	47.4245	33.5737	26.7036	22.6253	19.9424	18.0563	16.6677
12.875%	89.2586	47.4831	33.6338	26.7655	22.6891	20.0082	18.1241	16.7374
13.000%	89.3173	47.5418	33.6940	26.8275	22.7531	20.0741	18.1920	16.8073
13.125%	89.3759	47.6006	33.7542	26.8896	22.8171	20.1401	18.2600	16.8773
13.250%	89.4346	47.6593	33.8145	26.9517	22.8813	20.2063	18.3282	16.9474
13.375%	89.4933	47.7182	33.8749	27.0140	22.9455	20.2726	18.3965	17.0177
13.500%	89.5520	47.7770	33.9353	27.0763	23.0098	20.3390	18.4649	17.0882
13.625%	89.6108	47.8359	33.9958	27.1387	23.0743	20.4055	18.5335	17.1588
13.750%	89.6695	47.8949	34.0563	27.2012	23.1388	20.4721	18.6022	17.2295
13.875%	89.7283	47.9539	34.1169	27.2638	23.2035	20.5389	18.6710	17.3004
14.000%	89.7871	48.0129	34.1776	27.3265	23.2683	20.6057	18.7400	17.3715
14.125%	89.8459	48.0720	34.2384	27.3892	23.3331	20.6727	18.8091	17.4427
14.250%	89.9048	48.1311	34.2992	27.4520	23.3981	20.7398	18.8784	17.5141
14.375%	89.9637	48.1902	34.3600	27.5150	23.4631	20.8071	18.9478	17.5856
14.500%	90.0225	48.2494	34.4210	27.5780	23.5283	20.8744	19.0173	17.6573
14.625%	90.0815	48.3087	34.4820	27.6410	23.5935	20.9419	19.0870	17.7291
14.750%	90.1404	48.3680	34.5430	27.7042	23.6589	21.0095	19.1568	17.8010
14.875%	90.1993	48.4273	34.6041	27.7674	23.7244	21.0772	19.2267	17.8731
15.000%	90.2583	48.4866	34.6653	27.8307	23.7899	21.1450	19.2968	17.9454
15.125%	90.3173	48.5461	34.7266	27.8942	23.8556	21.2130	19.3670	18.0178
15.250%	90.3763	48.6055	34.7879	27.9576	23.9214	21.2810	19.4373	18.0904
15.375%	90.4354	48.6650	34.8492	28.0212	23.9872	21.3492	19.5077	18.1631
15.500%	90.4944	48.7245	34.9107	28.0849	24.0532	21.4175	19.5783	18.2359
15.625%	90.5535	48.7841	34.9722	28.1486	24.1193	21.4859	19.6491	18.3089
15.750%	90.6126	48.8437	35.0337	28.2124	24.1854	21.5544	19.7199	18.3821
15.875%	90.6717	48.9034	35.0954	28.2763	24.2517	21.6231	19.7909	18.4554
16.000%	90.7309	48.9631	35.1570	28.3403	24.3181	21.6918	19.8621	18.5288
16.125%	90.7900	49.0229	35.2188	28.4043	24.3845	21.7607	19.9333	18.6024
16.250%	90.8492	49.0826	35.2806	28.4685	24.4511	21.8297	20.0047	18.6761
16.375%	90.9084	49.1425	35.3425	28.5327	24.5178	21.8988	20.0762	18.7500
16.500%	90.9676	49.2024	35.4044	28.5970	24.5845	21.9681	20.1479	18.8240
16.625%	91.0269	49.2623	35.4664	28.6614	24.6514	22.0374	20.2197	18.8981
16.750%	91.0862	49.3222	35.5284	28.7259	24.7184	22.1069	20.2916	18.9724
16.875%	91.1454	49.3822	35.5905	28.7904	24.7854	22.1764	20.3636	19.0469

MONTHLY PAYMENT TO AMORTIZE A LOAN OF $1,000

Term of Loan

Interest Rate	9 Years	10 Years	11 Years	12 Years	13 Years	14 Years	15 Years	16 Years
12.000%	15.1842	14.3471	13.6779	13.1342	12.6867	12.3143	12.0017	11.7373
12.125%	15.2548	14.4194	13.7520	13.2100	12.7641	12.3933	12.0822	11.8193
12.250%	15.3256	14.4920	13.8263	13.2860	12.8417	12.4725	12.1630	11.9015
12.375%	15.3965	14.5647	13.9007	13.3622	12.9196	12.5520	12.2440	11.9840
12.500%	15.4676	14.6376	13.9754	13.4386	12.9977	12.6317	12.3252	12.0667
12.625%	15.5388	14.7107	14.0503	13.5152	13.0760	12.7116	12.4067	12.1496
12.750%	15.6102	14.7840	14.1254	13.5920	13.1545	12.7917	12.4884	12.2328
12.875%	15.6818	14.8574	14.2006	13.6690	13.2332	12.8721	12.5703	12.3162
13.000%	15.7536	14.9311	14.2761	13.7463	13.3121	12.9526	12.6524	12.3999
13.125%	15.8255	15.0049	14.3518	13.8237	13.3912	13.0334	12.7348	12.4837
13.250%	15.8976	15.0789	14.4276	13.9013	13.4706	13.1144	12.8174	12.5678
13.375%	15.9699	15.1531	14.5036	13.9791	13.5502	13.1956	12.9002	12.6521
13.500%	16.0423	15.2274	14.5799	14.0572	13.6299	13.2771	12.9832	12.7367
13.625%	16.1149	15.3020	14.6563	14.1354	13.7099	13.3587	13.0664	12.8214
13.750%	16.1877	15.3767	14.7329	14.2138	13.7901	13.4406	13.1499	12.9064
13.875%	16.2606	15.4516	14.8097	14.2925	13.8704	13.5226	13.2335	12.9916
14.000%	16.3337	15.5266	14.8867	14.3713	13.9510	13.6049	13.3174	13.0770
14.125%	16.4070	15.6019	14.9638	14.4503	14.0318	13.6874	13.4015	13.1626
14.250%	16.4804	15.6773	15.0412	14.5295	14.1128	13.7701	13.4858	13.2484
14.375%	16.5540	15.7529	15.1187	14.6089	14.1940	13.8529	13.5703	13.3345
14.500%	16.6277	15.8287	15.1964	14.6885	14.2754	13.9360	13.6550	13.4207
14.625%	16.7016	15.9046	15.2743	14.7683	14.3570	14.0193	13.7399	13.5071
14.750%	16.7757	15.9807	15.3524	14.8483	14.4387	14.1028	13.8250	13.5938
14.875%	16.8499	16.0570	15.4307	14.9284	14.5207	14.1865	13.9104	13.6806
15.000%	16.9243	16.1335	15.5091	15.0088	14.6029	14.2704	13.9959	13.7677
15.125%	16.9989	16.2101	15.5878	15.0893	14.6852	14.3545	14.0816	13.8549
15.250%	17.0736	16.2869	15.6666	15.1700	14.7678	14.4388	14.1675	13.9424
15.375%	17.1485	16.3639	15.7456	15.2509	14.8505	14.5232	14.2536	14.0300
15.500%	17.2235	16.4411	15.8247	15.3320	14.9335	14.6079	14.3399	14.1179
15.625%	17.2987	16.5184	15.9041	15.4133	15.0166	14.6928	14.4264	14.2059
15.750%	17.3741	16.5958	15.9836	15.4948	15.0999	14.7778	14.5131	14.2941
15.875%	17.4496	16.6735	16.0633	15.5764	15.1834	14.8630	14.5999	14.3825
16.000%	17.5253	16.7513	16.1432	15.6583	15.2670	14.9485	14.6870	14.4711
16.125%	17.6011	16.8293	16.2232	15.7403	15.3509	15.0341	14.7743	14.5599
16.250%	17.6771	16.9074	16.3034	15.8224	15.4349	15.1199	14.8617	14.6488
16.375%	17.7532	16.9858	16.3838	15.9048	15.5192	15.2058	14.9493	14.7380
16.500%	17.8295	17.0642	16.4644	15.9873	15.6036	15.2920	15.0371	14.8273
16.625%	17.9059	17.1429	16.5451	16.0700	15.6881	15.3783	15.1251	14.9168
16.750%	17.9825	17.2217	16.6260	16.1529	15.7729	15.4648	15.2132	15.0065
16.875%	18.0593	17.3006	16.7071	16.2360	15.8578	15.5515	15.3015	15.0963

MONTHLY PAYMENT TO AMORTIZE A LOAN OF $1,000

Term of Loan

Interest Rate	17 Years	18 Years	19 Years	20 Years	21 Years	22 Years	23 Years	24 Years
12.000%	11.5122	11.3195	11.1539	11.0109	10.8870	10.7794	10.6856	10.6038
12.125%	11.5956	11.4043	11.2399	11.0981	10.9754	10.8689	10.7762	10.6954
12.250%	11.6792	11.4893	11.3262	11.1856	11.0641	10.9587	10.8670	10.7872
12.375%	11.7631	11.5745	11.4127	11.2734	11.1530	11.0487	10.9581	10.8792
12.500%	11.8473	11.6600	11.4995	11.3614	11.2422	11.1390	11.0494	10.9714
12.625%	11.9316	11.7457	11.5865	11.4496	11.3316	11.2294	11.1409	11.0639
12.750%	12.0162	11.8317	11.6738	11.5381	11.4212	11.3202	11.2326	11.1566
12.875%	12.1011	11.9179	11.7613	11.6268	11.5111	11.4111	11.3246	11.2495
13.000%	12.1861	12.0043	11.8490	11.7158	11.6011	11.5023	11.4168	11.3427
13.125%	12.2714	12.0910	11.9369	11.8049	11.6915	11.5937	11.5092	11.4360
13.250%	12.3570	12.1779	12.0251	11.8943	11.7820	11.6853	11.6018	11.5296
13.375%	12.4427	12.2650	12.1135	11.9839	11.8727	11.7771	11.6946	11.6233
13.500%	12.5287	12.3523	12.2021	12.0737	11.9637	11.8691	11.7876	11.7173
13.625%	12.6149	12.4399	12.2910	12.1638	12.0549	11.9613	11.8808	11.8114
13.750%	12.7013	12.5276	12.3800	12.2541	12.1463	12.0538	11.9743	11.9058
13.875%	12.7879	12.6156	12.4693	12.3445	12.2379	12.1464	12.0679	12.0003
14.000%	12.8748	12.7038	12.5588	12.4352	12.3297	12.2393	12.1617	12.0950
14.125%	12.9618	12.7922	12.6485	12.5261	12.4217	12.3323	12.2557	12.1900
14.250%	13.0491	12.8809	12.7384	12.6172	12.5139	12.4256	12.3500	12.2851
14.375%	13.1366	12.9697	12.8285	12.7085	12.6063	12.5190	12.4443	12.3803
14.500%	13.2242	13.0587	12.9188	12.8000	12.6989	12.6126	12.5389	12.4758
14.625%	13.3121	13.1480	13.0093	12.8917	12.7917	12.7065	12.6337	12.5714
14.750%	13.4002	13.2374	13.1000	12.9836	12.8847	12.8004	12.7286	12.6672
14.875%	13.4885	13.3271	13.1909	13.0756	12.9778	12.8946	12.8237	12.7632
15.000%	13.5770	13.4169	13.2820	13.1679	13.0712	12.9890	12.9190	12.8593
15.125%	13.6657	13.5069	13.3733	13.2603	13.1647	13.0835	13.0144	12.9556
15.250%	13.7546	13.5972	13.4647	13.3530	13.2584	13.1782	13.1100	13.0520
15.375%	13.8437	13.6876	13.5564	13.4458	13.3523	13.2731	13.2058	13.1486
15.500%	13.9329	13.7782	13.6483	13.5388	13.4464	13.3681	13.3018	13.2454
15.625%	14.0224	13.8690	13.7403	13.6320	13.5406	13.4633	13.3979	13.3423
15.750%	14.1120	13.9600	13.8325	13.7253	13.6350	13.5587	13.4941	13.4394
15.875%	14.2019	14.0511	13.9249	13.8189	13.7296	13.6542	13.5905	13.5366
16.000%	14.2919	14.1425	14.0175	13.9126	13.8243	13.7499	13.6871	13.6339
16.125%	14.3821	14.2340	14.1102	14.0064	13.9192	13.8457	13.7838	13.7314
16.250%	14.4725	14.3257	14.2031	14.1005	14.0143	13.9417	13.8806	13.8290
16.375%	14.5630	14.4176	14.2962	14.1946	14.1095	14.0379	13.9776	13.9268
16.500%	14.6538	14.5096	14.3894	14.2890	14.2048	14.1342	14.0747	14.0247
16.625%	14.7447	14.6018	14.4829	14.3835	14.3004	14.2306	14.1720	14.1227
16.750%	14.8358	14.6942	14.5764	14.4782	14.3960	14.3272	14.2694	14.2208
16.875%	14.9270	14.7868	14.6702	14.5730	14.4919	14.4239	14.3669	14.3191

MONTHLY PAYMENT TO AMORTIZE A LOAN OF $1,000

Term of Loan

Interest Rate	25 Years	26 Years	27 Years	28 Years	29 Years	30 Years	35 Years	40 Years
12.000%	10.5322	10.4695	10.4145	10.3661	10.3236	10.2861	10.1555	10.0850
12.125%	10.6247	10.5629	10.5087	10.4611	10.4192	10.3824	10.2545	10.1859
12.250%	10.7174	10.6565	10.6030	10.5562	10.5151	10.4790	10.3537	10.2869
12.375%	10.8104	10.7503	10.6977	10.6516	10.6112	10.5757	10.4531	10.3880
12.500%	10.9035	10.8443	10.7925	10.7471	10.7074	10.6726	10.5525	10.4892
12.625%	10.9969	10.9385	10.8875	10.8429	10.8039	10.7697	10.6522	10.5905
12.750%	11.0905	11.0329	10.9827	10.9388	10.9005	10.8669	10.7520	10.6920
12.875%	11.1843	11.1276	11.0781	11.0350	10.9973	10.9644	10.8519	10.7935
13.000%	11.2784	11.2224	11.1738	11.1313	11.0943	11.0620	10.9519	10.8951
13.125%	11.3726	11.3175	11.2696	11.2279	11.1915	11.1598	11.0521	10.9969
13.250%	11.4670	11.4127	11.3656	11.3246	11.2888	11.2577	11.1524	11.0987
13.375%	11.5616	11.5082	11.4618	11.4214	11.3864	11.3558	11.2529	11.2006
13.500%	11.6564	11.6038	11.5581	11.5185	11.4841	11.4541	11.3534	11.3026
13.625%	11.7515	11.6996	11.6547	11.6157	11.5819	11.5525	11.4541	11.4047
13.750%	11.8467	11.7956	11.7514	11.7131	11.6799	11.6511	11.5549	11.5069
13.875%	11.9420	11.8917	11.8483	11.8107	11.7781	11.7498	11.6557	11.6091
14.000%	12.0376	11.9881	11.9453	11.9084	11.8764	11.8487	11.7567	11.7114
14.125%	12.1334	12.0846	12.0425	12.0062	11.9749	11.9477	11.8578	11.8138
14.250%	12.2293	12.1813	12.1399	12.1043	12.0735	12.0469	11.9590	11.9162
14.375%	12.3254	12.2781	12.2375	12.2024	12.1722	12.1461	12.0603	12.0187
14.500%	12.4216	12.3751	12.3351	12.3007	12.2711	12.2456	12.1617	12.1213
14.625%	12.5181	12.4723	12.4330	12.3992	12.3701	12.3451	12.2632	12.2240
14.750%	12.6146	12.5696	12.5310	12.4978	12.4693	12.4448	12.3647	12.3267
14.875%	12.7114	12.6671	12.6291	12.5965	12.5686	12.5445	12.4664	12.4294
15.000%	12.8083	12.7647	12.7274	12.6954	12.6680	12.6444	12.5681	12.5322
15.125%	12.9054	12.8625	12.8258	12.7944	12.7675	12.7445	12.6699	12.6351
15.250%	13.0026	12.9604	12.9243	12.8935	12.8672	12.8446	12.7718	12.7380
15.375%	13.0999	13.0584	13.0230	12.9928	12.9669	12.9448	12.8738	12.8410
15.500%	13.1975	13.1566	13.1218	13.0922	13.0668	13.0452	12.9758	12.9440
15.625%	13.2951	13.2550	13.2208	13.1916	13.1668	13.1456	13.0780	13.0471
15.750%	13.3929	13.3534	13.3198	13.2913	13.2669	13.2462	13.1801	13.1502
15.875%	13.4908	13.4520	13.4190	13.3910	13.3671	13.3468	13.2824	13.2533
16.000%	13.5889	13.5507	13.5183	13.4908	13.4674	13.4476	13.3847	13.3565
16.125%	13.6871	13.6496	13.6178	13.5908	13.5679	13.5484	13.4871	13.4597
16.250%	13.7854	13.7485	13.7173	13.6908	13.6684	13.6493	13.5895	13.5630
16.375%	13.8839	13.8476	13.8169	13.7910	13.7690	13.7504	13.6920	13.6663
16.500%	13.9824	13.9468	13.9167	13.8912	13.8697	13.8515	13.7945	13.7696
16.625%	14.0811	14.0461	14.0166	13.9916	13.9705	13.9527	13.8971	13.8730
16.750%	14.1800	14.1456	14.1165	14.0921	14.0714	14.0540	13.9998	13.9764
16.875%	14.2789	14.2451	14.2166	14.1926	14.1724	14.1553	14.1025	14.0798

MONTHLY PAYMENT TO AMORTIZE A LOAN OF $1,000

Term of Loan

Interest Rate	1 Year	2 Years	3 Years	4 Years	5 Years	6 Years	7 Years	8 Years
17.000%	91.2048	49.4423	35.6527	28.8550	24.8526	22.2461	20.4358	19.1215
17.125%	91.2641	49.5023	35.7150	28.9198	24.9198	22.3159	20.5081	19.1962
17.250%	91.3234	49.5625	35.7773	28.9845	24.9872	22.3859	20.5805	19.2710
17.375%	91.3828	49.6226	35.8396	29.0494	25.0547	22.4559	20.6531	19.3461
17.500%	91.4422	49.6828	35.9021	29.1144	25.1222	22.5260	20.7258	19.4212
17.625%	91.5016	49.7431	35.9646	29.1794	25.1899	22.5963	20.7986	19.4965
17.750%	91.5611	49.8034	36.0271	29.2445	25.2576	22.6667	20.8716	19.5719
17.875%	91.6205	49.8637	36.0897	29.3097	25.3255	22.7372	20.9446	19.6475
18.000%	91.6800	49.9241	36.1524	29.3750	25.3934	22.8078	21.0178	19.7232
18.125%	91.7395	49.9845	36.2151	29.4404	25.4615	22.8785	21.0912	19.7991
18.250%	91.7990	50.0450	36.2779	29.5058	25.5296	22.9493	21.1646	19.8751
18.375%	91.8586	50.1055	36.3408	29.5713	25.5979	23.0203	21.2382	19.9512
18.500%	91.9181	50.1660	36.4037	29.6369	25.6662	23.0914	21.3119	20.0274
18.625%	91.9777	50.2266	36.4667	29.7026	25.7346	23.1625	21.3858	20.1038
18.750%	92.0373	50.2872	36.5297	29.7684	25.8032	23.2338	21.4597	20.1804
18.875%	92.0969	50.3479	36.5929	29.8342	25.8718	23.3052	21.5338	20.2571
19.000%	92.1566	50.4086	36.6560	29.9001	25.9406	23.3767	21.6080	20.3339

MONTHLY PAYMENT TO AMORTIZE A LOAN OF $1,000

Term of Loan

Interest Rate	9 Years	10 Years	11 Years	12 Years	13 Years	14 Years	15 Years	16 Years
17.000%	18.1362	17.3798	16.7883	16.3192	15.9430	15.6384	15.3900	15.1863
17.125%	18.2132	17.4591	16.8697	16.4026	16.0282	15.7254	15.4787	15.2765
17.250%	18.2905	17.5385	16.9513	16.4862	16.1137	15.8126	15.5676	15.3669
17.375%	18.3678	17.6181	17.0330	16.5700	16.1993	15.9000	15.6566	15.4574
17.500%	18.4453	17.6979	17.1149	16.6539	16.2851	15.9876	15.7458	15.5481
17.625%	18.5230	17.7778	17.1970	16.7380	16.3711	16.0753	15.8351	15.6390
17.750%	18.6008	17.8579	17.2792	16.8222	16.4572	16.1632	15.9247	15.7300
17.875%	18.6788	17.9381	17.3616	16.9066	16.5435	16.2513	16.0144	15.8212
18.000%	18.7569	18.0185	17.4442	16.9912	16.6300	16.3395	16.1042	15.9126
18.125%	18.8351	18.0991	17.5269	17.0759	16.7166	16.4279	16.1942	16.0041
18.250%	18.9136	18.1798	17.6098	17.1608	16.8034	16.5165	16.2844	16.0957
18.375%	18.9921	18.2606	17.6928	17.2459	16.8904	16.6052	16.3747	16.1875
18.500%	19.0708	18.3417	17.7760	17.3311	16.9775	16.6941	16.4652	16.2795
18.625%	19.1497	18.4228	17.8593	17.4165	17.0648	16.7831	16.5559	16.3716
18.750%	19.2287	18.5041	17.9428	17.5021	17.1523	16.8723	16.6467	16.4639
18.875%	19.3078	18.5856	18.0265	17.5878	17.2399	16.9616	16.7376	16.5564
19.000%	19.3871	18.6672	18.1103	17.6736	17.3276	17.0511	16.8288	16.6489

MONTHLY PAYMENT TO AMORTIZE A LOAN OF $1,000

Term of Loan

Interest Rate	17 Years	18 Years	19 Years	20 Years	21 Years	22 Years	23 Years	24 Years
17.000%	15.0184	14.8795	14.7641	14.6680	14.5878	14.5208	14.4646	14.4175
17.125%	15.1100	14.9724	14.8581	14.7631	14.6839	14.6178	14.5624	14.5160
17.250%	15.2018	15.0654	14.9524	14.8584	14.7802	14.7149	14.6603	14.6147
17.375%	15.2937	15.1586	15.0467	14.9538	14.8766	14.8122	14.7584	14.7134
17.500%	15.3858	15.2519	15.1412	15.0494	14.9731	14.9095	14.8565	14.8123
17.625%	15.4780	15.3455	15.2359	15.1451	15.0698	15.0071	14.9548	14.9113
17.750%	15.5704	15.4391	15.3307	15.2410	15.1666	15.1047	15.0532	15.0104
17.875%	15.6630	15.5329	15.4257	15.3370	15.2635	15.2025	15.1518	15.1096
18.000%	15.7557	15.6269	15.5208	15.4331	15.3605	15.3004	15.2504	15.2089
18.125%	15.8486	15.7210	15.6160	15.5294	15.4577	15.3984	15.3492	15.3083
18.250%	15.9416	15.8153	15.7114	15.6258	15.5550	15.4965	15.4480	15.4078
18.375%	16.0348	15.9097	15.8069	15.7223	15.6525	15.5948	15.5470	15.5074
18.500%	16.1281	16.0042	15.9026	15.8190	15.7500	15.6931	15.6461	15.6071
18.625%	16.2216	16.0989	15.9984	15.9158	15.8477	15.7916	15.7452	15.7069
18.750%	16.3152	16.1938	16.0943	16.0127	15.9455	15.8902	15.8445	15.8068
18.875%	16.4090	16.2887	16.1904	16.1097	16.0434	15.9889	15.9439	15.9068
19.000%	16.5029	16.3838	16.2866	16.2068	16.1414	16.0876	16.0434	16.0069

MONTHLY PAYMENT TO AMORTIZE A LOAN OF $1,000

Term of Loan

Interest Rate	25 Years	26 Years	27 Years	28 Years	29 Years	30 Years	35 Years	40 Years
17.000%	14.3780	14.3447	14.3168	14.2933	14.2734	14.2568	14.2053	14.1832
17.125%	14.4771	14.4445	14.4171	14.3940	14.3746	14.3583	14.3081	14.2867
17.250%	14.5764	14.5443	14.5174	14.4948	14.4758	14.4599	14.4109	14.3902
17.375%	14.6758	14.6443	14.6179	14.5957	14.5771	14.5615	14.5138	14.4938
17.500%	14.7753	14.7443	14.7184	14.6967	14.6785	14.6633	14.6168	14.5973
17.625%	14.8749	14.8445	14.8191	14.7978	14.7800	14.7651	14.7197	14.7009
17.750%	14.9746	14.9447	14.9198	14.8989	14.8815	14.8669	14.8228	14.8045
17.875%	15.0744	15.0451	15.0206	15.0002	14.9831	14.9689	14.9258	14.9082
18.000%	15.1743	15.1455	15.1215	15.1015	15.0848	15.0709	15.0289	15.0118
18.125%	15.2743	15.2460	15.2225	15.2029	15.1865	15.1729	15.1321	15.1155
18.250%	15.3744	15.3466	15.3235	15.3043	15.2883	15.2750	15.2352	15.2192
18.375%	15.4746	15.4473	15.4247	15.4059	15.3902	15.3772	15.3384	15.3229
18.500%	15.5748	15.5481	15.5259	15.5075	15.4922	15.4794	15.4417	15.4266
18.625%	15.6752	15.6489	15.6272	15.6091	15.5942	15.5817	15.5449	15.5304
18.750%	15.7757	15.7499	15.7285	15.7109	15.6962	15.6841	15.6483	15.6342
18.875%	15.8762	15.8509	15.8300	15.8127	15.7983	15.7865	15.7516	15.7379
19.000%	15.9768	15.9520	15.9315	15.9145	15.9005	15.8889	15.8549	15.8417

APPENDIX

B

Remaining Principal Balance

If you arrange a balloon mortgage, monthly payments will be set on a long-term schedule. At some point during the life of the loan, though, the entire remaining balance will suddenly become due and payable.

How much will that final (balloon) payment be? In the early years of a loan, interest charges absorb most of the monthly payment, and little is left to reduce the principal. It is not unusual for the final payment to be almost as much as the original debt.

To calculate the amount:

1. Find the table with the interest rate on your mortgage.
2. Follow across the top line until you find the original term of the loan (the number of years used to calculate the monthly payment).
3. Go down the left-hand column until you find the number of years the loan will actually last (the age of the loan when you will make that balloon payment).
4. Find the spot where the two lines intersect.

   Example: On the chart for 10 percent loans, with an original term of 25 years, a ten-year balloon has a factor of .846. Almost 85 percent of the original loan is still due.

5. Multiply the original loan amount by the factor.
   Example: A loan of $74,500 × .846 (84.6%) = $63,027. This represents the remaining balance after ten years' payments have been made, and it represents the final balloon payment.

Remaining Principal Balance Factors

For Mortgages with an Interest Rate of 6.00% and an Original Term of:

Age of Loan in Years	5 Years	6 Years	7 Years	8 Years	9 Years	10 Years	11 Years	12 Years	15 Years	20 Years	25 Years	30 Years	35 Years	40 Years
1	0.823	0.857	0.881	0.900	0.914	0.925	0.934	0.941	0.958	0.973	0.982	0.988	0.991	0.994
2	0.635	0.706	0.756	0.793	0.822	0.845	0.864	0.879	0.913	0.945	0.963	0.975	0.982	0.987
3	0.436	0.545	0.622	0.680	0.724	0.760	0.789	0.813	0.865	0.915	0.943	0.961	0.972	0.980
4	0.225	0.374	0.480	0.560	0.621	0.670	0.710	0.743	0.814	0.883	0.922	0.946	0.962	0.973
5	0.000	0.193	0.330	0.432	0.511	0.574	0.626	0.668	0.760	0.849	0.899	0.931	0.951	0.965
6		0.000	0.170	0.297	0.395	0.473	0.536	0.589	0.703	0.813	0.875	0.914	0.939	0.957
7			0.000	0.153	0.271	0.365	0.441	0.505	0.642	0.775	0.850	0.896	0.927	0.948
8				0.000	0.139	0.250	0.341	0.416	0.578	0.734	0.823	0.878	0.914	0.938
9					0.000	0.129	0.234	0.321	0.509	0.691	0.794	0.858	0.900	0.928
10						0.000	0.120	0.220	0.436	0.645	0.764	0.837	0.885	0.918
11							0.000	0.113	0.359	0.597	0.731	0.815	0.869	0.906
12								0.000	0.277	0.545	0.697	0.791	0.852	0.894
15									0.000	0.371	0.580	0.710	0.796	0.854
20										0.000	0.333	0.540	0.676	0.768
25											0.000	0.310	0.514	0.652
30												0.000	0.295	0.496
35													0.000	0.285
40														0.000

For Mortgages with an Interest Rate of 6.25% and an Original Term of:

Age of Loan in Years	5 Years	6 Years	7 Years	8 Years	9 Years	10 Years	11 Years	12 Years	15 Years	20 Years	25 Years	30 Years	35 Years	40 Years
1	0.824	0.858	0.882	0.901	0.915	0.926	0.935	0.942	0.958	0.974	0.983	0.988	0.992	0.994
2	0.637	0.707	0.757	0.795	0.824	0.847	0.865	0.881	0.914	0.946	0.965	0.976	0.983	0.988
3	0.438	0.547	0.624	0.682	0.727	0.762	0.791	0.815	0.867	0.917	0.945	0.963	0.974	0.981
4	0.226	0.376	0.482	0.562	0.624	0.673	0.713	0.746	0.817	0.886	0.925	0.948	0.964	0.974
5	0.000	0.194	0.331	0.434	0.514	0.577	0.629	0.671	0.764	0.852	0.903	0.933	0.953	0.967
6		0.000	0.171	0.299	0.397	0.476	0.540	0.592	0.707	0.817	0.879	0.917	0.942	0.959
7			0.000	0.154	0.273	0.368	0.445	0.508	0.646	0.779	0.854	0.900	0.930	0.951
8				0.000	0.141	0.253	0.344	0.419	0.582	0.739	0.828	0.882	0.918	0.942
9					0.000	0.130	0.236	0.324	0.514	0.696	0.799	0.863	0.904	0.932
10						0.000	0.122	0.223	0.441	0.651	0.769	0.842	0.890	0.922
11							0.000	0.115	0.363	0.603	0.737	0.821	0.875	0.911
12								0.000	0.281	0.551	0.703	0.797	0.858	0.900
15									0.000	0.376	0.588	0.718	0.803	0.861
20										0.000	0.339	0.548	0.685	0.777
25											0.000	0.317	0.523	0.662
30												0.000	0.302	0.506
35													0.000	0.292
40														0.000

Remaining Principal Balance Factors

For Mortgages with an Interest Rate of 6.50% and an Original Term of:

Age of Loan in Years	5 Years	6 Years	7 Years	8 Years	9 Years	10 Years	11 Years	12 Years	15 Years	20 Years	25 Years	30 Years	35 Years	40 Years
1	0.825	0.859	0.883	0.901	0.915	0.927	0.936	0.943	0.959	0.975	0.983	0.989	0.992	0.995
2	0.638	0.709	0.759	0.796	0.825	0.848	0.867	0.882	0.916	0.948	0.966	0.977	0.984	0.989
3	0.439	0.548	0.626	0.684	0.729	0.765	0.794	0.818	0.869	0.919	0.947	0.964	0.975	0.983
4	0.227	0.377	0.484	0.564	0.626	0.675	0.715	0.748	0.820	0.889	0.927	0.951	0.966	0.976
5	0.000	0.195	0.333	0.437	0.517	0.580	0.632	0.675	0.767	0.856	0.906	0.936	0.956	0.969
6		0.000	0.172	0.301	0.400	0.479	0.543	0.596	0.711	0.821	0.883	0.921	0.945	0.962
7			0.000	0.155	0.275	0.370	0.448	0.512	0.651	0.784	0.858	0.904	0.934	0.954
8				0.000	0.142	0.255	0.347	0.422	0.587	0.744	0.832	0.887	0.922	0.945
9					0.000	0.132	0.238	0.327	0.518	0.702	0.805	0.868	0.909	0.936
10						0.000	0.123	0.225	0.445	0.657	0.775	0.848	0.895	0.926
11							0.000	0.116	0.367	0.608	0.744	0.826	0.880	0.916
12								0.000	0.284	0.557	0.710	0.804	0.864	0.905
15									0.000	0.381	0.595	0.726	0.810	0.867
20										0.000	0.345	0.557	0.694	0.785
25											0.000	0.323	0.532	0.672
30												0.000	0.309	0.516
35													0.000	0.299
40														0.000

For Mortgages with an Interest Rate of 6.75% and an Original Term of:

Age of Loan in Years	5 Years	6 Years	7 Years	8 Years	9 Years	10 Years	11 Years	12 Years	15 Years	20 Years	25 Years	30 Years	35 Years	40 Years
1	0.826	0.860	0.884	0.902	0.916	0.927	0.937	0.944	0.960	0.976	0.984	0.989	0.993	0.995
2	0.640	0.710	0.761	0.798	0.827	0.850	0.869	0.884	0.917	0.949	0.967	0.978	0.985	0.990
3	0.441	0.550	0.628	0.686	0.731	0.767	0.796	0.820	0.872	0.921	0.949	0.966	0.977	0.984
4	0.228	0.379	0.487	0.567	0.629	0.678	0.718	0.751	0.823	0.891	0.929	0.953	0.968	0.978
5	0.000	0.196	0.335	0.439	0.520	0.583	0.635	0.678	0.771	0.859	0.909	0.939	0.958	0.971
6		0.000	0.173	0.303	0.402	0.482	0.546	0.600	0.715	0.825	0.886	0.924	0.948	0.964
7			0.000	0.156	0.277	0.373	0.451	0.516	0.655	0.788	0.863	0.908	0.937	0.956
8				0.000	0.143	0.257	0.350	0.426	0.591	0.749	0.837	0.891	0.925	0.948
9					0.000	0.133	0.241	0.330	0.523	0.707	0.810	0.873	0.913	0.940
10						0.000	0.124	0.227	0.450	0.662	0.781	0.853	0.899	0.930
11							0.000	0.117	0.371	0.614	0.750	0.832	0.885	0.920
12								0.000	0.288	0.563	0.716	0.810	0.870	0.910
15									0.000	0.386	0.602	0.733	0.817	0.873
20										0.000	0.351	0.565	0.702	0.794
25											0.000	0.330	0.541	0.682
30												0.000	0.316	0.525
35													0.000	0.307
40														0.000

Remaining Principal Balance Factors

For Mortgages with an Interest Rate of 7.00% and an Original Term Of:

Age of Loan in Years	5 Years	6 Years	7 Years	8 Years	9 Years	10 Years	11 Years	12 Years	15 Years	20 Years	25 Years	30 Years	35 Years	40 Years
1	0.827	0.861	0.885	0.903	0.917	0.928	0.937	0.945	0.961	0.976	0.985	0.990	0.993	0.995
2	0.641	0.712	0.762	0.800	0.829	0.852	0.870	0.886	0.919	0.951	0.968	0.979	0.986	0.990
3	0.442	0.552	0.630	0.689	0.734	0.769	0.798	0.822	0.874	0.923	0.951	0.967	0.978	0.985
4	0.229	0.381	0.489	0.569	0.632	0.681	0.721	0.754	0.826	0.894	0.932	0.955	0.969	0.979
5	0.000	0.197	0.337	0.442	0.522	0.586	0.638	0.681	0.774	0.863	0.912	0.941	0.960	0.973
6		0.000	0.174	0.305	0.405	0.485	0.550	0.603	0.719	0.829	0.890	0.927	0.950	0.966
7			0.000	0.158	0.279	0.376	0.455	0.519	0.659	0.793	0.867	0.911	0.940	0.959
8				0.000	0.145	0.259	0.352	0.429	0.596	0.754	0.842	0.895	0.929	0.951
9					0.000	0.134	0.243	0.333	0.527	0.712	0.815	0.877	0.917	0.943
10						0.000	0.126	0.230	0.454	0.668	0.786	0.858	0.904	0.934
11							0.000	0.119	0.375	0.620	0.756	0.838	0.890	0.925
12								0.000	0.291	0.569	0.723	0.816	0.875	0.914
15									0.000	0.392	0.609	0.740	0.824	0.879
20										0.000	0.357	0.573	0.711	0.802
25											0.000	0.336	0.550	0.691
30												0.000	0.323	0.535
35													0.000	0.314
40														0.000

For Mortgages with an Interest Rate of 7.25% and an Original Term of:

Age of Loan in Years	5 Years	6 Years	7 Years	8 Years	9 Years	10 Years	11 Years	12 Years	15 Years	20 Years	25 Years	30 Years	35 Years	40 Years
1	0.828	0.862	0.886	0.904	0.918	0:929	0.938	0.946	0.962	0.977	0.985	0.990	0.994	0.996
2	0.643	0.714	0.764	0.801	0.830	0.853	0.872	0.887	0.921	0.952	0.969	0.980	0.987	0.991
3	0.444	0.554	0.632	0.691	0.736	0.772	0.801	0.825	0.876	0.925	0.952	0.969	0.979	0.986
4	0.230	0.383	0.491	0.572	0.634	0.684	0.724	0.757	0.829	0.897	0.934	0.957	0.971	0.980
5	0.000	0.198	0.339	0.444	0.525	0.589	0.642	0.685	0.778	0.866	0.915	0.944	0.962	0.974
6		0.000	0.176	0.307	0.408	0.488	0.553	0.607	0.723	0.833	0.893	0.930	0.953	0.968
7			0.000	0.159	0.281	0.379	0.458	0.523	0.663	0.797	0.871	0.915	0.943	0.961
8				0.000	0.146	0.262	0.355	0.433	0.600	0.759	0.846	0.899	0.932	0.954
9					0.000	0.136	0.245	0.336	0.532	0.718	0.820	0.882	0.921	0.946
10						0.000	0.127	0.232	0.458	0.673	0.792	0.863	0.908	0.938
11							0.000	0.120	0.379	0.626	0.761	0.843	0.895	0.929
12								0.000	0.295	0.574	0.729	0.822	0.880	0.919
15									0.000	0.397	0.616	0.747	0.831	0.885
20										0.000	0.363	0.581	0.719	0.809
25											0.000	0.342	0.559	0.701
30												0.000	0.330	0.545
35													0.000	0.321
40														0.000

Remaining Principal Balance Factors

For Mortgages with an Interest Rate of 7.50% and an Original Term of:

Age of Loan in Years	5 Years	6 Years	7 Years	8 Years	9 Years	10 Years	11 Years	12 Years	15 Years	20 Years	25 Years	30 Years	35 Years	40 Years
1	0.829	0.863	0.887	0.905	0.919	0.930	0.939	0.947	0.962	0.978	0.986	0.991	0.994	0.996
2	0.644	0.715	0.765	0.803	0.832	0.855	0.874	0.889	0.922	0.953	0.971	0.981	0.987	0.991
3	0.445	0.556	0.634	0.693	0.738	0.774	0.803	0.827	0.878	0.927	0.954	0.970	0.980	0.987
4	0.231	0.384	0.493	0.574	0.637	0.687	0.727	0.760	0.832	0.899	0.936	0.959	0.973	0.982
5	0.000	0.199	0.341	0.446	0.528	0.592	0.645	0.688	0.781	0.869	0.917	0.946	0.964	0.976
6		0.000	0.177	0.309	0.410	0.491	0.556	0.610	0.726	0.836	0.897	0.933	0.955	0.970
7			0.000	0.160	0.284	0.382	0.461	0.527	0.668	0.801	0.875	0.918	0.946	0.964
8				0.000	0.147	0.264	0.358	0.436	0.604	0.763	0.851	0.903	0.935	0.957
9					0.000	0.137	0.248	0.339	0.536	0.723	0.825	0.886	0.924	0.949
10						0.000	0.128	0.234	0.463	0.679	0.797	0.868	0.912	0.941
11							0.000	0.122	0.383	0.631	0.767	0.848	0.899	0.932
12								0.000	0.298	0.580	0.735	0.827	0.886	0.923
15									0.000	0.402	0.623	0.754	0.837	0.890
20										0.000	0.369	0.589	0.727	0.817
25											0.000	0.349	0.568	0.710
30												0.000	0.336	0.554
35													0.000	0.328
40														0.000

For Mortgages with an Interest Rate of 7.75% and an Original Term of:

Age of Loan in Years	5 Years	6 Years	7 Years	8 Years	9 Years	10 Years	11 Years	12 Years	15 Years	20 Years	25 Years	30 Years	35 Years	40 Years
1	0.830	0.864	0.888	0.906	0.920	0.931	0.940	0.947	0.963	0.978	0.986	0.991	0.994	0.996
2	0.646	0.717	0.767	0.805	0.834	0.857	0.875	0.891	0.924	0.955	0.972	0.982	0.988	0.992
3	0.447	0.558	0.636	0.695	0.740	0.776	0.805	0.829	0.881	0.929	0.956	0.971	0.981	0.988
4	0.232	0.386	0.495	0.577	0.639	0.689	0.730	0.763	0.834	0.902	0.939	0.960	0.974	0.983
5	0.000	0.200	0.343	0.449	0.531	0.595	0.648	0.691	0.784	0.872	0.920	0.948	0.966	0.978
6		0.000	0.178	0.311	0.413	0.494	0.560	0.614	0.730	0.840	0.900	0.936	0.958	0.972
7			0.000	0.161	0.286	0.384	0.464	0.530	0.672	0.806	0.878	0.922	0.949	0.966
8				0.000	0.148	0.266	0.361	0.440	0.609	0.768	0.855	0.907	0.939	0.959
9					0.000	0.138	0.250	0.342	0.541	0.728	0.830	0.890	0.928	0.952
10						0.000	0.130	0.237	0.467	0.684	0.802	0.873	0.916	0.944
11							0.000	0.123	0.387	0.637	0.773	0.854	0.904	0.936
12								0.000	0.301	0.586	0.741	0.833	0.890	0.927
15									0.000	0.407	0.629	0.761	0.843	0.896
20										0.000	0.375	0.597	0.735	0.824
25											0.000	0.355	0.577	0.719
30												0.000	0.343	0.564
35													0.000	0.336
40														0.000

Remaining Principal Balance Factors

For Mortgages with an Interest Rate of 8.00% and an Original Term of:

Age of Loan in Years	5 Years	6 Years	7 Years	8 Years	9 Years	10 Years	11 Years	12 Years	15 Years	20 Years	25 Years	30 Years	35 Years	40 Years
1	0.831	0.865	0.889	0.907	0.921	0.932	0.941	0.948	0.964	0.979	0.987	0.992	0.995	0.996
2	0.647	0.718	0.769	0.806	0.835	0.858	0.877	0.892	0.925	0.956	0.973	0.983	0.989	0.993
3	0.448	0.560	0.638	0.697	0.743	0.778	0.808	0.831	0.883	0.931	0.957	0.973	0.982	0.988
4	0.233	0.388	0.497	0.579	0.642	0.692	0.732	0.766	0.837	0.904	0.941	0.962	0.975	0.984
5	0.000	0.202	0.345	0.451	0.533	0.598	0.651	0.694	0.788	0.875	0.923	0.951	0.968	0.979
6		0.000	0.179	0.313	0.415	0.497	0.563	0.617	0.734	0.844	0.903	0.938	0.960	0.974
7			0.000	0.163	0.288	0.387	0.468	0.534	0.676	0.810	0.882	0.925	0.951	0.968
8				0.000	0.150	0.268	0.364	0.443	0.613	0.773	0.859	0.910	0.942	0.962
9					0.000	0.139	0.252	0.345	0.545	0.733	0.834	0.894	0.931	0.955
10						0.000	0.131	0.239	0.471	0.689	0.808	0.877	0.920	0.948
11							0.000	0.124	0.391	0.642	0.779	0.859	0.908	0.940
12								0.000	0.305	0.592	0.747	0.839	0.895	0.931
15									0.000	0.413	0.636	0.768	0.849	0.901
20										0.000	0.381	0.605	0.743	0.831
25											0.000	0.362	0.585	0.728
30												0.000	0.350	0.573
35													0.000	0.343
40														0.000

For Mortgages with an Interest Rate of 8.25% and an Original Term of:

Age of Loan in Years	5 Years	6 Years	7 Years	8 Years	9 Years	10 Years	11 Years	12 Years	15 Years	20 Years	25 Years	30 Years	35 Years	40 Years
1	0.831	0.866	0.890	0.908	0.922	0.933	0.942	0.949	0.965	0.979	0.987	0.992	0.995	0.997
2	0.648	0.720	0.770	0.808	0.837	0.860	0.878	0.894	0.927	0.957	0.974	0.983	0.989	0.993
3	0.450	0.561	0.640	0.699	0.745	0.781	0.810	0.834	0.885	0.933	0.959	0.974	0.983	0.989
4	0.234	0.389	0.500	0.581	0.645	0.695	0.735	0.769	0.840	0.907	0.943	0.964	0.977	0.985
5	0.000	0.203	0.347	0.454	0.536	0.601	0.654	0.698	0.791	0.878	0.925	0.953	0.970	0.980
6		0.000	0.180	0.315	0.418	0.500	0.566	0.621	0.738	0.847	0.906	0.941	0.962	0.975
7			0.000	0.164	0.290	0.390	0.471	0.537	0.680	0.814	0.886	0.928	0.954	0.970
8				0.000	0.151	0.271	0.367	0.447	0.617	0.777	0.863	0.914	0.945	0.964
9					0.000	0.141	0.255	0.349	0.549	0.738	0.839	0.898	0.935	0.958
10						0.000	0.133	0.242	0.476	0.695	0.813	0.882	0.924	0.951
11							0.000	0.126	0.395	0.648	0.784	0.864	0.912	0.943
12								0.000	0.308	0.597	0.753	0.844	0.900	0.935
15									0.000	0.418	0.643	0.774	0.855	0.906
20										0.000	0.387	0.613	0.751	0.838
25											0.000	0.368	0.594	0.736
30												0.000	0.357	0.582
35													0.000	0.250
40														0.000

Remaining Principal Balance Factors

For Mortgages with an Interest Rate of 8.50% and an Original Term of:

Age of Loan in Years	5 Years	6 Years	7 Years	8 Years	9 Years	10 Years	11 Years	12 Years	15 Years	20 Years	25 Years	30 Years	35 Years	40 Years
1	0.832	0.867	0.891	0.909	0.923	0.934	0.943	0.950	0.966	0.980	0.988	0.992	0.995	0.997
2	0.650	0.721	0.772	0.810	0.839	0.861	0.880	0.895	0.928	0.958	0.975	0.984	0.990	0.994
3	0.451	0.563	0.642	0.701	0.747	0.783	0.812	0.836	0.887	0.935	0.960	0.975	0.984	0.990
4	0.235	0.391	0.502	0.584	0.647	0.697	0.738	0.771	0.843	0.909	0.945	0.966	0.978	0.986
5	0.000	0.204	0.348	0.456	0.539	0.604	0.657	0.701	0.794	0.881	0.928	0.955	0.971	0.982
6		0.000	0.182	0.317	0.421	0.503	0.570	0.624	0.742	0.851	0.909	0.943	0.964	0.977
7			0.000	0.165	0.292	0.393	0.474	0.541	0.684	0.818	0.889	0.931	0.956	0.972
8				0.000	0.152	0.273	0.370	0.450	0.622	0.782	0.867	0.917	0.947	0.966
9					0.000	0.142	0.257	0.352	0.554	0.743	0.844	0.902	0.938	0.960
10						0.000	0.134	0.244	0.480	0.700	0.818	0.886	0.928	0.953
11							0.000	0.127	0.400	0.654	0.790	0.868	0.916	0.946
12								0.000	0.312	0.603	0.759	0.849	0.904	0.938
15									0.000	0.423	0.649	0.781	0.861	0.910
20										0.000	0.392	0.620	0.758	0.845
25											0.000	0.375	0.602	0.744
30												0.000	0.364	0.591
35													0.000	0.357
40														0.000

For Mortgages with an Interest Rate of 8.75% and an Original Term of:

Age of Loan in Years	5 Years	6 Years	7 Years	8 Years	9 Years	10 Years	11 Years	12 Years	15 Years	20 Years	25 Years	30 Years	35 Years	40 Years
1	0.833	0.867	0.892	0.910	0.924	0.935	0.943	0.951	0.966	0.981	0.988	0.993	0.995	0.997
2	0.651	0.723	0.773	0.811	0.840	0.863	0.882	0.897	0.929	0.960	0.976	0.985	0.991	0.994
3	0.453	0.565	0.645	0.704	0.749	0.785	0.814	0.838	0.889	0.937	0.962	0.976	0.985	0.991
4	0.236	0.393	0.504	0.586	0.650	0.700	0.741	0.774	0.845	0.912	0.947	0.967	0.979	0.987
5	0.000	0.205	0.350	0.458	0.541	0.607	0.660	0.704	0.797	0.884	0.930	0.957	0.973	0.983
6		0.000	0.183	0.319	0.423	0.506	0.573	0.628	0.745	0.854	0.912	0.946	0.966	0.978
7			0.000	0.166	0.294	0.396	0.477	0.545	0.688	0.822	0.893	0.934	0.958	0.973
8				0.000	0.154	0.275	0.373	0.454	0.626	0.786	0.871	0.920	0.950	0.968
9					0.000	0.144	0.259	0.355	0.558	0.747	0.848	0.906	0.941	0.962
10						0.000	0.135	0.247	0.484	0.705	0.823	0.890	0.931	0.956
11							0.000	0.129	0.404	0.659	0.795	0.873	0.920	0.949
12								0.000	0.315	0.609	0.765	0.854	0.908	0.942
15									0.000	0.428	0.656	0.787	0.866	0.915
20										0.000	0.398	0.628	0.766	0.851
25											0.000	0.381	0.611	0.753
30												0.000	0.371	0.600
35													0.000	0.364
40														0.000

Remaining Principal Balance Factors

For Mortgages with an Interest Rate of 9.00% and an Original Term of:

Age of Loan in Years	5 Years	6 Years	7 Years	8 Years	9 Years	10 Years	11 Years	12 Years	15 Years	20 Years	25 Years	30 Years	35 Years	40 Years
1	0.834	0.868	0.893	0.911	0.924	0.935	0.944	0.951	0.967	0.981	0.989	0.993	0.996	0.997
2	0.653	0.724	0.775	0.813	0.842	0.865	0.883	0.898	0.931	0.961	0.977	0.986	0.991	0.994
3	0.454	0.567	0.647	0.706	0.751	0.787	0.816	0.840	0.891	0.938	0.963	0.978	0.986	0.991
4	0.237	0.395	0.506	0.589	0.652	0.703	0.743	0.777	0.848	0.914	0.949	0.969	0.980	0.988
5	0.000	0.206	0.352	0.461	0.544	0.610	0.664	0.707	0.801	0.887	0.933	0.959	0.974	0.984
6		0.000	0.184	0.321	0.426	0.509	0.576	0.631	0.749	0.858	0.915	0.948	0.968	0.980
7			0.000	0.168	0.296	0.398	0.481	0.548	0.692	0.826	0.896	0.936	0.960	0.975
8				0.000	0.155	0.277	0.376	0.457	0.630	0.791	0.875	0.924	0.952	0.970
9					0.000	0.145	0.262	0.358	0.563	0.752	0.852	0.910	0.944	0.965
10						0.000	0.137	0.249	0.489	0.710	0.827	0.894	0.934	0.959
11							0.000	0.130	0.408	0.664	0.800	0.878	0.924	0.952
12								0.000	0.319	0.614	0.770	0.859	0.912	0.945
15									0.000	0.433	0.662	0.793	0.871	0.919
20										0.000	0.404	0.635	0.773	0.857
25											0.000	0.388	0.619	0.761
30												0.000	0.378	0.609
35													0.000	0.372
40														0.000

For Mortgages with an Interest Rate of 9.25% and an Original Term of:

Age of Loan in Years	5 Years	6 Years	7 Years	8 Years	9 Years	10 Years	11 Years	12 Years	15 Years	20 Years	25 Years	30 Years	35 Years	40 Years
1	0.835	0.869	0.893	0.911	0.925	0.936	0.945	0.952	0.968	0.982	0.989	0.994	0.996	0.998
2	0.654	0.726	0.777	0.814	0.843	0.866	0.885	0.900	0.932	0.962	0.978	0.986	0.992	0.995
3	0.456	0.569	0.649	0.708	0.753	0.790	0.819	0.842	0.893	0.940	0.965	0.979	0.987	0.992
4	0.238	0.396	0.508	0.591	0.655	0.705	0.746	0.780	0.851	0.916	0.951	0.970	0.982	0.989
5	0.000	0.207	0.354	0.463	0.547	0.613	0.667	0.710	0.804	0.890	0.935	0.961	0.976	0.985
6		0.000	0.185	0.323	0.428	0.512	0.579	0.635	0.753	0.861	0.918	0.950	0.969	0.981
7			0.000	0.169	0.299	0.401	0.484	0.552	0.696	0.830	0.899	0.939	0.962	0.977
8				0.000	0.156	0.280	0.379	0.461	0.635	0.795	0.879	0.927	0.955	0.972
9					0.000	0.146	0.264	0.361	0.567	0.757	0.857	0.913	0.947	0.967
10						0.000	0.138	0.252	0.493	0.715	0.832	0.898	0.937	0.961
11							0.000	0.132	0.412	0.670	0.805	0.882	0.927	0.955
12								0.000	0.322	0.620	0.776	0.864	0.916	0.948
15									0.000	0.439	0.669	0.799	0.876	0.923
20										0.000	0.410	0.643	0.780	0.863
25											0.000	0.394	0.627	0.768
30												0.000	0.384	0.618
35													0.000	0.379
40														0.000

Remaining Principal Balance Factors

For Mortgages with an Interest Rate of 9.50% and an Original Term of:

Age of Loan in Years	5 Years	6 Years	7 Years	8 Years	9 Years	10 Years	11 Years	12 Years	15 Years	20 Years	25 Years	30 Years	35 Years	40 Years
1	0.836	0.870	0.894	0.912	0.926	0.937	0.946	0.953	0.968	0.982	0.990	0.994	0.996	0.998
2	0.656	0.727	0.778	0.816	0.845	0.868	0.886	0.901	0.934	0.963	0.978	0.987	0.992	0.995
3	0.457	0.570	0.651	0.710	0.756	0.792	0.821	0.845	0.895	0.942	0.966	0.980	0.988	0.992
4	0.240	0.398	0.510	0.594	0.658	0.708	0.749	0.782	0.853	0.918	0.952	0.971	0.983	0.989
5	0.000	0.208	0.356	0.465	0.550	0.616	0.670	0.714	0.807	0.893	0.937	0.962	0.977	0.986
6		0.000	0.186	0.325	0.431	0.515	0.583	0.638	0.756	0.864	0.921	0.953	0.971	0.982
7			0.000	0.170	0.301	0.404	0.487	0.555	0.700	0.833	0.903	0.942	0.964	0.978
8				0.000	0.157	0.282	0.382	0.464	0.639	0.799	0.883	0.930	0.957	0.974
9					0.000	0.148	0.267	0.364	0.571	0.762	0.861	0.917	0.949	0.969
10						0.000	0.140	0.254	0.497	0.720	0.837	0.902	0.940	0.963
11							0.000	0.133	0.416	0.675	0.810	0.886	0.931	0.957
12								0.000	0.326	0.625	0.781	0.869	0.920	0.951
15									0.000	0.444	0.675	0.805	0.881	0.927
20										0.000	0.416	0.650	0.787	0.869
25											0.000	0.400	0.635	0.776
30												0.000	0.391	0.626
35													0.000	0.386
40														0.000

For Mortgages with an Interest Rate of 9.75% and an Original Term of:

Age of Loan in Years	5 Years	6 Years	7 Years	8 Years	9 Years	10 Years	11 Years	12 Years	15 Years	20 Years	25 Years	30 Years	35 Years	40 Years
1	0.837	0.871	0.895	0.913	0.927	0.938	0.947	0.954	0.969	0.983	0.990	0.994	0.996	0.998
2	0.657	0.729	0.780	0.818	0.846	0.869	0.888	0.903	0.935	0.964	0.979	0.988	0.993	0.995
3	0.459	0.572	0.653	0.712	0.758	0.794	0.823	0.847	0.897	0.943	0.967	0.981	0.988	0.993
4	0.241	0.400	0.512	0.596	0.660	0.711	0.751	0.785	0.856	0.921	0.954	0.973	0.984	0.990
5	0.000	0.210	0.358	0.468	0.552	0.619	0.673	0.717	0.810	0.895	0.940	0.964	0.978	0.987
6		0.000	0.188	0.327	0.434	0.518	0.586	0.642	0.760	0.868	0.923	0.955	0.973	0.983
7			0.000	0.171	0.303	0.407	0.490	0.559	0.704	0.837	0.906	0.944	0.966	0.980
8				0.000	0.159	0.284	0.385	0.468	0.643	0.803	0.886	0.933	0.959	0.975
9					0.000	0.149	0.269	0.367	0.576	0.766	0.865	0.920	0.952	0.971
10						0.000	0.141	0.257	0.501	0.725	0.841	0.906	0.943	0.966
11							0.000	0.134	0.420	0.680	0.815	0.890	0.934	0.960
12								0.000	0.330	0.631	0.786	0.873	0.924	0.954
15									0.000	0.449	0.681	0.811	0.886	0.931
20										0.000	0.422	0.657	0.793	0.875
25											0.000	0.407	0.643	0.783
30												0.000	0.398	0.634
35													0.000	0.393
40														0.000

Remaining Principal Balance Factors

For Mortgages with an Interest Rate of 10.00% and an Original Term of:

Age of Loan in Years	5 Years	6 Years	7 Years	8 Years	9 Years	10 Years	11 Years	12 Years	15 Years	20 Years	25 Years	30 Years	35 Years	40 Years
1	0.838	0.872	0.896	0.914	0.928	0.939	0.947	0.955	0.970	0.983	0.991	0.994	0.997	0.998
2	0.658	0.730	0.781	0.819	0.848	0.871	0.889	0.904	0.936	0.965	0.980	0.988	0.993	0.996
3	0.460	0.574	0.655	0.714	0.760	0.796	0.825	0.849	0.899	0.945	0.969	0.982	0.989	0.993
4	0.242	0.401	0.514	0.598	0.663	0.713	0.754	0.788	0.858	0.923	0.956	0.974	0.985	0.991
5	0.000	0.211	0.360	0.470	0.555	0.622	0.676	0.720	0.813	0.898	0.942	0.966	0.980	0.988
6		0.000	0.189	0.329	0.436	0.521	0.589	0.645	0.763	0.871	0.926	0.957	0.974	0.984
7			0.000	0.173	0.305	-0.410	0.494	0.562	0.708	0.841	0.909	0.946	0.968	0.981
8				0.000	0.160	0.286	0.388	0.471	0.647	0.807	0.890	0.935	0.961	0.977
9					0.000	0.150	0.271	0.370	0.580	0.771	0.869	0.923	0.954	0.972
10						0.000	0.142	0.259	0.506	0.730	0.846	0.909	0.946	0.968
11							0.000	0.136	0.424	0.685	0.820	0.894	0.937	0.962
12								0.000	0.333	0.636	0.792	0.878	0.927	0.956
15									0.000	0.454	0.688	0.817	0.891	0:934
20										0.000	0.428	0.664	0.800	0.880
25											0.000	0.413	0.651	0.790
30												0.000	0.405	0.643
35													0.000	0.400
40														0.000

For Mortgages with an Interest Rate of 10.25% and an Original Term of:

Age of Loan in Years	5 Years	6 Years	7 Years	8 Years	9 Years	10 Years	11 Years	12 Years	15 Years	20 Years	25 Years	30 Years	35 Years	40 Years
1	0.839	0.873	0.897	0.915	0.929	0.939	0.948	0.955	0.970	0.984	0.991	0.995	0.997	0.998
2	0.660	0.732	0.783	0.821	0.850	0.872	0.891	0.906	0.937	0.966	0.981	0.989	0.993	0.996
3	0.462	0.576	0.657	0.716	0.762	0.798	0.827	0.851	0.901	0.947	0.970	0.982	0.990	0.994
4	0.243	0.403	0.517	0.601	0.665	0.716	0.757	0.790	0.861	0.925	0.957	0.975	0.985	0.991
5	0.000	0.212	0.362	0.473	0.558	0.625	0.679	0.723	0.816	0.901	0.944	0.967	0.981	0.989
6		0.000	0.190	0.331	0.439	0.524	0.592	0.648	0.767	0.874	0.929	0.959	0.976	0.986
7			0.000	0.174	0.307	0.412	0.497	0.566	0.712	0.844	0.912	0.949	0.970	0.982
8				0.000	0.161	0.289	0.391	0.475	0.651	0.812	0.893	0.938	0.964	0.978
9					0.000	0.152	0.274	0.373	0.584	0.775	0.873	0.926	0.956	0.974
10						0.000	0.144	0.261	0.510	0.735	0.850	0.913	0.949	0.970
11							0.000	0.137	0.428	0.691	0.825	0.898	0.940	0.964
12								0.000	0.337	0.641	0.797	0.882	0.931	0.959
15									0.000	0.459	0.694	0.822	0.895	0.938
20										0.000	0.433	0.671	0.806	0.885
25											0.000	0.419	0.658	0.797
30												0.000	0.411	0.651
35													0.000	0.407
40														0.000

Remaining Principal Balance Factors

For Mortgages with an Interest Rate of 10.50% and an Original Term of:

Age of Loan in Years	5 Years	6 Years	7 Years	8 Years	9 Years	10 Years	11 Years	12 Years	15 Years	20 Years	25 Years	30 Years	35 Years	40 Years
1	0.839	0.874	0.898	0.916	0.929	0.940	0.949	0.956	0.971	0.984	0.991	0.995	0.997	0.998
2	0.661	0.733	0.784	0.822	0.851	0.874	0.892	0.907	0.939	0.967	0.982	0.989	0.994	0.996
3	0.463	0.578	0.659	0.718	0.764	0.800	0.829	0.853	0.903	0.948	0.971	0.983	0.990	0.994
4	0.244	0.405	0.519	0.603	0.668	0.719	0.759	0.793	0.863	0.927	0.959	0.976	0.986	0.992
5	0.000	0.213	0.364	0.475	0.561	0.628	0.682	0.726	0.819	0.903	0.946	0.969	0.982	0.989
6		0.000	0.191	0.333	0.442	0.527	0.596	0.652	0.770	0.877	0.931	0.960	0.977	0.986
7			0.000	0.175	0.309	0.415	0.500	0.570	0.716	0.848	0.915	0.951	0.971	0.983
8				0.000	0.163	0.291	0.394	0.478	0.656	0.816	0.897	0.941	0.965	0.980
9					0.000	0.153	0.276	0.377	0.589	0.780	0.876	0.929	0.959	0.976
10						0.000	0.145	0.264	0.514	0.740	0.854	0.916	0.951	0.971
11							0.000	0.139	0.432	0.696	0.829	0.902	0.943	0.967
12								0.000	0.340	0.647	0.802	0.886	0.934	0.961
15									0.000	0.464	0.700	0.828	0.900	0.941
20										0.000	0.439	0.678	0.812	0.890
25											0.000	0.426	0.666	0.804
30												0.000	0.418	0.659
35													0.000	0.413
40														0.000

For Mortgages with an Interest Rate of 10.75% and an Original Term of:

Age of Loan in Years	5 Years	6 Years	7 Years	8 Years	9 Years	10 Years	11 Years	12 Years	15 Years	20 Years	25 Years	30 Years	35 Years	40 Years
1	0.840	0.875	0.899	0.917	0.930	0.941	0.950	0.957	0.972	0.985	0.992	0.995	0.997	0.998
2	0.663	0.735	0.786	0.824	0.853	0.875	0.894	0.909	0.940	0.968	0.982	0.990	0.994	0.997
3	0.465	0.580	0.661	0.720	0.766	0.802	0.831	0.855	0.905	0.950	0.972	0.984	0.991	0.995
4	0.245	0.407	0.521	0.605	0.670	0.721	0.762	0.795	0.866	0.929	0.960	0.978	0.987	0.993
5	0.000	0.214	0.365	0.477	0.563	0.631	0.685	0.729	0.822	0.906	0.948	0.970	0.983	0.990
6		0.000	0.193	0.335	0.444	0.530	0.599	0.655	0.774	0.880	0.933	0.962	0.978	0.987
7			0.000	0.176	0.312	0.418	0.503	0.573	0.720	0.851	0.918	0.953	0.973	0.984
8				0.000	0.164	0.293	0.397	0.482	0.660	0.820	0.900	0.943	0.967	0.981
9					0.000	0.154	0.279	0.380	0.593	0.784	0.880	0.932	0.961	0.977
10						0.000	0.147	0.266	0.519	0.745	0.858	0.919	0.954	0.973
11							0.000	0.140	0.436	0.701	0.834	0.906	0.946	0.969
12								0.000	0.344	0.652	0.807	0.890	0.937	0.963
15									0.000	0.470	0.706	0.833	0.904	0.944
20										0.000	0.445	0.685	0.819	0.895
25											0.000	0.432	0.673	0.810
30												0.000	0.424	0.666
35													0.000	0.420
40														0.000

Remaining Principal Balance Factors

For Mortgages with an Interest Rate of 11.00% and an Original Term of:

Age of Loan in Years	5 Years	6 Years	7 Years	8 Years	9 Years	10 Years	11 Years	12 Years	15 Years	20 Years	25 Years	30 Years	35 Years	40 Years
1	0.841	0.875	0.900	0.917	0.931	0.942	0.950	0.957	0.972	0.985	0.992	0.995	0.997	0.999
2	0.664	0.736	0.788	0.825	0.854	0.877	0.895	0.910	0.941	0.969	0.983	0.990	0.995	0.997
3	0.466	0.581	0.662	0.722	0.768	0.805	0.833	0.857	0.907	0.951	0.973	0.985	0.991	0.995
4	0.246	0.408	0.523	0.608	0.673	0.724	0.765	0.798	0.868	0.931	0.962	0.979	0.988	0.993
5	0.000	0.215	0.367	0.480	0.566	0.634	0.688	0.732	0.825	0.908	0.950	0.972	0.984	0.991
6		0.000	0.194	0.337	0.447	0.533	0.602	0.659	0.777	0.883	0.936	0.964	0.979	0.988
7			0.000	0.178	0.314	0.421	0.507	0.577	0.724	0.855	0.920	0.955	0.974	0.985
8				0.000	0.165	0.296	0.400	0.485	0.664	0.823	0.903	0.945	0.969	0.982
9					0.000	0.156	0.281	0.383	0.597	0.788	0.884	0.935	0.963	0.979
10						0.000	0.148	0.269	0.523	0.749	0.862	0.923	0.956	0.975
11							0.000	0.142	0.440	0.706	0.838	0.909	0.948	0.970
12								0.000	0.347	0.657	0.812	0.894	0.940	0.965
15									0.000	0.475	0.712	0.838	0.908	0.947
20										0.000	0.451	0.691	0.824	0.899
25											0.000	0.438	0.680	0.817
30												0.000	0.431	0.674
35													0.000	0.427
40														0.000

For Mortgages with an Interest Rate of 11.25% and an Original Term of:

Age of Loan in Years	5 Years	6 Years	7 Years	8 Years	9 Years	10 Years	11 Years	12 Years	15 Years	20 Years	25 Years	30 Years	35 Years	40 Years
1	0.842	0.876	0.900	0.918	0.932	0.943	0.951	0.958	0.973	0.986	0.992	0.996	0.998	0.999
2	0.666	0.738	0.789	0.827	0.856	0.878	0.897	0.911	0.942	0.970	0.984	0.991	0.995	0.997
3	0.468	0.583	0.664	0.725	0.770	0.807	0.836	0.859	0.909	0.952	0.974	0.986	0.992	0.995
4	0.247	0.410	0.525	0.610	0.675	0.726	0.767	0.801	0.871	0.933	0.963	0.980	0.989	0.994
5	0.000	0.217	0.369	0.482	0.569	0.636	0.691	0.735	0.828	0.911	0.951	0.973	0.985	0.991
6		0.000	0.195	0.339	0.449	0.536	0.605	0.662	0.780	0.886	0.938	0.966	0.981	0.989
7			0.000	0.179	0.316	0.424	0.510	0.580	0.727	0.858	0.923	0.957	0.976	0.986
8				0.000	0.167	0.298	0.403	0.488	0.668	0.827	0.906	0.948	0.971	0.983
9					0.000	0.157	0.283	0.386	0.601	0.793	0.887	0.937	0.965	0.980
10						0.000	0.150	0.271	0.527	0.754	0.866	0.926	0.958	0.976
11							0.000	0.143	0.444	0.711	0.843	0.913	0.951	0.972
12								0.000	0.351	0.662	0.816	0.898	0.943	0.967
15									0.000	0.480	0.717	0.843	0.912	0.950
20										0.000	0.456	0.698	0.830	0.904
25											0.000	0.444	0.687	0.823
30												0.000	0.437	0.681
35													0.000	0.434
40														0.000

Remaining Principal Balance Factors

For Mortgages with an Interest Rate of 11.50% and an Original Term of:

Age of Loan in Years	5 Years	6 Years	7 Years	8 Years	9 Years	10 Years	11 Years	12 Years	15 Years	20 Years	25 Years	30 Years	35 Years	40 Years
1	0.843	0.877	0.901	0.919	0.933	0.943	0.952	0.959	0.973	0.986	0.993	0.996	0.998	0.999
2	0.667	0.739	0.791	0.828	0.857	0.880	0.898	0.913	0.944	0.971	0.984	0.991	0.995	0.997
3	0.470	0.585	0.666	0.727	0.773	0.809	0.838	0.861	0.910	0.954	0.975	0.986	0.992	0.996
4	0.248	0.412	0.527	0.612	0.678	0.729	0.770	0.803	0.873	0.935	0.965	0.981	0.989	0.994
5	0.000	0.218	0.371	0.485	0.571	0.639	0.694	0.738	0.831	0.913	0.953	0.974	0.986	0.992
6		0.000	0.196	0.341	0.452	0.539	0.609	0.665	0.784	0.889	0.940	0.967	0.982	0.990
7			0.000	0.180	0.318	0.426	0.513	0.584	0.731	0.861	0.925	0.959	0.977	0.987
8				0.000	0.168	0.300	0.406	0.492	0.672	0.831	0.909	0.950	0.972	0.984
9					0.000	0.159	0.286	0.389	0.606	0.797	0.891	0.940	0.967	0.981
10						0.000	0.151	0.274	0.531	0.759	0.870	0.929	0.960	0.978
11							0.000	0.145	0.448	0.716	0.847	0.916	0.953	0.974
12								0.000	0.354	0.667	0.821	0.902	0.945	0.969
15									0.000	0.485	0.723	0.848	0.915	0.953
20										0.000	0.462	0.704	0.836	0.908
25											0.000	0.450	0.694	0.829
30												0.000	0.444	0.689
35													0.000	0.440
40														0.000

For Mortgages with an Interest Rate of 11.75% and an Original Term of:

Age of Loan in Years	5 Years	6 Years	7 Years	8 Years	9 Years	10 Years	11 Years	12 Years	15 Years	20 Years	25 Years	30 Years	35 Years	40 Years
1	0.844	0.878	0.902	0.920	0.933	0.944	0.953	0.960	0.974	0.987	0.993	0.996	0.998	0.999
2	0.668	0.741	0.792	0.830	0.859	0.881	0.899	0.914	0.945	0.972	0.985	0.992	0.996	0.998
3	0.471	0.587	0.668	0.729	0.775	0.811	0.840	0.863	0.912	0.955	0.976	0.987	0.993	0.996
4	0.249	0.414	0.529	0.615	0.680	0.731	0.772	0.806	0.875	0.936	0.966	0.982	0.990	0.994
5	0.000	0.219	0.373	0.487	0.574	0.642	0.697	0.741	0.834	0.915	0.955	0.975	0.987	0.993
6		0.000	0.197	0.343	0.455	0.542	0.612	0.669	0.787	0.891	0.942	0.969	0.983	0.990
7			0.000	0.182	0.320	0.429	0.516	0.587	0.735	0.865	0.928	0.961	0.978	0.988
8				0.000	0.170	0.302	0.409	0.495	0.676	0.835	0.912	0.952	0.974	0.985
9					0.000	0.160	0.288	0.392	0.610	0.801	0.894	0.942	0.968	0.982
10						0.000	0.152	0.276	0.535	0.763	0.874	0.931	0.962	0.979
11							0.000	0.146	0.452	0.720	0.851	0.919	0.956	0.975
12								0.000	0.358	0.672	0.826	0.905	0.948	0.971
15									0.000	0.490	0.729	0.852	0.919	0.955
20										0.000	0.468	0.711	0.841	0.912
25											0.000	0.456	0.701	0.835
30												0.000	0.450	0.696
35													0.000	0.447
40														0.000

Remaining Principal Balance Factors

For Mortgages with an Interest Rate of 12.00% and an Original Term of:

Age of Loan in Years	5 Years	6 Years	7 Years	8 Years	9 Years	10 Years	11 Years	12 Years	15 Years	20 Years	25 Years	30 Years	35 Years	40 Years
1	0.845	0.879	0.903	0.921	0.934	0.945	0.953	0.960	0.975	0.987	0.993	0.996	0.998	0.999
2	0.670	0.742	0.794	0.831	0.860	0.883	0.901	0.915	0.946	0.973	0.986	0.992	0.996	0.998
3	0.473	0.589	0.670	0.731	0.777	0.813	0.842	0.865	0.914	0.956	0.977	0.988	0.993	0.996
4	0.250	0.415	0.531	0.617	0.683	0.734	0.775	0.808	0.877	0.938	0.967	0.982	0.990	0.995
5	0.000	0.220	0.375	0.489	0.577	0.645	0.700	0.744	0.837	0.917	0.957	0.977	0.987	0.993
6		0.000	0.199	0.345	0.457	0.545	0.615	0.672	0.790	0.894	0.944	0.970	0.984	0.991
7			0.000	0.183	0.323	0.432	0.519	0.590	0.738	0.868	0.930	0.963	0.980	0.989
8				0.000	0.171	0.305	0.412	0.499	0.680	0.838	0.915	0.954	0.975	0.986
9					0.000	0.161	0.291	0.395	0.614	0.805	0.897	0.945	0.970	0.984
10						0.000	0.154	0.279	0.540	0.767	0.878	0.934	0.964	0.980
11							0.000	0.148	0.456	0.725	0.855	0.922	0.958	0.977
12								0.000	0.361	0.677	0.830	0.909	0.950	0.973
15									0.000	0.495	0.734	0.857	0.922	0.958
20										0.000	0.473	0.717	0.846	0.916
25											0.000	0.462	0.708	0.840
30												0.000	0.457	0.703
35													0.000	0.453
40														0.000

APPENDIX C

Seller's Property Disclosure Statement

REAL ESTATE TRANSFER DISCLOSURE STATEMENT

(CALIFORNIA CIVIL CODE 1102, ET SEQ.)

CALIFORNIA ASSOCIATION OF REALTORS® (CAR) STANDARD FORM

☐

THIS DISCLOSURE STATEMENT CONCERNS THE REAL PROPERTY SITUATED IN THE CITY OF________________ ____, COUNTY OF____, STATE OF CALIFORNIA, DESCRIBED AS____.

THIS STATEMENT IS A DISCLOSURE OF THE CONDITION OF THE ABOVE DESCRIBED PROPERTY IN COMPLIANCE WITH SECTION 1102 OF THE CIVIL CODE AS OF __________________________________, 19_____. IT IS NOT A WARRANTY OF ANY KIND BY THE SELLER(S) OR ANY AGENT(S) REPRESENTING ANY PRINCIPAL(S) IN THIS TRANSACTION, AND IS NOT A SUBSTITUTE FOR ANY INSPECTIONS OR WARRANTIES THE PRINCIPAL(S) MAY WISH TO OBTAIN.

I

COORDINATION WITH OTHER DISCLOSURE FORMS

This Real Estate Transfer Disclosure Statement is made pursuant to Section 1102 of the Civil Code. Other statutes require disclosures, depending upon the details of the particular real estate transaction (for example: special study zone and purchase-money liens on residential property).

Substituted Disclosures: The following disclosures have or will be in connection with this real estate transfer, and are intended to satisfy the disclosure obligations on this form, where the subject matter is the same: ____

(LIST ALL SUBSTITUTED DISCLOSURE FORMS TO BE USED IN CONNECTION WITH THIS TRANSACTION)

II

SELLER'S INFORMATION

The Seller discloses the following information with the knowledge that even though this is not a warranty, prospective Buyers may rely on this information in deciding whether and on what terms to purchase the subject property. Seller hereby authorizes any agent(s) representing any principal(s) in this transaction to provide a copy of this statement to any person or entity in connection with any actual or anticipated sale of the property.

THE FOLLOWING ARE REPRESENTATIONS MADE BY THE SELLER(S) AND ARE NOT THE REPRESENTATIONS OF THE AGENT(S), IF ANY. THIS INFORMATION IS A DISCLOSURE AND IS NOT INTENDED TO BE PART OF ANY CONTRACT BETWEEN THE BUYER AND SELLER.

Seller ☐ is ☐ is not occupying the property.

A. The subject property has the items checked below (read across):

☐ Range	☐ Oven	☐ Microwave
☐ Dishwasher	☐ Trash Compactor	☐ Garbage Disposal
☐ Washer/Dryer Hookups	☐ Window Screens	☐ Rain Gutters
☐ Burglar Alarms	☐ Smoke Detector(s)	☐ Fire Alarm
☐ T.V. Antenna	☐ Satellite Dish	☐ Intercom
☐ Central Heating	☐ Central Air Conditioning	☐ Evaporator Cooler(s)
☐ Wall/Window Air Conditioning	☐ Sprinklers	☐ Public Sewer System
☐ Septic Tank	☐ Sump Pump	☐ Water Softener
☐ Patio/Decking	☐ Built-in Barbeque	☐ Gazebo
☐ Sauna	☐ Pool	☐ Spa ☐ Hot Tub
☐ Security Gate(s)	☐ Automatic Garage Door Opener(s)*	☐ Number of Remote Controls ________
Garage: ☐ Attached	☐ Not Attached	☐ Carport
Pool/Spa Heater: ☐ Gas	☐ Solar	☐ Electric
Water Heater: ☐ Gas	☐ Solar	☐ Electric
Water Supply: ☐ City	☐ Well	☐ Private Utility ☐ Other________
Gas Supply: ☐ Utility	☐ Bottled	

Exhaust Fan(s) in ________________ 220 Volt Wiring in ________________

Fireplace(s) in ________________ ☐ Gas Starter

☐ Roof(s): Type: ________________ Age: ________________ (approx.)

☐ Other: ________________

Are there, to the best of your (Seller's) knowledge, any of the above that are not in operating condition? ☐ Yes ☐ No If yes, then describe. (Attach additional sheets if necessary.): ________________

____

____

B. Are you (Seller) aware of any significant defects/malfunctions in any of the following? ☐ Yes ☐ No If yes, check appropriate space(s) below.

☐ Interior Walls ☐ Ceilings ☐ Floors ☐ Exterior Walls ☐ Insulation ☐ Roof(s) ☐ Windows ☐ Doors ☐ Foundation ☐ Slab(s) ☐ Driveways ☐ Sidewalks ☐ Walls/Fences ☐ Electrical Systems ☐ Plumbing/Sewers/Septics ☐ Other Structural Components

(Describe: ________________

____

________________)

If any of the above is checked, explain. (Attach additional sheets if necessary): ________________

____

____

____

*This garage door opener may not be in compliance with the safety standards relating to automatic reversing devices as set forth in Chapter 12.5 (commencing with Section 19890) of Part 3 of Division 13 of the Health and Safety Code.

Buyer and Seller acknowledge receipt of copy of this page, which constitutes Page 1 of 2 Pages.

Buyer's Initials (________) (________) Seller's Initials (________) (________)

BROKER'S COPY

OFFICE USE ONLY

Reviewed by Broker or Designee ________

Date ________________

EQUAL HOUSING OPPORTUNITY

M-PM-5/94

REAL ESTATE TRANSFER DISCLOSURE STATEMENT (TDS-14 PAGE 1 OF 2)

☐

Subject Property Address: ______________________ ______________, 19____

C. Are you (Seller) aware of any of the following:

1. Substances, materials, or products which may be an environmental hazard such as, but not limited to, asbestos, formaldehyde, radon gas, lead-based paint, fuel or chemical storage tanks, and contaminated soil or water on the subject property. . . . . ☐ Yes ☐ No
2. Features of the property shared in common with adjoining landowners, such as walls, fences, and driveways, whose use or responsibility for maintenance may have an effect on the subject property. . . . . ☐ Yes ☐ No
3. Any encroachments, easements or similar matters that may affect your interest in the subject property. . . . . ☐ Yes ☐ No
4. Room additions, structural modifications, or other alterations or repairs made without necessary permits. . . . . ☐ Yes ☐ No
5. Room additions, structural modifications, or other alterations or repairs not in compliance with building codes. . . . ☐ Yes ☐ No
6. Landfill (compacted or otherwise) on the property or any portion thereof. . . . . ☐ Yes ☐ No
7. Any settling from any cause, or slippage, sliding, or other soil problems. . . . . ☐ Yes ☐ No
8. Flooding, drainage or grading problems. . . . . ☐ Yes ☐ No
9. Major damage to the property or any of the structures from fire, earthquake, floods, or landslides. . . . . ☐ Yes ☐ No
10. Any zoning violations, nonconforming uses, violations of "setback" requirements. . . . . ☐ Yes ☐ No
11. Neighborhood noise problems or other nuisances. . . . . ☐ Yes ☐ No
12. CC&R's or other deed restrictions or obligations. . . . . ☐ Yes ☐ No
13. Homeowners' Association which has any authority over the subject property. . . . . ☐ Yes ☐ No
14. Any "common area" (facilities such as pools, tennis courts, walkways, or other areas co-owned in undivided interest with others). . . . . ☐ Yes ☐ No
15. Any notices of abatement or citations against the property. . . . . ☐ Yes ☐ No
16. Any lawsuits against the seller threatening to or affecting this real property. . . . . ☐ Yes ☐ No

If the answer to any of these is yes, explain. (Attach additional sheets if necessary.): ______________________

____

____

____

Seller certifies that the information herein is true and correct to the best of the Seller's knowledge as of the date signed by the Seller.

Seller______________________________ Date______________

Seller______________________________ Date______________

III

AGENT'S INSPECTION DISCLOSURE

(To be completed only if the seller is represented by an agent in this transaction.)

THE UNDERSIGNED, BASED ON THE ABOVE INQUIRY OF THE SELLER(S) AS TO THE CONDITION OF THE PROPERTY AND BASED ON A REASONABLY COMPETENT AND DILIGENT VISUAL INSPECTION OF THE ACCESSIBLE AREAS OF THE PROPERTY IN CONJUNCTION WITH THAT INQUIRY, STATES THE FOLLOWING:

____

____

____

Agent (Broker
Representing Seller)______________ (PLEASE PRINT) By______________ (ASSOCIATE LICENSEE OR BROKER-SIGNATURE) Date______________

IV

AGENT'S INSPECTION DISCLOSURE

(To be completed only if the agent who has obtained the offer is other than the agent above.)

THE UNDERSIGNED, BASED ON A REASONABLY COMPETENT AND DILIGENT VISUAL INSPECTION OF THE ACCESSIBLE AREAS OF THE PROPERTY, STATES THE FOLLOWING:

____

____

____

Agent (Broker obtaining the Offer) ____________ (PLEASE PRINT) By ____________ (ASSOCIATE LICENSEE OR BROKER-SIGNATURE) Date ____________

V

BUYER(S) AND SELLER(S) MAY WISH TO OBTAIN PROFESSIONAL ADVICE AND/OR INSPECTIONS OF THE PROPERTY AND TO PROVIDE FOR APPROPRIATE PROVISIONS IN A CONTRACT BETWEEN BUYER AND SELLER(S) WITH RESPECT TO ANY ADVICE/INSPECTIONS/DEFECTS.

I/WE ACKNOWLEDGE RECEIPT OF A COPY OF THIS STATEMENT.

Seller ____________ Date ________ Buyer ____________ Date ________

Seller ____________ Date ________ Buyer ____________ Date ________

Agent (Broker Representing Seller) ____________ (PLEASE PRINT) By ____________ (ASSOCIATE LICENSEE OR BROKER-SIGNATURE) Date ____________

Agent (Broker obtaining the Offer) ____________ (PLEASE PRINT) By ____________ (ASSOCIATE LICENSEE OR BROKER-SIGNATURE) Date ____________

A REAL ESTATE BROKER IS QUALIFIED TO ADVISE ON REAL ESTATE. IF YOU DESIRE LEGAL ADVICE, CONSULT YOUR ATTORNEY.

BUYER'S COPY

Page 2 of ________ Pages.

OFFICE USE ONLY

Reviewed by Broker or Designee ________

Date ________

EQUAL HOUSING OPPORTUNITY

M-PM-5/94

REAL ESTATE TRANSFER DISCLOSURE STATEMENT (TDS-14 PAGE 2 OF 2)

APPENDIX

D

EPA Lead Paint Disclosure Brochure

Are You Planning To Buy, Rent, or Renovate a Home Built Before 1978?

Many houses and apartments built before 1978 have paint that contains lead (called lead-based paint). Lead from paint, chips, and dust can pose serious health hazards if not taken care of properly.

By 1996, federal law will require that individuals receive certain information before renting, buying, or renovating pre-1978 housing:

LANDLORDS will have to disclose known information on lead-based paint hazards before leases take effect. Leases will include a federal form about lead-based paint.

SELLERS will have to disclose known information on lead-based paint hazards before selling a house. Sales contracts will include a federal form about lead-based paint in the building. Buyers will have up to 10 days to check for lead hazards.

RENOVATORS will have to give you this pamphlet before starting work.

IF YOU WANT MORE INFORMATION on these requirements, call the National Lead Information Clearinghouse at **1-800-424-LEAD**.

IMPORTANT!

Lead From Paint, Dust, and Soil Can Be Dangerous If Not Managed Properly

FACT: Lead exposure can harm young children and babies even before they are born.

FACT: Even children that seem healthy can have high levels of lead in their bodies.

FACT: People can get lead in their bodies by breathing or swallowing lead dust, or by eating soil or paint chips with lead in them.

FACT: People have many options for reducing lead hazards. In most cases, lead-based paint that is in good condition is not a hazard.

FACT: Removing lead-based paint improperly can increase the danger to your family.

If you think your home might have lead hazards, read this pamphlet to learn some simple steps to protect your family.

Lead Gets in the Body in Many Ways

1 out of every 11 children in the United States has dangerous levels of lead in the blood-stream.

Even children who appear healthy can have dangerous levels of lead.

People can get lead in their body if they:

- Put their hands or other objects covered with lead dust in their mouths.
- Eat paint chips or soil that contains lead.
- Breathe in lead dust (especially during renovations that disturb painted surfaces).

Lead is even more dangerous to children than adults because:

- Babies and young children often put their hands and other objects in their mouths. These objects can have lead dust on them.
- Children's growing bodies absorb more lead.
- Children's brains and nervous systems are more sensitive to the damaging effects of lead.

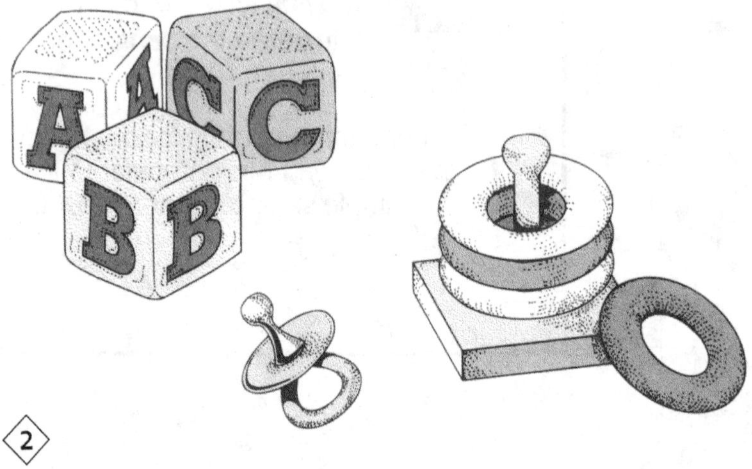

Lead's Effects

If not detected early, children with high levels of lead in their bodies can suffer from:

- Damage to the brain and nervous system
- Behavior and learning problems (such as hyperactivity)
- Slowed growth
- Hearing problems
- Headaches

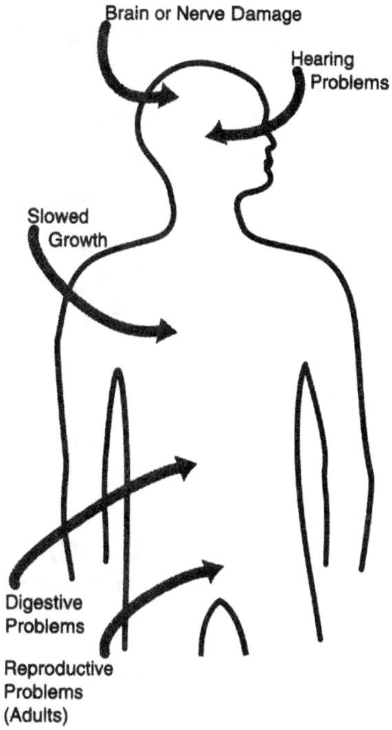

Lead is also harmful to adults. Adults can suffer from:

- Difficulties during pregnancy
- Other reproductive problems (in both men and women)
- High blood pressure
- Digestive problems
- Nerve disorders
- Memory and concentration problems
- Muscle and joint pain

Lead affects the body in many ways.

Checking Your Family for Lead

Get your children tested if you think your home has high levels of lead.

A simple blood test can detect high levels of lead. Blood tests are important for:

- Children who are 6 months to 1 year old (6 months if you live in an older home with cracking or peeling paint).
- Family members that you think might have high levels of lead.

If your child is older than 1 year, talk to your doctor about whether your child needs testing.

Your doctor or health center can do blood tests. They are inexpensive and sometimes free. Your doctor will explain what the test results mean. *Treatment can range from changes in your diet to medication or a hospital stay.*

Where Lead-Based Paint Is Found

In general, the older your home, the more likely it has lead-based paint.

Many homes built before 1978 have lead-based paint. The federal government banned lead-based paint from housing in 1978. Some states stopped its use even earlier. Lead can be found:

- In homes in the city, country, or suburbs.
- In apartments, single-family homes, and both private and public housing.
- Inside *and* outside of the house.
- In soil around a home. (Soil can pick up lead from exterior paint, or other sources such as past use of leaded gas in cars.)

Where Lead Is Likely To Be a Hazard

Lead-based paint that is in good condition is usually not a hazard.

Peeling, chipping, chalking, or cracking lead-based paint is a hazard and needs immediate attention.

Lead-based paint may also be a hazard when found on surfaces that children can chew or that get a lot of wear-and-tear. These areas include:

- Windows and window sills.
- Doors and door frames.
- Stairs, railings, and banisters.
- Porches and fences.

Lead from paint chips, which you can see, and lead dust, which you can't always see, can both be serious hazards

Lead dust can form when lead-based paint is dry scraped, dry sanded, or heated. Dust also forms when painted surfaces bump or rub together. Lead chips and dust can get on surfaces and objects that people touch. Settled lead dust can reenter the air when people vacuum, sweep, or walk through it.

Lead in soil can be a hazard when children play in bare soil or when people bring soil into the house on their shoes. Call your state agency (see page 12) to find out about soil testing for lead.

Checking Your Home for Lead Hazards

Just knowing that a home has lead-based paint may not tell you if there is a hazard.

You can get your home checked for lead hazards in one of two ways, or both:

- A paint **inspection** tells you the lead content of every painted surface in your home. It won't tell you whether the paint is a hazard or how you should deal with it.
- A **risk assessment** tells you if there are any sources of serious lead exposure (such as peeling paint and lead dust). It also tells you what actions to take to address these hazards.

Have qualified professionals do the work. *The federal government is writing standards for inspectors and risk assessors. Some states might already have standards in place.* Call your state agency for help with locating qualified professionals in your area (see page 12).

Trained professionals use a range of methods when checking your home, including:

- Visual inspection of paint condition and location.
- Lab tests of paint samples.
- Surface dust tests.
- A portable x-ray fluorescence machine.

Home test kits for lead are available, but recent studies suggest that they are not always accurate. Consumers should not rely on these tests before doing renovations or to assure safety.

What You Can Do Now To Protect Your Family

If you suspect that your house has lead hazards, you can take some immediate steps to reduce your family's risk:

- **If you rent, notify your landlord of peeling or chipping paint.**
- **Clean up paint chips immediately.**
- **Clean floors, window frames, window sills, and other surfaces weekly.** Use a mop or sponge with warm water and a general all-purpose cleaner or a cleaner made specifically for lead. REMEMBER: NEVER MIX AMMONIA AND BLEACH PRODUCTS TOGETHER SINCE THEY CAN FORM A DANGEROUS GAS.

- **Thoroughly rinse sponges and mop heads after cleaning dirty or dusty areas.**
- **Wash children's hands often, especially before they eat and before nap time and bed time.**
- **Keep play areas clean.** Wash bottles, pacifiers, toys, and stuffed animals regularly.
- **Keep children from chewing window sills or other painted surfaces.**
- **Clean or remove shoes before entering your home to avoid tracking in lead from soil.**
- **Make sure children eat nutritious, low-fat meals high in iron and calcium,** such as spinach and low-fat dairy products. Children with good diets absorb less lead.

How To Significantly Reduce Lead Hazards

Removing lead improperly can increase the hazard to your family by spreading even more lead dust around the house.

Always use a professional who is trained to remove lead hazards safely.

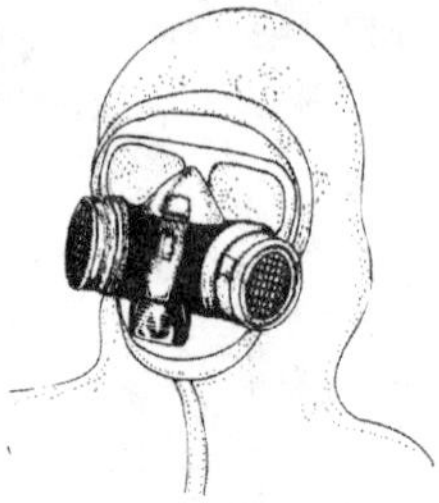

In addition to day-to-day cleaning and good nutrition:

- You can **temporarily** reduce lead hazards by taking actions such as repairing damaged painted surfaces and planting grass to cover soil with high lead levels. These actions (called "interim controls") are not permanent solutions and will need ongoing attention.
- To **permanently** remove lead hazards, you must hire a lead "abatement" contractor. Abatement (or permanent hazard elimination) methods include removing, sealing, or enclosing lead-based paint with special materials. Just painting over the hazard with regular paint is not enough.

Always hire a person with special training for correcting lead problems—someone who knows how to do this work safely and has the proper equipment to clean up thoroughly. If possible, hire a certified lead abatement contractor. Certified contractors will employ qualified workers and follow strict safety rules as set by their state or by the federal government.

Call your state agency (see page 12) for help with locating qualified contractors in your area and to see if financial assistance is available.

Remodeling or Renovating a Home With Lead-Based Paint

Take precautions before you begin remodeling or renovations that disturb painted surfaces (such as scraping off paint or tearing out walls):

- **Have the area tested for lead-based paint.**
- **Do not use a dry scraper, belt-sander, propane torch, or heat gun** to remove lead-based paint. These actions create large amounts of lead dust and fumes. Lead dust can remain in your home long after the work is done.
- **Temporarily move your family** (especially children and pregnant women) out of the apartment or house until the work is done and the area is properly cleaned. If you can't move your family, at least completely seal off the work area.
- **Follow other safety measures to reduce lead hazards.** You can find out about other safety measures by calling 1-800-424-LEAD. Ask for the brochure "Reducing Lead Hazards When Remodeling Your Home." This brochure explains what to do before, during, and after renovations.

If not conducted properly, certain types of renovations can release lead from paint and dust into the air.

If you have already completed renovations or remodeling that could have released lead-based paint or dust, get your young children tested and follow the steps outlined on page 7 of this brochure.

Other Sources of Lead

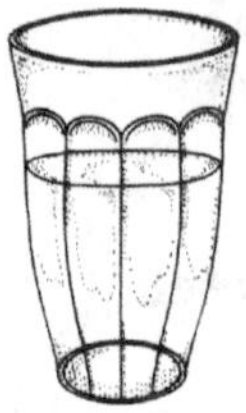

While paint, dust, and soil are the most common lead hazards, other lead sources also exist.

- **Drinking water.** Your home might have plumbing with lead or lead solder. Call your local health department or water supplier to find out about testing your water. You cannot see, smell, or taste lead, and boiling your water will not get rid of lead. If you think your plumbing might have lead in it:
    - Use only cold water for drinking and cooking.
    - Run water for 15 to 30 seconds before drinking it, especially if you have not used your water for a few hours.
- **The job.** If you work with lead, you could bring it home on your hands or clothes. Shower and change clothes before coming home. Launder your clothes separately from the rest of your family's.
- Old painted **toys** and **furniture.**
- Food and liquids stored in **lead crystal** or **lead-glazed pottery or porcelain.**
- **Lead smelters** or other industries that release lead into the air.
- **Hobbies** that use lead, such as making pottery or stained glass, or refinishing furniture.
- **Folk remedies** that contain lead, such as "greta" and "azarcon" used to treat an upset stomach.

For More Information

The National Lead Information Center

Call **1-800-LEAD-FYI** to learn how to protect children from lead poisoning.

For other information on lead hazards, call the center's clearinghouse at **1-800-424-LEAD.** For the hearing impaired, call, **TDD 1-800-526-5456** (FAX: **202-659-1192,** Internet: **EHC@CAIS.COM**).

EPA's Safe Drinking Water Hotline

Call **1-800-426-4791** for information about lead in drinking water.

Consumer Product Safety Commission Hotline

To request information on lead in consumer products, or to report an unsafe consumer product or a product-related injury call **1-800-638-2772**. (Internet: info@cpsc.gov). For the hearing impaired, call **TDD 1-800-638-8270**.

Local Sources of Information

State Health and Environmental Agencies

Some cities and states have their own rules for lead-based paint activities. Check with your state agency (listed below) to see if state or local laws apply to you. Most state agencies can also provide information on finding a lead abatement firm in your area, and on possible sources of financial aid for reducing lead hazards.

State/Region	Phone Number
Alabama	(205) 242-5661
Alaska	(907) 465-5152
Arkansas	(501) 661-2534
Arizona	(602) 542-7307
California	(510) 450-2424
Colorado	(303) 692-3012
Connecticut	(203) 566-5808
Washington, DC	(202) 727-9850
Delaware	(302) 739-4735
Florida	(904) 488-3385
Georgia	(404) 657-6514
Hawaii	(808) 832-5860
Idaho	(208) 332-5544
Illinois	(800) 545-2200
Indiana	(317) 382-6662
Iowa	(800) 972-2026
Kansas	(913) 296-0189
Kentucky	(502) 564-2154
Louisiana	(504) 765-0219
Massachusetts	(800) 532-9571
Maryland	(410) 631-3859
Maine	(207) 287-4311
Michigan	(517) 335-8885
Minnesota	(612) 627-5498
Mississippi	(601) 960-7463
Missouri	(314) 526-4911
Montana	(406) 444-3671
Nebraska	(402) 471-2451
Nevada	(702) 687-6615
New Hampshire	(603) 271-4507
New Jersey	(609) 633-2043
New Mexico	(505) 841-8024
New York	(800) 458-1158
North Carolina	(919) 715-3293
North Dakota	(701) 328-5188
Ohio	(614) 466-1450
Oklahoma	(405) 271-5220
Oregon	(503) 248-5240
Pennsylvania	(717) 782-2884
Rhode Island	(401) 277-3424
South Carolina	(803) 935-7945
South Dakota	(605) 773-3153
Tennessee	(615) 741-5683
Texas	(512) 834-6600
Utah	(801) 536-4000
Vermont	(802) 863-7231
Virginia	(800) 523-4019
Washington	(206) 753-2556
West Virginia	(304) 558-2981
Wisconsin	(608) 266-5885
Wyoming	(307) 777-7391

EPA Regional Offices

Your Regional EPA Office can provide further information regarding regulations and lead protection programs.

EPA Regional Offices

Region 1 (Connecticut, Massachusetts, Maine, New Hampshire, Rhode Island, Vermont)
John F. Kennedy Federal Building
One Congress Street
Boston, MA 02203
(617) 565-3420

Region 2 (New Jersey, New York, Puerto Rico, Virgin Islands)
Building 5
2890 Woodbridge Avenue
Edison, NJ 08837-3679
(908) 321-6671

Region 3 (Delaware, Washington DC, Maryland, Pennsylvania, Virginia, West Virginia)
841 Chestnut Building
Philadelphia, PA 19107
(215) 597-9800

Region 4 (Alabama, Florida, Georgia, Kentucky, Mississippi, North Carolina, South Carolina, Tennessee)
345 Courtland Street, NE
Atlanta, GA 30365
(404) 347-4727

Region 5 (Illinois, Indiana, Michigan, Minnesota, Ohio, Wisconsin)
77 West Jackson Boulevard
Chicago, IL 60604-3590
(312) 886-6003

Region 6 (Arkansas, Louisiana, New Mexico, Oklahoma, Texas)
First Interstate Bank Tower
1445 Ross Avenue, 12th Floor, Suite 1200
Dallas, TX 75202-2733
(214) 665-7244

Region 7 (Iowa, Kansas, Missouri, Nebraska)
726 Minnesota Avenue
Kansas City, KS 66101
(913) 551-7020

Region 8 (Colorado, Montana, North Dakota, South Dakota, Utah, Wyoming)
999 18th Street, Suite 500
Denver, CO 80202-2405
(303) 293-1603

Region 9 (Arizona, California, Hawaii, Nevada)
75 Hawthorne Street
San Francisco, CA 94105
(415) 744-1124

Region 10 (Idaho, Oregon, Washington, Alaska)
1200 Sixth Avenue
Seattle, WA 98101
(206) 553-1200

CPSC Regional Offices

Eastern Regional Center
6 World Trade Center
Vesey Street, Room 350
New York, NY 10048
(212) 466-1612

Central Regional Center
230 South Dearborn Street
Room 2944
Chicago, IL 60604-1601
(312) 353-8260

Western Regional Center
600 Harrison Street, Room 245
San Francisco, CA 94107
(415) 744-2966

Simple Steps To Protect Your Family From Lead Hazards

If you think your home has high levels of lead:

- Get your young children tested for lead, even if they seem healthy.
- Wash children's hands, bottles, pacifiers, and toys often.
- Make sure children eat healthy, low-fat foods.
- Get your home checked for lead hazards.
- Regularly clean floors, window sills, and other surfaces.
- Wipe soil off shoes before entering house.
- Talk to your landlord about fixing surfaces with peeling or chipping paint.
- Take precautions to avoid exposure to lead dust when remodeling or renovating (call 1-800-424-LEAD for guidelines).
- Don't use a belt-sander, propane torch, dry scraper, or dry sandpaper on painted surfaces that may contain lead.
- Don't try to remove lead-based paint yourself.

APPENDIX

E

Helpful Web Sites for Homesellers

The ever-changing and competitive cyber-world gives us no guarantee that Web sites listed here will stand the test of time. These sites, however, have been among the most reliable over the past few years.

Professional Real Estate Listings

- Realtor.com
- HomeAdvisor.com
- HomeSeekers.com
- Yahoo!RealEstate.com
- Cyberhomes.com

Home Improvement Sites

- Improve.net
- Remodel.com
- Builderonline.com

For Sale By Owner and Discount Broker Sites

- Help-u-sell.com
- Owners.com
- Americas-real-estate.com
- iOwn.com
- eBay.com
- FSBONET.com

Real Estate News and Advice Sites

- RealtyTimes.com
- Inman.com
- RealtorMag.com
- Rismedia.com
- HomeStore.com

Professional Organizers and Movers

- NAPO.net
- iMove.com
- HomeFair.com

Retirement Information and Support

- AARP.org
- NCOA.org
- SocialSecurity.com

Directory of Real Estate Sites

- IRED.com

Glossary

abstract of title (abstract) History of a parcel of real estate, compiled from public records, listing transfers of ownership and claims against the property

acceleration clause Provision in a mortgage document stating that if a payment is missed or any other provision violated, the whole debt becomes immediately due and payable

acknowledgment Formal declaration before a public official that one has signed a document

acre Land measure equal to 43,560 square feet

addendum Document attached to and accompanying the purchase agreement that, once signed by both buyer and seller, becomes a part of the agreement

adjustable-rate mortgage (ARM) A loan with an interest rate that changes periodically to keep pace with current levels

adjusted basis Original cost of property plus any later improvements and minus a figure for depreciation claimed

adjusted sales price Sales price minus commissions, legal fees, and other costs of selling

agent Person authorized to act on behalf of another in dealings with third parties

agreement of sale (purchase agreement, sales agreement, contract to purchase) Written contract detailing terms under which buyer agrees to buy and seller agrees to sell

alienation clause (due-on-sale, nonassumption) Provision in a mortgage document stating that the loan must be paid in full if ownership is transferred; sometimes contingent upon other occurrences

amortization Gradual payment of a debt through regular installments that cover both principal and interest

appraisal Estimate of value of real estate, presumably by an expert

appreciation Increase in value or worth of property

"as is" Present condition of property being transferred, with no guaranty or warranty provided by the seller

assessed valuation Value placed on property as a basis for levying property taxes; not identical with appraised or market value

assignment Transfer of a contract from one party to another

assumable mortgage Loan that may be passed to the next owner of the property

assumption Takeover of a loan by any qualified buyer (available for FHA and VA loans)

automatic renewal clause Provision that allows a listing contract to be renewed indefinitely unless canceled by the property owner

balloon loan Mortgage in which the remaining balance becomes fully due and payable at a predetermined time

balloon payment Final payment on a balloon loan

bidding war Where two or more potential buyers try to outbid one another for the same property

bill of sale Written document transferring personal property

binder Preliminary agreement of sale, usually accompanied by earnest money (term also used with property insurance)

bond Roughly the same as *promissory note;* a written promise to repay a loan, often with an accompanying mortgage that pledges real estate as security

broker Person licensed by the state to represent another for a fee in real estate transactions

builder warranty agreement Limited guarantee, usually up to ten years in duration, requiring a builder to tend to any structural defects that may occur in its homes

building code Regulations of local government stipulating requirements and standards for building and construction

buydown The payment of additional points to a mortgage lender in return for a lower interest rate on the loan

buyer's broker Agent who takes the buyer as client, is obligated to put the buyer's interests above all others, and owes specific fiduciary duties to the buyer

buyer's market Situation in which supply of homes for sale exceeds demand

cap Limit (typically about 2 percent) by which an adjustable mortgage rate might be raised at any one time

capital gain Taxable profit on the sale of an appreciated asset

caveat emptor Let the buyer beware

ceiling Also known as *lifetime cap;* limit beyond which an adjustable mortgage rate may never be raised

certificate of occupancy Document issued by local governmental agency stating that property meets standards for occupancy

chattel Personal property

client The broker's principal, to whom fiduciary duties are owed

closing (settlement, escrow, passing papers) Conclusion of a real estate sale, at which time title is transferred and necessary funds change hands

closing costs One-time charges paid by buyer and seller on the day property changes hands

closing statement Statement prepared for buyer and seller listing debits and credits, completed by the person in charge of the closing

cloud (on title) Outstanding claim or encumbrance that challenges the owner's clear title

commission Fee paid (usually by a seller) for a broker's services in securing a buyer for property; commonly a percentage of sales price

commitment (letter) Written promise to grant a mortgage loan

common elements Parts of a condominium development in which each owner holds an interest (swimming pool, etc.)

comparable Recently sold similar property, used to estimate market value

comparative market analysis Method of valuing homes using study of comparables, property that failed to sell, and other property currently on the market

conditional commitment Lender's promise to make a loan subject to the fulfillment of specified conditions

conditional offer Purchase offer in which the buyer proposes to purchase only after certain occurrences (sale of another home, securing of financing, etc.)

condominium Type of ownership involving individual ownership of dwelling units and common ownership of shared areas

consideration Something of value given to induce another to enter into a contract

contingency Condition (inserted into the contract) that must be satisfied before the buyer purchases a house

contract Legally enforceable agreement to do (or not to do) a particular thing

contract for deed (land contract) Method of selling whereby the buyer receives possession but the seller retains title

conventional mortgage Loan arranged between lender and borrower with no governmental guarantee or insurance

cost basis Accounting figure that includes original cost of property plus certain expenses to purchase, money spent on permanent improvements and other costs, minus any depreciation claimed on tax returns over the years

curtesy In some states, rights a widower obtains to a portion of his deceased wife's real property

customer Typically, the buyer, as opposed to the principal (seller)

days on market (DOM) Number of days between the time a house is put on the market and the date of a firm sales contract

deed Formal written document transferring title to real estate; a new deed is used for each transfer

deed of trust Document by which title to property is held by a neutral third party until a debt is paid; used instead of a mortgage in some states

deed restriction (restrictive covenant) Provision placed in a deed to control use and occupancy of the property by future owners

default Failure to make mortgage payment

deferred maintenance Needed repairs that have been put off

deficiency judgment Personal claim against the debtor when foreclosed property does not yield enough at sale to pay off loans against it

delivery Legal transfer of a deed to the new property owner; the moment at which transfer of title occurs

depreciation Decrease in value of property because of deterioration or obsolescence; sometimes, an artificial bookkeeping concept valuable as a tax shelter

direct endorsement Complete processing of an FHA mortgage application by an authorized local lender

discount broker Broker who operates at reduced commissions for sellers who wish to handle many of the marketing tasks for their own homes

documentary tax stamp Charge levied by state or local governments when real estate is transferred or mortgaged

double-ended sale Sale where the listing and sale (seller and buyer) are both handled and represented by the same broker, and the agent receives the full commission

dower In some states, the rights of a widow to a portion of her deceased husband's property

down payment Cash to be paid by the buyer at closing

earnest money Buyer's good faith deposit accompanying purchase offer

easement A permanent right to use another's property (telephone lines, common driveway, footpath, etc.)

encroachment Unauthorized intrusion of a building or improvement onto another's land

encumbrance Claim against another's real estate (unpaid tax, mortgage, easement, etc.)

equity The money realized when property is sold and all the claims against it are paid; commonly, sales price minus present mortgage

escrow Funds given to a third party to be held pending some occurrence; may refer to earnest money; funds collected by a lender for the payment of taxes and insurance charges; funds withheld at closing to insure uncompleted repairs; or, in some states, the entire process of closing

exclusive agency Listing agreement under which only the listing office can sell the property and keep the commission, except if the owner sells the house, in which case no commission is paid

exclusive right to sell Listing agreement under which the owner promises to pay a commission if the property is sold during the listing period by anyone, even the owner

facilitator One who offers real estate services without owing special fiduciary duties to either seller or buyer (See also **transaction broker**)

fair market value See **market value**

fee-for-services broker Broker who sells each of his or her list of professional real estate services separately, or unbundled

fee simple (absolute) Highest possible degree of ownership of land

FHA Federal Housing Administration (HUD), which insures mortgages to protect the lending institution in case of default

FHA mortgage Loan made by a local lending institution and insured by the FHA, with the borrower paying the premium

fiduciary A person in a position of trust or responsibility with specific duties to act in the best interest of the client

first mortgage Mortgage holding priority over the claims of subsequent lenders against the same property

fixture Personal property that has become part of the real estate

foreclosure Legal procedure for enforcing payment of a debt by seizing and selling the mortgaged property

front foot Measurement of land along a street or waterfront—each front foot is one foot wide and extends to the depth of the lot

functional obsolescence Phenomenon of improving a home beyond its capacity to function and blend with the existing structure

grantee The buyer, who receives a deed

grantor The seller, who gives a deed

guaranteed sale Promise by the listing broker that if the property cannot be sold by a specific date, the broker will buy it, usually at a sharply discounted price

hazard insurance Insurance on a property against fire and similar risks

homeowners policy Policy that puts many kinds of insurance together into one package

improvements Permanent additions that increase the value of a home

index Benchmark measure of current interest levels, used to calculate periodic changes in rates charged on adjustable-rate mortgages

joint tenancy Ownership by two or more persons, each with an undivided ownership—if one dies, the property goes automatically to the survivor

junior mortgage A mortgage subordinate to another

land contract Type of layaway installment plan for buying a house; sought by a buyer who does not have enough down payment to qualify for a bank loan or to persuade the seller to turn over title

lien A claim against property for the payment of a debt: mechanic's lien, mortgage, unpaid taxes, judgments

lis pendens Notice that litigation is pending on property

listing agreement (listing) Written employment agreement between a property owner and a real estate broker, authorizing the broker to find a buyer

listing presentation Proposal submitted orally or in writing by a real estate agent who seeks to put a prospective seller's property on the market

loan servicing Handling paperwork of collecting loan payments, checking property tax and insurance coverage, handling delinquencies

lock-in Guarantee that the borrower will receive the rate in effect at the time of loan application

maintenance fees Payments made by the unit owner of a condominium to the homeowners association for expenses incurred in upkeep of the common areas

margin Percentage (typically about 2.5 percent) added to index to calculate mortgage rate adjustment

marketable title Title free of liens, clouds, and defects; a title that will be freely accepted by a buyer

market value The most likely price a given property will bring if widely exposed on the market, assuming fully informed buyer and seller

mechanic's lien Claim placed against property by unpaid workers or suppliers

meeting of the minds Agreement by buyer and seller on the provisions of a contract

mortgage A lien or claim against real property given as security for a loan; the homeowner gives the mortgage; the lender takes it

mortgagee The lender

mortgagor The borrower

Multiple Listing Service (MLS) An arrangement by which brokers work together on the sale of each others' listed homes, with shared commissions

negative amortization Arrangement under which the shortfall in a mortgage payment is added to the amount borrowed; gradual raising of a debt

net listing Arrangement under which the seller receives a specific sum from the sales price and the agent keeps the rest as sales commission (open to abuses; illegal in most states)

note See **bond**

PITI Abbreviation for principal, interest, taxes, and insurance, often lumped together in a monthly mortgage payment

plat Map or chart of a lot, subdivision, or community, showing boundary lines, buildings, and easements

PMI Private mortgage insurance

point (discount point) 1 percent of a new mortgage being placed, paid in a one-time lump sum to the lender

portfolio loans Loans made by a bank that keeps its mortgages as assets in its own portfolio (also called *nonconforming loans*)

prepayment Payment of a mortgage loan before its due date

prepayment penalty Charge levied by the lender for paying off a mortgage before its maturity date

principal Party (typically the seller) who hires and pays an agent

procuring cause Actions by a broker that bring about the desired results

prorations Expenses that are fairly divided between buyer and seller at closing

purchase-money mortgage Mortgage for the purchase of real property, commonly a mortgage taken back by the seller

quitclaim deed Deed that completely transfers whatever ownership the grantor may have had, but makes no claim of ownership in the first place

real property Land and the improvements on it

Realtist Member of the National Association of Real Estate Brokers

REALTOR® Registered name for a member of the National Association of REALTORS®

REALTOR-ASSOCIATE® Salesperson associated with a broker who is a member of a Board of REALTORS®

redlining The practice of refusing to provide loans or insurance in certain neighborhoods

RESPA Real Estate Settlement Procedures Act, requiring advance disclosure to the borrower of information pertinent to the loan

restrictive covenant See **deed restriction**

reverse mortgage Arrangement under which an elderly homeowner, who does not need to meet income or credit requirements, can draw against the equity in the home with no immediate repayment

salesperson Holder of an entry-level license who is allowed to assist a broker who is legally responsible for the salesperson's activities (synonymous in some areas with *agent*)

seller's broker Agent who takes the seller as a client, is legally obligated to a set of fiduciary duties, and is required to put the seller's interests above all others'

sellers' market Situation in which demand for homes exceeds the supply offered for sale

settlement See **closing**

specific performance Lawsuit requesting that a contract be exactly carried out, usually asking that the seller be ordered to convey the property as previously agreed

subagency Legal process by which the seller who lists property for sale with a broker takes on the broker's associates and cooperating firms in a multiple listing system as agents

subprime lenders Sometimes referred to as B or C paper lenders; lenders that offer mortgage funds at higher-than-going rates to borrowers who have difficulties qualifying for mortgage financing at conventional rates

survey Map made by a licensed surveyor who measures the land and charts its boundaries, improvements, and relationship to the property surrounding it

time is of the essence Legal phrase in a contract, requiring punctual performance of all obligations

title Rights of ownership, control, and possession of property

title insurance Policy protecting the insured against loss or damage due to defects in title: the owner's policy protects the buyer, the mortgagee's policy protects the lender; paid with a one-time premium

title search Check of the public records, usually at the local courthouse, to make sure that no adverse claims affect the value of the title

transaction broker Broker who offers services without owing fiduciary duties to either party, as defined by law in various states

VA Department of Veterans Affairs (formerly Veterans Administration), which guarantees a veteran's mortgage so that a lender is willing to make the loan with little or no down payment

vendee The buyer

vendor The seller

warranty deed Most valuable type of deed, in which the grantor makes formal assurance of title

zoning Laws of local government establishing building codes and regulations on usage of property

Index

B

C

D

E

F

P

Q

R

U

V

W–Z